Alienation
and Freedom

See p. 183 "alienate"

— quote Bob's stuff
for work for husband? —

marriage

1) Callerwork
2) setting after for family
   advance. + etc.
3)

R. Blamer doesn't answer: what are
the expectation a man brings
to work??

X for end. for
"work" as central force —
— cite studies on
workers on
extended strike →
demoralization

Alienation
and Freedom

The Factory Worker and His Industry

ROBERT BLAUNER

Chicago and London
THE UNIVERSITY OF CHICAGO PRESS

Library of Congress Catalog Card Number: 64-15820

THE UNIVERSITY OF CHICAGO PRESS, CHICAGO 60637

The University of Chicago Press Ltd., London W. C. 1

Published 1964

Fourth Impression 1968

Printed in the United States of America

*To Dan Casey's gang
in Department 13-C
Emeryville, California, 1952–56*

PREFACE

This book is about factory workers who are employed in industrial situations that vary considerably from one another—the print shop, the textile mill, the automobile assembly line, and the automated chemical plant. It is chiefly about their work, both in its objective features and in its subjective meanings. In the broadest sense, it is a sociological study of the relationships between technology, social structure, and personal experience. I attempt to show that the worker's relation to the technological organization of the work process and to the social organization of the factory determines whether or not he characteristically experiences in that work a sense of control rather than domination, a sense of meaningful purpose rather than futility, a sense of social connection rather than isolation, and a sense of spontaneous involvement and self-expression rather than detachment and discontent.

Domination, futility, isolation, and discontent are each aspects of experience that have been identified as elements of the general condition of *alienation,* a leading perspective in modern social thought. This, then, is a book about alienation in the work process and its opposite condition, freedom. The principal question I attempt to answer is, Under what conditions are the alienating tendencies of modern factory technology and work organization intensified, and under what conditions are they minimized and counteracted? Such an investigation has brought together two modes of inquiry that have usually stayed somewhat apart—the abstract, even philosophical, speculation of the alienation concept, and empirical research, with its sensitivity to concrete social life and scientific procedures. Our journey then proceeds from a broad theoretical discussion to the detailed description of factory workers' jobs to the consideration of data embedded in statistical tables. The most basic assumption of this book has been the idea that the alienation perspective can be used scientifically—rather than polemically—to elucidate the complex realities of present-day industrial society.

Among these realities, the nature of the work a man does eight hours a day is of paramount significance. The importance of work in the total life-experience is a further assumption of this study, one that runs counter to much current thinking. In industrial sociology, a recent tendency has been to view the range of possibilities for happiness and unhappiness on the job as defined chiefly within the sphere of "human relations." The crucial variables to be studied and manipulated are, then, the general social climate of the enterprise and the quality of interpersonal contact among employees and between employees and their supervisors—rather than the worker's relation to technology and the division of labor. Similarly, social commentators look at the offices and factories of today and perceive a mass of undifferentiated jobs that lack the potential for meaning and fulfilment, and they therefore place their bets on the burgeoning area of leisure as the main hope for individuality and self-expression. But, if—as I believe the findings of this study suggest—the nature of a man's work affects his social character and personality, the manner in which he participates or fails to participate as a citizen in the larger community, and his over-all sense of worth and dignity, then we had better not "give up" on work as a major interest of industrial and public policy.

Perhaps it is curious to be concerned with meaning in work when the basic anxiety of factory workers is the job itself. With technological and population trends ever threatening to increase the already high levels of unemployment, the most serious and immediate social problem of our industrial economy is clearly not the nature of work but the very existence of sufficient jobs. From one point of view, freedom, meaning, and self-expression in work are luxuries whose absence is experienced as a deprivation only by those who have had steady employment at adequate wages for a considerable period of time. This book worries, then, about the icing, when many of its principals are wondering whether they will have any cake at all.

This paradox is most apparent in my treatment of automation. I have little to say about its impact on the number of jobs and the problems of retraining displaced workers. Instead, the case study of a chemical plant in chapters 6 and 7 focuses on the nature of work for those who remain on the job in automated industrial environments. What emerges there is a picture of automation made up of positive components, which are necessarily de-emphasized by those who have concentrated on its immediate consequences for employment. The worker in the automated factory "regains" a sense of control over his complex technological environment that is usually absent in mass-production factories. He is not rushed, but has free time, can move around the plant, experience the factory as a whole, and socialize with his fellow employees. The work of monitoring automatic controls demands and encourages individual responsibility, and the decentralized organization of chemical operations gives him a sense of function in an industrial environment that is socially integrated. These findings must be checked through studies of automation in other industries, but they do give hope that there may be far-reaching positive, as well as negative, consequences resulting from the central technological trend of our era.

Possibly it would be more appropriate to study the problem of freedom and self-expression in work among white-collar and professional people, whose higher education has awakened the aspirations for fulfilment and creativity that often lie dormant among the mass of less-educated manual workers. Here I plead the continuity of intellectual tradition and my own personal history to defend my choice. The concept of alienation, in its classical form, was an attempt to explain the changes in the nature of manual work brought about by the industrial revolution. And it is in the factory that the impact of technology on social structure and the consequences of both on the experience of alienation and freedom are revealed most clearly. Hopefully my approach in this book will encourage others to undertake similar investigations of employees in those non-manual occupations and work environments that have become numerically dominant and most characteristic of employment in advanced industrial societies.

Further, my own greater familiarity with industrial work made the choice of factory workers as the subject of this inquiry more feasible. The first debt that I must acknowledge is to the employees of two California factories—one in the electrical, the other in the automotive truck industry—with whom I worked from 1952 to 1956 as an assembler and a laborer. It is to these early colleagues that the book is dedicated. They not only kindled my interest in the human meaning of factory work; they taught me much about human relations in general and gave specific lessons on the character of the working class in an affluent society.

My second debt is to three former teachers, now colleagues, in the Department of Sociology of the University of California, at Berkeley—William Kornhauser, Seymour Martin Lipset, and Philip Selznick. Kornhauser's instruction in political sociology contributed immensely to the process of re-education begun by the workers in the factory. Lipset awakened my interest in the relationship between social structure and behavior through the example of his own work and encouraged the present study with many ideas and continuous moral support. The outcome of this project would have been considerably inferior without Selznick's critical acuteness and his insistence on standards of excellence.

In the early stages of the research I profited from the suggestions of many friends and fellow sociologists, including Robert Alford, Bennett Berger, Amitai Etzioni, Fred Goldner, John Spier, and Arthur Stinchcombe. To Professor Stinchcombe, of Johns Hopkins University, who filled an entire folder of my files with his original and always useful comments, I owe a special debt. For valuable reactions to the previous draft of this manuscript I am grateful to Chris Argyris, Sol Barkin, Ely Chinoy, Edward

Gross, Robert Guest, Harriet Herring, Morris Janowitz, Maurice Kilbridge, and Melvin Seeman.

Weekly seminars on the topic of the freedom of the employee in modern industry, sponsored by the Fund for the Republic's Trade Union Study in 1958 and 1959, provided important intellectual perspective; I am also grateful to the Trade Union Study and its director, Paul Jacobs, for financial aid. A liberal Social Science Research Council fellowship in 1960–61 supported the research in its most critical stages. Professor Philip K. Hastings, of the Roper Public Opinion Research Center, Williamstown, Massachusetts, was most co-operative in permitting me to analyze the materials in their library, particularly the Roper-*Fortune* survey; and William Rogan, of the Institute of Industrial Relations, Berkeley, helped in arranging plant visits.

The need to preserve research anonymity makes it unfortunately impossible to acknowledge directly the great help of the officials and employees of the Bay Chemical Company, whose plant served as the field laboratory for the observations made in chapters 6 and 7. Other workers, white-collar and blue-collar, whose labor contributed to the final product include the statistical tabulators at the Survey Research Center, Berkeley; Charmaine Davis, Laurel Fujishige, and Jane Street, typists; and the typesetters and proofreaders at the Colonial Press, Clinton, Massachusetts. And although I attempted from time to time to farm out major and minor tasks to my wife Rena, without much success, her initial enthusiastic response to the manuscript and her continued belief in the enterprise has been very important to me.

CONTENTS

ILLUSTRATIONS

TABLES

1

THE DIVERSITY
OF INDUSTRIAL ENVIRONMENTS

In recent years there has been an increasing interest in the concept of alienation. In the advanced industrial societies an absolute increase in wealth and
a relatively more equal distribution of income has pushed economic problems
into the background. In the abundance of an affluent society, intellectuals
are now concerned with the cultural and spiritual malaise. Except for the
new nations in the early stages of industrialization, the focus has shifted
from a concern with economic and social justice to a concern with the quality
of the inner life.

A further stimulus to the discussion of alienation is the belated discovery
and publication of the early works of Karl Marx in which this idea is most
fully developed.[1] Curiously enough, it was the very young Marx (writing in
the early 1840's) who developed ideas very much in the mood of other
systems of thought that have such great appeal to the mentality of the 1950's
and 1960's: psychoanalysis, existentialism, and Zen Buddhism. And con-
trariwise, the work of the mature Marx, which stressed economic and political
analysis, has been less compelling to intellectuals of the advanced Western
nations since the end of World War II.[2]

[1] Especially the *Economic and Philosophical Manuscripts of 1844* (Moscow: Foreign Languages
Publishing House, 1961). The major sections have also been translated by T. B. Bottomore
and appear in Erich Fromm, *Marx's Concept of Man* (New York: Frederick Ungar Publishing
Co., 1961), which contains a long discussion of the alienation thesis.

Other recent treatments of the early Marx may be found in Hannah Arendt, *The Human
Condition* (Chicago: University of Chicago Press, 1958); Fritz Pappenheim, *The Alienation of
Modern Man* (New York: Monthly Review Press, 1959); Daniel Bell, *The End of Ideology*
(Glencoe, Ill.: Free Press, 1960), pp. 335–68; Michael Harrington, "Marx Versus Marx," in
New Politics, I (1961), 112–23; and Robert Tucker, *Philosophy and Myth in Karl Marx*
(Cambridge: Cambridge University Press, 1961).

Lewis Feuer has recently argued that the concept of alienation in the early writings of
Marx can best be understood in terms of its *sexual* connotations. See his "What Is Alienation?
The Career of a Concept," *New Politics,* II (1962), 116–34.

[2] Bell points out how the moral, humanist concept of alienation was replaced by the
economic concept of exploitation in Marx's later work (*op. cit.*). This interpretation has aroused
controversy among Marxian scholars. See Harrington, *op. cit.*

As a concept that is concerned with the inner life and involves a moral critique of the mechanization and spiritual isolation of modern society, alienation is particularly suited to the present-day mood. In fact, as Robert Nisbet has noted in his study of the historical forces which brought about modern "mass society," the hypothesis of alienation "has become nearly as prevalent as the doctrine of enlightened self-interest was two generations ago."[3] Not surprisingly, the term, now very fashionable, is bandied about; modern man is said to be alienated from himself, from other human beings, from political life, from work, from his intellectual and artistic productions, from religion, belief, and culture.[4]

The notion that the *industrial worker* is alienated in his work has long been a central idea in the Marxian analysis of modern society. The orthodox Marxist believed that the lack of meaningful self-fulfilment in a work relationship without control over the product and the process of work would push the proletarian toward a revolutionary outlook. Today few students of American society still believe in the revolutionary potential of the working class. Yet the idea that the present-day worker is alienated—basically Marxian in origin—is quite widespread, even among non-Marxist intellectuals and social scientists.

The alienation thesis has become the intellectual's shorthand interpretation of the impact of the industrial revolution on the manual worker. Non-Marxists and even anti-Marxists have followed Marx in the view that factory technology, increasing division of labor, and capitalist property institutions brought about the estrangement of the industrial worker from his work.

With the coming of the industrial revolution, highly mechanized systems replaced craft methods of production in which the artisan had been master of his tools and materials. In the new factories, the intelligence and skill previously expressed by craftsmen were "built into" the machines. Workers were left with routine and monotonous jobs. In the preindustrial period both craftsmen and peasants had considerable control over the rhythms and movements of work. But the machine system now controlled the pace of work and restricted the employee's free movements. Factory technology dominated the workers, whose alienation was expressed in their relative *powerlessness* before the machine system.

Similarly, the increasing division of labor within the factory made jobs simpler, and each employee's area of responsibility diminished. This resulted not only from technological developments as such but also from the organization of work in line with managerial and engineering concepts of effi-

[3] Robert Nisbet, *The Quest for Community* (New York: Oxford University Press, 1953), p. 15.

[4] A collection of readings has appeared recently which attempts to portray the all-inclusiveness of the alienation of modern man. See *Man Alone*, edited with an introduction by Eric and Mary Josephson (New York: Dell Publishing Co., 1962).

ciency. In rationalizing production, the total work process was broken down into minutely subdivided tasks. A job made up of only one or a few operations involved no real responsibility, nor did it require an understanding of the factory's total productive process. Responsibility, problem-solving, and decision-making, removed from the ranks of the employees by the systematic division of labor, became the concern of supervisors, engineers, and other technical staff. The fragmented relation of the individual to his work robbed him of a sense of purpose. Thus the alienation of *meaninglessness* was added to that of powerlessness.

According to Marx, it was the property relations of capitalist society which most basically contributed to the alienation of the employee. The factory belonged to the entrepreneur who had the legal and social power to hire labor, to sell the products of the enterprise on the market, and personally to appropriate its profits. The worker was propertyless and had nothing to sell but his labor power. Because he had no legal or social claim to the product which he and hundreds of other workmen produced, he was alienated from the product of his labor. Because the factory and its machines belonged to the capitalist, the worker was not likely to identify psychologically with the fortunes of the enterprise. And because the profits from his work would not benefit him personally, but only the capitalist, what motivation was there to work with energy and intelligence? From the property institutions of capitalism arose, then, a third aspect of alienation, the employee's sense of *isolation* from the system of organized production and its goals.

Proponents of the alienation thesis argue that capitalist economic institutions and modern factory technology have deprived the employee of a truly human relation to his work. Loss of control means loss of freedom, initiative, and creativity. Specialization is so elaborate that the goals of the enterprise become remote, and the work itself is deprived of any co-operative meaning. The worker does not identify with the productive organization, but feels himself apart, or alienated, from its purposes. When work activity does not permit control, evoke a sense of purpose, or encourage larger identifications, employment becomes simply a means to the end of making a living. For Marx himself this was *self-estrangement*, the very heart of the alienation idea. Productive work, which he believed to be the expression of man's essential human nature, had become simply an instrumental activity subordinated to the most animal needs for food and shelter.

Today, most social scientists would say that alienation is not a consequence of capitalism per se but of employment in the large-scale organizations and impersonal bureaucracies that pervade all industrial societies. Its incorporation into the more general theory of bureaucracy indicates how extremely influential the Marxian hypothesis of the alienated worker has become.

OUTLOOK OF THE PRESENT STUDY

Nevertheless, this hypothesis has inspired fruitless polemics more often than serious scientific research. Too often the question—is the modern employee alienated or not?—joins the issue in simplistic fashion, and understanding is obscured in the waving of political banners. On the one side, there are those who uncritically accept Marxian perspectives and fortify their position with a minimum of empirical materials, usually taken from the most oppressive work situations. On the other side are the proponents of what Harvey Swados has called "the myth of the happy worker." [5] They point to the lack of overt discontent and militant revolutionary activity among American workers. Or they cite the impressive evidence from hundreds of job-attitude surveys that culminate in the generalization that the vast majority of employees, including factory workers, report at least moderate satisfaction with their jobs and work situations.[6] Important as these findings are, their "face-value" acceptance implies a radical empiricism that denies itself the theoretical insights of the Marxian perspective.

The present study rejects the two extreme positions but accepts the Marxian premise that there are powerful alienating tendencies in modern factory technology and industrial organization. Recasting a politically loaded controversy into a manageable scientific question, the problem becomes to determine under what conditions these tendencies are intensified in modern industry, what situations give rise to different forms of alienation, and what consequences develop for workers and for productive systems. Rejecting an a priori extreme position that workers either are or are not alienated, one expects to find work situations where alienation is absent, as well as those where it is present. In this investigation, then, the alienation concept is taken seriously; an attempt is made to develop its theoretical assumptions and to test them through the consideration of empirical evidence.

Another basic assumption of the present approach is the existence of critically different types of work environments within modern industry. These diverse industrial environments result in large variations in the form and the intensity of alienation. Because of Marx's historical scope and polemical purpose, he stressed the homogeneity of the capitalist mode of production. Since his goal was to analyze how its distinctive property relations and technological base differed from feudal and socialist societies and affected societal arrangements and workers' experiences he was not primarily in-

---

[5] Harvey Swados, "The Myth of the Happy Worker," *Nation,* CLXXXV (August 17, 1957), 65–69.

[6] For a discussion of this research, see Robert Blauner, "Work Satisfaction and Industrial Trends in Modern Society," in Walter Galenson and Seymour Martin Lipset eds., *Labor and Trade Unionism* (New York: John Wiley & Sons, 1960), pp. 339–60.

terested in the diversity of relations between employees and sociotechnical systems within capitalist industry.

Yet, within modern industry a vast process of "structural differentiation" has taken place. Although some common features link all modern employment situations, more striking are the differences between the work settings of the coal miner, the truck driver, the television repairman, and the factory operative. Even within the manufacturing sector (a declining component of the total economy in contrast to the growing and highly differentiated service industries), modern factories vary considerably in technology, in division of labor, in economic structure, and in organizational character. These differences produce sociotechnical systems in which the objective conditions and the inner life of employees are strikingly variant. In some industrial environments the alienating tendencies that Marx emphasized are present to a high degree. In others they are relatively undeveloped or have been countered by new technical, economic, and social forces. As a result, the industrial system distributes alienation unevenly among its blue-collar labor force, just as our economic system distributes income unevenly.

Curiously enough, that work environment with the most alienating consequences, the automobile assembly line, has been the favorite research laboratory for the sociologist of the manual worker. There have been at least seven book-length studies on automobile workers by sociologists, more than for any other industrial group in the United States. Possibly because the assembly line calls up such dramatic images, social commentators have been more than likely to use the example of the automobile worker when considering the situation of the American factory worker.[7] If the most alienated workers are viewed as typical workers, it is no wonder that there is a persistent tendency to view manual workers in general as alienated.[8] Yet assembly-line workers in all industries probably constitute no more than 5 per cent of the entire labor force. And comparisons of the job attitudes of automobile workers with factory employees in other industries suggest that their level of alienation is not typical.

In a study of 3,000 factory workers in sixteen different industries, the job attitudes of automobile workers reveal greater alienation than those in any other industry. Among the lowest skilled male workers, 61 per cent of the automobile workers felt their jobs were monotonous all or most of the time, in contrast to 38 per cent of the unskilled men in the entire sample. Compared to factory workers in general, automobile workers were more

---

[7] At present the even more dramatic image of the automated factory is in the air, and we can expect that popular writers will more and more use this example. A similar result, already discernible, is to exaggerate the numerical incidence of automated work environments.

[8] Gladys L. Palmer is one of the few social scientists who has criticized the tendency to generalize from case studies of the automobile worker. See her "Attitudes toward Work in an Industrial Community," *American Journal of Sociology*, LXIII (1957), 17–26.

likely to feel that their jobs made them work too fast, that they were too simple for their best abilities, that they would not lead to any higher positions within the company. Whereas 33 per cent of the automobile workers complained of excessive job pressures, only 6 per cent of oil refining workers, employed in a very different technological setting—automated continuous-process plants—had to work too fast. Less than half of the auto workers felt they could try out their own ideas on the job, yet more than three-fourths of the printers, working in a craft industry, had the possibility for personal initiative. Sixty-two per cent of the automobile employees felt their company was as good or the best place to work in the industry; in contrast, 92 per cent of the chemical workers felt this identification with their employer.[9]

The present investigation is an attempt to demonstrate and to explain the uneven distribution of alienation among factory workers in American industry. Viewing an industry as a complex of firms devoted to the manufacture of the same or similar products, I attempt to show that the industry a man works in is *fateful,* because the conditions of work and existence in various industrial environments are quite different. Through a comparison of four factory industries—printing, textiles, automobiles, and chemicals—I shall illustrate the far-reaching diversity of American industrial life, as well as analyze the technological, economic, and social sources of alienation.

TECHNOLOGY AND INDUSTRIAL DIVERSITY

The most important single factor that gives an industry a distinctive character is its *technology.* Technology refers to the complex of physical objects and technical operations (both manual and machine) regularly employed in turning out the goods and services produced by an industry. Technology signifies primarily the machine system, the level and type of mechanization, but it includes also the technical "know-how" and mechanical skills involved in production. Three main factors determine the kind of technology utilized in the manufacturing operations of a particular industry: the over-all state of the industrial arts, that is, the existing level and variety of mechanical and scientific processes; the economic and engineering resources of individual firms; and most important, the nature of the product manufactured. An industry's products may be relatively unique and individuated as are the homes, buildings, and roads constructed by the building industry, or they may be as standardized as the products of the television and appliance industries. Unique-product manufacturing limits the use of complex machine processes so that many of the basic operations must be

---

[9] These data come from a study conducted by Elmo Roper for *Fortune* magazine that is described in more detail later in this chapter (see pp. 11–12 and nn. 12, 13, below). In the body of the present volume there is a more thorough presentation and analysis of the findings of the Roper research.

carried out manually. A standardized product makes possible a more mechanized mass-production technology, in one of its various forms.

The structural character of the product further conditions the type of technology utilized. If a standardized product is fluid or homogeneous in texture, it more readily lends itself to automated continuous-process techniques. If the product is a solid, is heterogeneous in texture, and made up of a number of discrete parts, some form of assembly production is necessary and continuous-process technology is not possible. Assuming then the norm of technological and economic rationality, the most efficient method of producing finished motor vehicles involves a technology—the conveyer-belt assembly line—very different from the most efficient means of producing gasoline—the continuous-process operation of an oil refinery. Similarly, the nature of cloth, compared to that of steel or newspapers, means that textile mills will have a technology far different from steel mills or print shops.

Of course, no industry has a completely homogeneous technology. Even within the same factory there may be different technological processes that carry out various stages of production.[10] Yet most individual industries have their characteristic forms of production. The four compared in this study have distinctive technological arrangements. Since relatively unique products are manufactured in printing, there is little standardization of production. The level of mechanization is low. Much work is done by hand rather than by machines. These are the characteristics of a *craft* technology. The textile industry is more highly mechanized and its work processes are more standardized. Since the bulk of the productive process is carried out by workers who "mind" machines, it may be called a *machine-tending* technology. The automobile industry is dominated by an *assembly-line* technology and highly rationalized work organization. The conveyer belt carries cars in the process of completion past lines of "semiskilled" operatives, each of whom makes his contribution to the assembly of a particular part on the body or chassis. The industrial chemical industry is based on the most advanced kind of technology, *continuous-process* production, a form of automation. Since all production processes are carried out automatically in a series of chemical reactors through which the product flows continuously, the relatively few blue-collar workers in this industry either monitor instruments on panel boards or repair the automatic machinery when necessary.

Because technical and scientific innovations in manufacturing accumulate, there is a tendency for technology to become progressively more developed. Historically, manufacturing technologies have evinced higher and higher levels of mechanization. Yet this development has not taken place evenly in all industries, and technical systems with different levels of mechanization

---

[10] Alain Touraine's study of the Renault automobile plant in the Paris region focuses on the three stages of technology coexisting within this one factory. Alain Touraine, *L'évolution du travail ouvrier aux usines Renault* (Paris: Centre National de la Recherche Scientifique, 1955).

continue to operate side by side today. The industries compared in this book represent four different types of extant factory technology and also illustrate stages in the long-run trend toward increased mechanization. The craft technology in printing and the continuous-process technology in industrial chemicals typify the two extreme historical poles. The machine-tending and assembly-line technologies in textiles and automobile manufacturing are two intermediate forms of mechanized production.[11]

Variations in technology are of critical interest to students of the human meaning of work because technology, more than any other factor, determines the nature of the job tasks performed by blue-collar employees and has an important effect on a number of aspects of alienation. It is primarily the technological setting that influences the worker's powerlessness, limiting or expanding the amount of freedom and control he exercises in his immediate work environment. Technological factors are paramount also in their impact on self-estrangement, since the machine system largely decides whether the worker can become directly engrossed in the activity of work or whether detachment and monotony more commonly result. Since technological considerations often determine the size of an industrial plant, they markedly influence the social atmosphere and degree of cohesion among the work force. Technology also structures the existence and form of work groups, in this way influencing cohesion. Even the nature of discipline and supervision to some extent depends on technological factors. And technology largely determines the occupational structure and skill distribution within an enterprise, the basic factors in advancement opportunities, and normative integration.[12]

[11] The four technological types do not represent inevitable stages in a predetermined, unilinear course of industrial evolution. A particular industry or factory does not begin with craft production, introduce machines, then use assembly lines, and finally develop a fully automated continuous-process technology. On the contrary, there is a strong tendency for many companies and industries to maintain roughly the same kind of technology that characterized their "heyday" and that is why I speak of the uneven development of mechanization. The fact that industries do not "evolve" in any set, predetermined fashion does not negate the historical relevance of these industrial types. There is some tendency for some industries to develop in this manner, achieving at least one further developmental stage. Glass-making, which was once a craft, has become largely a mass-production industry, and the former craft industry of shoe manufacturing has developed both machine and assembly-line characteristics, although the former predominate. Cases of reverse development are very rare: characteristically, machine industries do not become craft industries; assembly-line technologies do not reinstitute craft or machine production; and continuous-process production does not give way to less mechanized forms, but continually proceeds in the direction of more automation. The result is a general tendency of the entire industrial structure to become more advanced in mechanization, even though no unilinear processes of technological evolution take place. (Maurice Kilbridge has called my attention to one exception. When automobile companies began using a wide variety of automobile frames rather than one standardized frame, the A. O. Smith Company was forced to revert from automated to hand manufacture because automation was no longer economically feasible.)

[12] The relation between technology, work organization, and workers' behavior has been a central interest of industrial sociology. Most important have been the research of William

DIVISION OF LABOR, SOCIAL ORGANIZATION, AND ECONOMIC STRUCTURE

Industries differ not only in technology but also in their characteristic methods of *division of labor*. This refers to the systematic manner in which the technical operations of men and machines are assigned to individual employees as work tasks—a bundle of work tasks constituting a "job." Whereas technology sets limits on the organization of work, it does not fully determine it, since a number of different organizations of the work process may be possible in the same technological system. On the whole, industrial development has brought about an increasingly elaborate division of labor within the factory. The four industries compared in this study illustrate diverse forms of the division of labor. These variations are important for alienation because they directly affect the amount of meaning and purpose manual workers experience in their jobs.

A third factor by which industries may be distinguished is *social organization*. Along with the trends toward an increasingly mechanized technology and more subdivided work organization, there has been an historic shift from traditional to bureaucratic principles of industrial social organization. This is reflected by the fact that a system of general standards and specific rules governing the situation of workers in economic organizations (including their relations with employers) has matured in advanced industrial societies, and the norm of universal or impartial application of these rules has become increasingly institutionalized.

Just as technological development has taken place unevenly, long-run changes in industrial social structure have also been uneven, so that "traditional" industries with old organizational forms coexist with the advanced "bureaucratic" industries that are most characteristic of the present era. In traditional industries, the norms of the employment relationship depend on custom or past practices and on special personal loyalties between workers and employers. In bureaucratic industries, the rules of the enterprise are regularly subjected to more or less systematic rationalization, and formal rules and procedures tend to replace personal considerations.[13]

Foote Whyte and Charles R. Walker and their students in the United States, the writings and research of Georges Friedmann and his students in France, and the work of the British industrial sociologists at the University of Liverpool. An excellent compendium of representative research and theory on the relation between technology and work organization is Charles R. Walker's recent *Modern Technology and Civilization* (New York: McGraw-Hill Book Co., 1962).

[13] Since old industries tend to maintain the structure and institutions associated with their period of origin, even when these forms may not be appropriate to modern conditions, the oldest industries are most likely to be traditional in their organizational character. Bureaucratic industries tend to be young, and their social institutions and characteristics therefore reflect modern conditions of production and economic organization. Traditional industries are usually made up of many small firms that are quite competitive, and many companies are marginal economically. Bureaucratic industries are typically dominated by a few large firms, and since

Both printing and textiles are traditional industries in the sense that the systematic rationalization of administration is prevented by the strength of past practices and customary expectations. There is a difference, however, in the basis of their traditionalism. In printing and other craft industries, the traditions of craft groups form the core of the normative system. Employers and their organizations are relatively uninfluential. In the southern textile industry, normative integration is based on the traditional institutions of the local "folk" community and the paternalistic authority of management. Automobile manufacturing and heavy chemicals are both bureaucratic industries in that their norms and practices are systematically organized and codified. These industries illustrate different types of bureaucratic social organization; one, in chemicals, based on a strong consensus and sense of industrial community; the other, in automobiles, based on conflict and a relative lack of community.

Finally, industries differ also in their *economic structure*. Such economic factors as competition in product markets, concentration, profit margins of firms, typical cost structures, growth rates, and trends in demand affect the alienation levels of manual workers, though usually in an indirect fashion. When an industry is economically profitable and progressive, workers are less likely to be subjected to intense pressure, more likely to be free from fears of unemployment and to have opportunities to advance. Economic prosperity therefore furthers a social climate in which the worker becomes more integrated in the company.

Technology, division of labor, social organization, and economic structure vary from industry to industry; and these four variables are the key underlying elements in comparative industrial analysis. Their unique constellation

---

both corporate size and youth are economic advantages, these modern industries are more likely to be financially prosperous and growing.

Since bureaucratization is little developed, companies in traditional industries rarely practice modern personnel methods and typically do not have the full complement of specialized departments, such as public relations, training, and industrial relations, common in bureaucratic industries. In the highly bureaucratized industries, the number of clerical and administrative employees tends to surpass the number of production workers, while in traditional industries that handle less paper work and keep fewer records, the proportion of white-collar employees in the labor force is quite small. The older industries carry on little scientific or industrial research and hire few professionals, whereas the newer industries tend to be research-oriented, innovating, and dynamic, and employ many professionals and scientists. Traditional and bureaucratic industries also differ in the character of their managerial elites. In traditional industries, executives tend to be "entrepreneurial," self-made men, with little education or tend to be related by kinship ties to officers or founders of the firm; in modern industries, the typical executive is a college-trained "organizational man." The most significant consequence of these differences is in over-all outlook; traditional industries are generally conservative, whereas bureaucratic industries have modern perspectives and are receptive to change. A number of important differences between these types and their consequences have been developed in two papers by Arthur L. Stinchcombe, "Bureaucratic and Craft Administration of Production: A Comparative Study," *Administrative Science Quarterly*, IV (1959), 168–87, and "The Sociology of Organization and the Theory of the Firm," *Pacific Sociological Review*, III (1960), 75–82.

in a specific case imparts to an individual industry its distinctive character and results in a work environment that is somewhat special in its impact on the blue-collar labor force.[14] But despite my emphasis on these four impersonal factors, this study does not follow a totally deterministic approach. In certain situations, the conscious organizational policies of industrial management may be critical in their effects on employee alienation. And the character of the labor force in particular industries and the personalities of individual employees influence their subjective and behavioral responses to objectively alienating conditions.

DATA AND METHODS

The present study brings together empirical evidence from a variety of sources. My most important source of comparative quantitative data on the alienation process in the four industries is a job-attitude survey carried out by Elmo Roper for *Fortune* magazine in 1947. This was a representative sample of 3,000 blue-collar factory workers in sixteen different factory industries. It is the only major study of workers I have seen that divides the sample according to specific industries, as compared to such general industrial categories as manufacturing, mining, construction, and transportation. The sample included 118 printing workers, 419 textile workers, 180 automobile workers, and 78 chemical workers. "Within the universe defined, the sample was stratified so as to contain the proper distribution of respondents by sex, geographic area, race, and age according to the Census of 1940." [15] Although not a random probability sample, it was, according to Elmo Roper, "a pretty carefully controlled quota sample," and therefore representative of a population much larger than the 3,000 workers interviewed.[16]

[14] Although both theory and empirical research in the sociology of work have generally neglected the importance of industrial variations, a few writers have been sensitive to this problem. In his insightful study, *The British Worker* ([Harmondsworth, England: Penguin Books, 1952], p. 42), Ferdynand Zweig devotes an entire chapter to the proposition that "every industry breeds its own type of men." A classic study based on the industrial variable is Clark Kerr and Abraham Siegel, "The Interindustry Propensity To Strike—an International Comparison," in Arthur Kornhauser, Robert Dubin, and Arthur Ross (eds.), *Industrial Conflict* (New York: McGraw-Hill Book Co., 1954), 189–212. Of all the empirical research in American industrial sociology, Charles R. Walker's studies of steel and automotive plants have probably contributed most to the understanding of industrial variation. See Charles R. Walker, *Steeltown* (New York: Harper & Bros., 1950) and Charles R. Walker and Robert Guest, *Man on the Assembly Line* (Cambridge, Mass.: Harvard University Press, 1952). The political sociological writings of Seymour Martin Lipset and Daniel Bell also show a sensitivity to the effect of industrial environment on the political and trade union behavior of workers. See Lipset's "The Political Process in Trade Unions," in Seymour Martin Lipset, *Political Man* (Garden City, N.Y.: Doubleday & Co., 1960), pp. 361–63 and Daniel Bell, *op. cit.*, especially pp. 159–61.

[15] From file report of Elmo Roper and Associates, *Fortune* survey #58, January, 1947, p. 1.

[16] Elmo Roper, personal correspondence, January 9, 1959. A copy of the Roper questionnaire is included in Appendix C. The over-all findings of the Roper survey were published in the May and June, 1947, issues of *Fortune* magazine under the headings: "The American Factory Worker. What's good about his job . . . What's bad about it? What makes him satisfied

There are difficulties in the secondary analysis of the Roper survey which require that it be utilized with caution. First, it is an old survey, conducted in 1947, and there is the problem of the extent to which conditions in various industries have changed since that date. Second, since I did not gather the data myself, I do not have full information on the survey. For example, I cannot know exactly what kind of chemical plants the 78 chemical employees worked in. Third, the other limitations of secondary analysis, familiar to the survey-oriented social scientist, exist. Although it was an extraordinarily valuable job-attitude questionnaire, I am limited to the questions asked, and it is therefore not possible to determine certain important data. In secondary analysis one does not always know what a particular question really means to the respondent.

Although the Roper survey provides the chief statistical attitude data, I have relied on industrial case studies and published accounts for additional descriptive and analytic material. Because of the lack of research on continuous-process workers,[17] I conducted a field study in a chemical plant in the California bay area, during the winter of 1961. The plant, which had 400 blue-collar and 250 white-collar employees, is a branch of a large national industrial company. It produces heavy industrial organic and inorganic chemicals and is therefore typical of the most advanced section of the industry, although the bay area plant is not as new and as highly automated as some chemical factories. I interviewed 21 blue-collar workers in this plant, which shall be referred to as the Bay Chemical Company. The respondents were chosen at random among employees in the three major divisions—operations, maintenance, and distribution—who had worked in other industries. The interviews lasted from one hour to an hour and a half and took place on company property, with the co-operation of the local union. In addition to formal interviews in 1961, I spent several days and nights in

with his company? What makes him happy in his type of job?" "The Fortune Survey," *Fortune,* May, 1947, pp. 5–6, 10, 12; June, 1947, pp. 5–6, 10. The reports of the survey in *Fortune* emphasized the general results, and very little statistical analysis was published. A few cross-tabulations, by union affiliation, sex, education, and race were reported; and an index of morale factors was constructed and analyzed. However, the *Fortune* articles contain no discussion of industrial differences in job attitudes. My statistical analysis of this study revealed that the variations in job conditions and attitudes among workers in different industries were strikingly larger than those accounted for by other variables; only the levels of training (skill) differences were of an equal magnitude.

[17] William Foote Whyte's suggestive paper on an aviation gasoline plant, "Engineers and Workers—a Case Study" (*Human Organization,* XIV [1956], 3–12), is the only analysis of the work situation in the oil or chemical industry available. Floyd Mann and L. R. Hoffman's *Automation and the Worker* (New York: Henry Holt & Co, 1960) deals with a related work environment, an electrical power plant, and is extremely useful. Other excellent sociological analyses of automated plants are Charles R. Walker, *Toward the Automatic Factory* (New Haven: Yale University Press, 1959), and William Faunce, "Automation in the Automobile Industry: Some Consequences for In-Plant Social Structure," *American Sociological Review,* XXIII (1958), 401–7, and "Automation and the Automobile Worker," *Social Problems,* VI (1958), 68–78.

various departments of the plant in the summer of 1962, observing the work process and discussing the operators' work situations.

Since I gathered relatively few interviews, it was especially valuable to supplement my findings on the Bay Chemical Company with those derived in a questionnaire survey conducted by Professor Louis Davis of the Department of Industrial Engineering of the University of California. Davis interviewed approximately 230 blue-collar workers in the same plant on a wide variety of job-attitude questions in 1959 in order to analyze the effects of a program of job redesign.[18] He has generously allowed me to make my own tabulations and analyses from his data.

Some limitations of this study should be emphasized. There was no over-all research design applied to the four industries which would have assured precisely equivalent materials for each case. The most directly comparable data come from the Roper interindustry survey, an extremely old study. When generalizations are made from case studies of plants in particular industries, it is not always certain how representative the firms are of the entire industry. For the automobile industry, I have relied heavily on Walker and Guest's account of the "X" plant,[19] a factory whose particularly low morale may overstate the alienation typical among automobile workers. The literature on textile manufacturing reveals considerable disagreement on workers' attitudes, probably because of the diversity of conditions within the industry.[20] In considering continuous-process production, I have used principally my own case study of the Bay chemical plant. Quite possibly the conditions in this highly integrated branch plant of a progressive company are more positive than in the chemical industry as a whole.

The four industries analyzed are each important, and their contrasting characteristics suggest the diversity of factory work environments. The four do not, however, comprise an exhaustive typology of factory industries. One cannot predict the level of alienation in another industry by direct analogy with one of my four cases. Although there are other industries that share many of the technological and economic characteristics of those analyzed in this study, many important factory industries have their own distinctive attributes. The critically important iron and steel industry, for example, defies classification into craft, machine-tending, assembly-line, or continuous-process technology. It has features of each type and its own special characteristics; the same can be said of many other factory industries. Since the four industries compared employ less than three million factory workers, the study does not tell us the over-all level of alienation in the industrial population.

[18] For an account of this study see Louis E. Davis and Richard Werling, "Job Design Factors," *Occupational Psychology*, XXXIV, No. 2 (1960), 109–32.

[19] Charles R. Walker and Robert Guest, *op. cit.*

[20] I visited a number of cotton mills in North Carolina in 1962 in an attempt to supplement the observations of students of the industry.

Because of these limitations, many of the generalizations that emerge from this research are only suggestive rather than conclusive. Yet I believe the evidence presented on industrial variations in work attitudes is more comprehensive than what has been previously available. The complete tables in Appendix B that provide job-attitude data for sixteen industries should be especially useful. And I hope that the method employed in this beginning investigation—the explanation of the conditions and consequences of alienation through an analytical comparison of industrial environments—will provide a starting point for further explorations.

In the next chapter, I look more closely at the meaning of alienation in industrial work and distinguish the four dimensions of the concept that shall be considered throughout the study. The following chapters are devoted to case studies of each of the four factory industries. Chapter 3 describes workers in the printing industry, the work environment closest to the non-alienated milieu of the preindustrial craftsman. Chapter 4 analyzes textile workers in a machine-tending industry where strong tendencies toward alienation stemming from technology and work organization coexist in the integrative milieux of small, traditional communities. The classic case of the automobile assembly-line industry in which technological, economic, and social factors combine to produce the most alienating work environment is considered in chapter 5. Chapters 6 and 7 treat the automated chemical industry, whose unique form of production, favorable economic environment, and new social structural features, reverse many of the alienating tendencies of modern factory technology and industrial organization. In the last chapter a synthesis of the four case studies is attempted through the placement of the industrial types in historical perspective. Here I consider how long-range developments in technology, division of labor, economic structure, and social organization have changed the relations between the factory worker and his work, with special emphasis on the implications of automation. The causal factors affecting the alienation process are isolated more clearly, and a number of policy measures that might infuse industrial work environments with more human dignity are discussed.

2

ALIENATION
AND MODERN INDUSTRY

No simple definition of alienation can do justice to the many intellectual traditions which have engaged this concept as a central explanatory idea. One basis of confusion is the fact that the idea of alienation has incorporated philosophical, psychological, sociological, and political orientations. In the literature on the theory of alienation, one finds statements of the desired state of human experience, assertions about the actual quality of personal experience, propositions which link attitudes and experience to social situations and social structures, and programs for the amelioration of the human condition. My own perspective in this investigation is chiefly sociological, or perhaps social-psychological, in that alienation is viewed as a quality of personal experience which results from specific kinds of social arrangements.[1]

This study also employs a multidimensional, rather than a unitary, conception of alienation. Alienation is a general syndrome made up of a number of different objective conditions and subjective feeling-states which emerge from certain relationships between workers and the sociotechnical settings of employment. Alienation exists when workers are unable to control their immediate work processes, to develop a sense of purpose and function which connects their jobs to the over-all organization of production, to belong to integrated industrial communities, and when they fail to become involved in the activity of work as a mode of personal self-expression. In modern industrial employment, control, purpose, social integration, and self-involvement are all problematic. In this chapter we discuss how various aspects of the technology, work organization, and social structure of modern industry

[1] Although my main approach is not philosophical, it will become clear that the problems which I analyze attain their relevancy from a personal value system. Along with Marx, Erich Fromm (*The Sane Society* [New York: Rinehart & Co., 1955]), and Chris Argyris (*Personality and Organization* [New York: Harper & Bros., 1957]), I assume that work which permits autonomy, responsibility, social connection, and self-actualization further the dignity of the human individual, whereas work without these characteristics limits the development of personal potential and is therefore to be negatively valued.

further the four types of alienation which correspond to these non-alienated states: powerlessness, meaninglessness, isolation, and self-estrangement.[2]

POWERLESSNESS: MODES OF FREEDOM
AND CONTROL IN INDUSTRY

A person is powerless when he is an object controlled and manipulated by other persons or by an impersonal system (such as technology), and when he cannot assert himself as a subject to change or modify this domination. Like an object, the powerless person reacts rather than acts. He is directed or dominated, rather than self-directing. The non-alienated pole of the powerlessness dimension is freedom and control. Freedom is the state which allows the person to remove himself from those dominating situations that make him simply a reacting object. Freedom may therefore involve the possibility of movement in a physical or social sense, the ability to walk away from a coercive machine process, or the opportunity of quitting a job because of the existence of alternative employment. Control is more positive than freedom, suggesting the assertion of the self-directing subject over such potentially dominating forces as employers or machine systems.

The degree of powerlessness a student imputes to manual workers in industry today depends not only on his sociological and political perspective but also on the aspects of freedom and control he selects as the most important. There are at least four modes of industrial powerlessness which have preoccupied writers on "the social question." These are (1) the separation from ownership of the means of production and the finished products, (2) the inability to influence general managerial policies, (3) the lack of control over the conditions of employment, and (4) the lack of control over the immediate work process. It is my contention that control over the condi-

---

[2] For identifying these dimensions of alienation I am indebted to a recent article by Melvin Seeman, "On the Meaning of Alienation," *American Sociological Review*, XXIV (1959), 783–91. The author helps clarify this confused area by distinguishing five different ways in which the alienation concept has been utilized in sociological theory and social thought. He attempts to restate the concepts of powerlessness, meaninglessness, normlessness, isolation, and self-estrangement in terms of a modern vocabulary of expectations and rewards. I have made a rather free adaptation of his discussion, redefining a number of his categories so that they better fit the industrial situation, an application Seeman does not himself make. I have not treated normlessness as a separate dimension but consider some of its implications in my discussion of isolation.

In the earliest discussion of alienated labor, Karl Marx also took a multidimensional approach and distinguished economic, psychological, sociological, and philosophical aspects of alienation. In the *Economic and Philosophical Manuscripts of 1844* (Moscow: Foreign Languages Publishing House, n.d.), the youthful Marx analyzed how the institutions of capitalism, private property, market economy, and money alienated the worker from the product of his work, in the process or activity of· work, from other human beings and from his own human nature.

Again, the connection between some of Marx's dimensions and those employed in the present chapter is clear.

tions of employment and control over the immediate work process are most salient for manual workers, who are most likely to value control over those matters which affect their immediate jobs and work tasks and least likely to be concerned with the more general and abstract aspects of powerlessness.

The very nature of employment in a large-scale organization means that workers have forfeited their claims on the finished product and that they do not own the factory, machines, or often their own tools. Unlike the absence of control over the immediate work process, "ownership powerlessness" is a constant in modern industry, and employees, therefore, normally do not develop expectations for influence in this area. Today the average worker no more desires to own his machines than modern soldiers their howitzers or government clerks their file cabinets.[3] Automobile and chemical workers, by and large, do not feel deprived because they cannot take home the Corvairs or sulfuric acid they produce.

Orthodox Marxism saw the separation from the means of production as the central fact of capitalism, the inevitable consequence of which would be the worker's general alienation from society. This has not happened: manual workers have required only steady jobs, reasonable wages, and employee benefits to put down at least moderate stakes in society and industry. Yet, despite the lack of any conscious desire for control in this area, we cannot know for certain whether or not the worker's alienation from ownership unconsciously colors the whole quality of his experience in the factory, as Erich Fromm, for one, argues.[4] The appeal of small-business ownership, stronger among manual than white-collar employees, suggests that there may be many workers like the automobile worker Ely Chinoy quotes, for whom employment itself is inherently alienating:

The main thing is to be independent and give your own orders and not have to take them from anybody else. That's the reason the fellows in the shop all want to start their own business. Then the profits are all for yourself. When you're in the shop, there's nothing for yourself in it. So you just do what you have to do in order to get along. A fellow would rather do it for himself. If you expend the energy, it's for your benefit then.[5]

Like the separation from ownership, another facet of industrial powerlessness, the lack of control over decision-making, is also common to the modern employment relationship. Large-scale organizations are hierarchical authority

[3] It was Max Weber in his classic analysis of bureaucracy who expanded Marx's concept of the industrial worker's separation from the means of production to all modern large-scale organizations. Civil servants are separated from the means of administration; soldiers from the means of violence; and scientists from the means of inquiry. Hans Gerth and C. W. Mills, *From Max Weber: Essays in Sociology* (New York: Oxford University Press, 1946), p. 50.

[4] Fromm, *op. cit.*

[5] Ely Chinoy, *Automobile Workers and the American Dream* (New York: Doubleday & Co., 1955), pp. xvi–xvii.

structures with power concentrated at the top, and manual workers have little opportunity to control the major decisions of the enterprise. And unlike the worker quoted above, most employees do not seem to resent this aspect of powerlessness, which they also tend to accept as a "given" of industry. The average worker does not want the responsibility for such decisions as what, for whom, and how much to produce; how to design the product; what machinery to buy; how to distribute jobs; or how to organize the flow of work. It is only when these decisions directly affect his immediate job and work load that he expects his labor organization to influence policy in his behalf—as the recent labor-management conflicts over work rules indicate.

A number of industrial reform movements have attempted to counteract this aspect of powerlessness. Early in the twentieth century, the classical advocates of workers' control—the socialist followers of Rosa Luxembourg in Germany, the American IWW, the French syndicalists, and the British shop-stewards' movements—raised the slogan of industrial democracy. But as labor reform movements became more sophisticated, they realized that large-scale production organizations cannot be governed directly and en masse. The sponsors of direct democracy gave way to the advocates of representative democracy and participation in management. The most important recent examples of this trend are "joint consultation" in England, codetermination in Germany, and the workers' councils of eastern Europe.[6] Yet the experience of these representative systems suggests that it is only the delegate or the participator, not the average worker, who actually feels he is influencing major decisions. Even those progressive firms which have encouraged mass participation in shop councils find that the average employee confines his interest to his own job and work group and leaves participation in the over-all plan to a select few.[7]

A third aspect of industrial powerlessness, the lack of control over conditions of employment, is considerably more meaningful to American workers. Selig Perlman's characterization of the American working class as more "job conscious" than "class conscious" suggests that control of the opportunity for work itself within the oligarchic industrial system has been historically more relevant than the two more "revolutionary" aspects of control discussed above.[8]

Under early capitalism, the worker could be hired and fired at will by

[6] Hugh Clegg, *A New Approach to Industrial Democracy* (Oxford: Basil Blackwell, 1960), p. 5.

[7] E. Jaques, *The Changing Culture of the Factory* (London: Tavistock Publications, 1951), and F. Blum, *Toward a Democratic Work Process* (New York: Harper & Bros., 1953). A most notable exception to this generalization seems to be the Scanlon plan which encourages workers to make suggestions for increasing efficiency, cutting costs, and raising profits through a system of company-wide meetings and a group bonus plan. Probably best suited for small companies, it has been remarkably successful in a number of cases. See, for example, Frederick Lesieur (ed.), *The Scanlon Plan* (New York: John Wiley & Sons, 1958).

[8] S. Perlman, *A Theory of the Labor Movement* (New York: August M. Kelley, 1949).

impersonal forces of the market and personal whims of the employer. As a commodity subject to supply and demand factors, his employment depended on the extent of his skills and the phase of the business cycle. This is no longer the case. The most important innovations sponsored by American labor unions have been aimed at reducing the historic inequality of power in the contractual situation of employment. Collective bargaining, the contract, grievance procedures, arbitration, seniority provisions, hiring halls, and now "guaranteed annual wages" have all been partially successful attempts to increase the control of employees over their conditions of employment.

In addition, a number of economic changes have greatly reduced the worker's powerlessness in this area. The severity of periodic economic crises has diminished as industry and government have imposed major checks on the anarchy of a free competitive system. Technological requirements have increased the need for more skilled and responsible workers. Thus, the large corporation has recognized the advantage of a more permanent work force to its pursuit of economic stability and higher productivity.

As a result of these changes in economic life, technology, corporation policy, and union power, the worker's control over his employment is increasing in what Ralf Dahrendorf calls "post-capitalist society." The *worker*, who in classical capitalism was considered virtually a commodity or a cost of production and treated as a *thing*, is giving way to the *employee*, a permanent worker who is viewed much more as a *human being*. Many employees have job security based on seniority provisions or a *de facto* "common law" right to their jobs. The employment relationship no longer reflects merely the balance of power; it is more and more determined by a system of institutional justice.[9]

Economic security is not distributed equally in the industrial structure, for the trends outlined above have not developed evenly. Some firms, industries, and specific occupations are extremely unstable in employment, whereas others provide virtual tenure in jobs. Empirical studies constantly emphasize the important part which regularity of employment plays in workers' evaluations of particular jobs and companies.[10] As an area of significant concern for manual workers, control over employment conditions will be analyzed in the four industrial comparisons, with the major emphasis on variations in control over the immediate work process.

Both sociologists and socialists, in their emphasis on the assembly-line work situation, have provided much data on the powerlessness of the worker in the

[9] This guiding idea informs the work of Philip Selznick, *From Power to Justice in Industry* (forthcoming). See also Howard Vollmer, *Employee Rights and the Employment Relationship* (Berkeley: University of California Press, 1960).

[10] Combining data from sixteen studies of employee attitudes, Herzberg and his collaborators found that security was the most important factor of ten job factors. See F. Herzberg, *et al.*, *Job Attitudes: Review of Research and Opinion* (Pittsburgh: Psychological Service of Pittsburgh, 1957), p. 44.

face of a dominating technological system. Despite the fact that the assembly line is not the representative work milieu, these scholars have rightly emphasized the central importance of the worker's relation to technology as a major condition of alienation. For when a worker is dominated and controlled by the machine system in the very process of his work, he, in effect, becomes reduced to a mechanical device. Reacting to the rhythms of technology rather than acting in some independent or autonomous manner, he approaches most completely the condition of *thingness,* the essence of alienation.

Studies of the assembly line show that workers greatly resent the dominance of technology and constantly try to devise ways to gain some measure of control over the machine system. The resentment against this kind of powerlessness may reflect an awareness of its special degrading and humiliating features, as well as the knowledge that there are many alternative kinds of work situations in factory employment.[11]

The variations in control over the immediate activity of work are a principal focus of the present study. We shall analyze each of the four factory work settings in terms of its characteristic tendency to impose restrictions and to permit freedom of action in a number of specific areas directly related to the job. Whether a worker controls his sociotechnical environment depends on his freedom of movement, freedom to make choices, and freedom from oppressive constraints. It is necessary to specify this final aspect of industrial powerlessness more precisely by distinguishing those individual freedoms which are the components or elements of control over the immediate activity of work. Of these, the most important is control over the *pace* of work.

A basic distinction can be made between those jobs which are machine-

---

[11] The high degree of importance which workers place on control of their immediate job conditions is attested to by numerous investigations. The economists Joseph Shister and Lloyd Reynolds found that among two large samples of workers, "independence and control" were the most important elements among eleven job characteristics accounting for both satisfaction and dissatisfaction with their present jobs. *Job Horizons* (New York: Harper & Bros., 1949), p. 7. In his study of a gypsum plant Alvin Gouldner attributed the outbreak of a wildcat strike to the company's abrogation of an "indulgency pattern," an informal situation in which the workers had maintained a great deal of freedom and control in their immediate job realm. *Wildcat Strike* (Yellow Springs, Ohio: Antioch Press, 1954). In a survey of the literature on occupational differences in job satisfaction, the present writer found that variations in the degree of control over the conditions of work was the most important single factor accounting for these differences. "Work Satisfaction and Industrial Trends in Modern Society," in Walter Galenson and Seymour Martin Lipset (eds.), *Labor and Trade Unionism* (New York: John Wiley & Sons, 1960), pp. 345–49.

Among other studies of workers' attitudes which confirm the importance of control are Theodore Purcell, *The Worker Speaks His Mind on Company and Union* (Cambridge, Mass.: Harvard University Press, 1954), p. 103; Gladys Palmer, "Attitudes toward Work in an Industrial Community," *American Journal of Sociology,* LXIII (1957), 24; and Nancy C. Morse and Robert S. Weiss, "The Function and Meaning of Work and the Job," *American Sociological Review,* XX (1955), 191–98.

paced, with the rhythms of work and the timing of the operator's action depending on the speed of the machine or machine process, and those which are man-paced, in which the worker himself can vary the rhythms of his actions.[12] This distinction can be seen in two occupations outside the factory. The man who takes money or issues tickets at the toll plaza of a bridge or highway has virtually no control over the pace of his work, since it is determined by the flow of traffic. He can only respond. An unskilled clerk in an office who adds columns of figures all day on an adding machine, however, has considerable control over his work pace. Often he can slow down, speed up, or take a break at his own discretion, although supervisors and other clerks might have some influence over his work pace.

Control over the pace of work is critical because it sets a man apart from the machine system of modern technology. The pace of work is probably the most insistent, the most basic, aspect of a job and retaining control in this area is a kind of affirmation of human dignity. This freedom is also crucial because it influences other work freedoms.

For example, when a man can control his work rhythm, he can usually regulate the degree of *pressure* exerted on him. Some work environments, like automobile and textile factories, are characterized by considerable pressure, while others, like print shops and chemical plants, have a relaxed atmosphere; in later chapters we shall be concerned with the factors that affect this. In addition, *freedom of physical movement* is much more likely when a worker controls his own work rhythm and also when he is relatively free from pressure. In American industry today many jobs require the worker to stay close to his station for eight hours a day, while others permit a great deal of moving around the plant. The automobile assembly line is again an extreme example of restricted physical movement, whereas the work milieu of the print shop permits a high degree of this freedom. Many manual workers consider free movement quite important; the rather common preference of manual workers for truck-driving, railroad, and construction work rather than factory jobs often represents an aversion to physically confining "inside" work.

Control over work pace generally brings some *freedom to control the quantity of production*. Of course, workers cannot keep their jobs without a minimum production. But many are able to vary the hourly and daily output greatly,[13] while others have no power at all to control this. Similar to this is the freedom to control the *quality* of one's work. When a man sets his own pace and is free from pressure, as are craft printers, he can take the

[12] John Dunlop, *Industrial Relations Systems* (New York: Henry Holt & Co., 1958), pp. 52–53.

[13] This has been a common research finding in industrial sociology since the Western Electric study dramatized the fact. See especially the studies of Donald Roy—for example, "Quota Restriction and Goldbricking in a Machine Shop," *American Journal of Sociology*, LVII (1952), 427–42.

pains to do a job up to his standards of workmanship; in machine-paced systems with high-speed production, a worker's desire to put out quality work is often frustrated, as is the case with many automobile assemblers.

A final component of control over the immediate work process refers to *techniques*. In mass production there is generally little opportunity to make choices as to how to do one's job, since these decisions have been already made by engineers, time-study men, and supervisors. In other industrial settings, however, jobs permit some selection of work methods. There, workers can solve problems and use their own ideas.

These individual task-related freedoms—control over pace, freedom from pressure, freedom of physical movement, and the ability to control the quantity and quality of production and to choose the techniques of work— together make up control over the immediate work process. When rationalized technology and work organization do not permit the active intervention of the worker at any of these points, the alienating tendencies of modern industry, which make the worker simply a responding object, an instrument of the productive process, are carried to their furthest extremes.

MEANINGLESSNESS: PURPOSE AND
FUNCTION IN MANUAL WORK

A second dimension of alienation in industrial employment is meaninglessness. Bureaucratic structures seem to encourage feelings of meaninglessness. As division of labor increases in complexity in large-scale organizations, individual roles may seem to lack organic connection with the whole structure of roles, and the result is that the employee may lack understanding of the co-ordinated activity and a sense of purpose in his work.

Karl Mannheim saw meaninglessness emerging in bureaucracies as a result of the tension between "functional rationalization" and "substantial rationality." Functional rationalization refers to the idea that in a modern organization everything is geared to the highest efficiency. The number of tasks and procedures required for a product or a service are analyzed, and the work is organized so that there is a smooth flow and a minimum of costs. The rationale of the technical and social organization is comprehended fully only by a few top managers (and engineers in the case of a factory), if indeed by anyone at all. But along with the greater efficiency and rationality of the whole, the substantial rationality of the individuals who make up the system declines. The man who has a highly subdivided job in a complex factory and the clerk working in a huge government bureau need only know very limited tasks. They need not know anyone else's job and may not even know what happens in the departments of the organization next to them. They need not know how their own small task fits into the entire operation. What results is a decline in the "capacity to act intelligently in a given situation on the basis of one's own insight into the inter-relations of events." [14]

Meaning in work depends largely on three aspects of the worker's relationship to the product, process, and organization of work. The first factor is the character of the product itself. Working on a unique and individuated product is almost inherently meaningful. It is more difficult to develop and maintain a sense of purpose in contributing toward a standardized product, since this inevitably involves repetitive work cycles. The second point is the scope of the product worked on. It is more meaningful to work on the whole, or a large part, of even a standardized product than to perform one's tasks on only a small part of the final product. Third, purpose and function increase when the employee's job makes him responsible for a large span of the production process, rather than a small restricted sphere.

Tendencies toward meaninglessness therefore stem from the nature of modern manufacturing, which is based on standardized production and a division of labor that reduces the size of the worker's contribution to the final product. Whereas many independent craftsmen of the preindustrial era made the entire product themselves, from the first step in the operations to the last, an automobile assembler may spend all his time putting on headlights and never have anything to do with any other operation. These alienating tendencies may be overcome when job design or technological developments result in a wide rather than a narrow scope of operations for the employee. Purpose may also be injected into relatively fractionized jobs when the worker develops an understanding of the organization's total function and of the relation of his own contribution to that larger whole. However, such understanding is less likely to lead toward a sense of purpose and function if the worker's responsibilities and scope of operations remain narrow.

Like powerlessness, meaninglessness is unequally distributed among manual workers in modern industry. The nature of an industry's technology and work organization affects the worker's ability to wrest a sense of purpose from his work task—substantial irrationality is not the fate of all modern factory employees. This mode of alienation is most intensified when production is carried out in large plants. In the small factory it is easier for the worker to see the relationship of his contribution to the enterprise as a whole. Team production also reduces meaninglessness. It is easier for factory workers to develop a sense of purpose when they are members of work crews which carry out the job jointly than for employees who do their work individually. Finally there is less alienation in process technology than in batch or assembly methods of production. In the former system, work is organized in terms of an integrated process rather than in terms of sub-

[14] K. Mannheim, *Man and Society in an Age of Reconstruction* (New York: Harcourt, Brace & Co., 1940), p. 59, cited in Seeman, *op. cit.*, p. 786.

divided tasks, and the worker's span of responsibility and job assignment is enlarged. An increased sense of purpose and function in work for the blue-collar employee may be one of the most important by-products of automation, since this technical system brings about smaller factories, production by teams rather than individuals, and integrated process operations.

SOCIAL ALIENATION: INTEGRATION AND MEMBERSHIP IN INDUSTRIAL COMMUNITIES

In contrast to Marx, who emphasized the powerlessness of workers in modern industry and saw the solution to the modern social problem in "restoring" control to the workers over their conditions of work, the French sociologist Emile Durkheim saw *anomie* (normlessness) and the breakup of integrated communities as the distinguishing feature of modern society. The massive social processes of industrialization and urbanization had destroyed the normative structure of a more traditional society and uprooted people from the local groups and institutions which had provided stability and security.

The transition to industrialism brought about tendencies toward social alienation, not only in the larger society but also in the factories and mills. Although the use of physical force and the threat of starvation as "incentives" expressed the callousness of many industrialists, it also reflected the fact that there was as yet no basis for an industrial community. With normative integration absent, machine-breaking, sabotage, strikes, and revolutionary activity not only represented protest against unbearable conditions but expressed the fact that workers had not yet developed a sense of loyalty to industrial enterprise or commitment to the new social role of factory employee.

In advanced industrial societies like the United States, the social alienation in factory employment characteristic of the early period has been greatly reduced. Even workers who lack control over their immediate work task and experience difficulty in achieving meaning and self-expression in the job may be spared the alienation of isolation, which implies the absence of a sense of membership in an industrial community. Membership in an industrial community involves commitment to the work role and loyalty to one or more centers of the work community. Isolation, on the other hand, means that the worker feels no sense of belonging in the work situation and is unable to identify or uninterested in identifying with the organization and its goals.

An industrial community is made up of a network of social relationships which are derived from a work organization and which are valued by the members of the community. For many factory workers the plant as a whole is a community, a center of belongingness and identification, which mitigates feelings of isolation. It is quite common for workers to come to a factory thirty minutes early every day to relax in the company of their friends. It has been argued that the human contacts of the plant community are critical in making work which is in other ways alienating bearable for mass production workers.[15] Beginning with the work of Elton Mayo and his associates, much research in industrial sociology has documented the role of informal work groups in providing a sense of belonging within the impersonal atmosphere of modern industry.

An industrial community also has a structure of norms, informal and formal rules, which guide the behavior of its members. Industrial organizations differ in the extent of normative integration, and this is important in determining the employee's sense of belonging to a cohesive work community. Industrial organizations are normatively integrated when there is consensus between the work force and management on standards of behavior, expectations of rewards, and definitions of fair play and justice, and when there are agreed-upon "rules of the game" which govern the relations between employees and employers. The norms and practices through which workers are disciplined and laid off, assigned wage rates relative to the earnings of others, and awarded promotions, are especially critical. These matters affect the worker's sense of equity with respect to the allocation of rewards and the standards of distributive justice and therefore often determine his sense of alienation from, or integration in, the industrial enterprise.

Although the maturation of industrial society has generally reduced the worker's isolation, the implications of bureaucratic organization for social alienation are somewhat mixed. Bureaucracy's norm of impersonal administration emphasizes formal procedures, and in many cases this creates a feeling of distance between workers and management. And the bureaucratic principle of the rational utilization of all resources to maximize organizational goals furthers the tendency to view employees as *labor,* as means to the ends of profit and company growth. But bureaucratic administration also enhances normative consensus through its emphasis on universalistic standards of justice and "fair treatment" and thus makes it possible for employees to acquire the status of industrial citizenship. It is probably the policy and practices of individual firms, unique historical and economic conditions, and particularly the technological setting,[16] that determines whether bureaucratization increases or decreases social integration in a specific situation.

[15] "Only the human contacts bring a touch of variety into the monotony of the daily work. . . . If you speak to a worker who has been sick for some time, and could not go to work, and he asks about the 'fellows' in the gang—then you realize the secret attraction which the plant has for many workers . . . . the shop community is a major factor making the experience of work more positive." Blum, *op. cit.,* p. 77.

[16] As suggested in chapter 1, technology has an important impact on social alienation because it determines a number of aspects of industrial structure that affect cohesion and integration: the occupational distribution of the blue-collar labor force, the economic cost structure of the enterprise, the typical size of plant, and the existence and structure of work groups.

Industries vary not only in the extent but also in the basis of normative integration and in the key institutions which are the center of the work community and the focus of worker loyalties. It is important to stress that the company need not be the major focus of the industrial community, as the advocates of what has been called "managerial sociology" tend to assume. In some cases, occupational groups and unions, in other situations, the local community as a whole, are more important presently and potentially. The analysis of the sources of normative integration and consensus in the four industries compared in the following chapters suggests that industries devise their own specific solutions to the problem of social alienation.

SELF-ESTRANGEMENT

Self-estrangement refers to the fact that the worker may become alienated from his inner self in the activity of work. Particularly when an individual lacks control over the work process and a sense of purposeful connection to the work enterprise, he may experience a kind of depersonalized detachment rather than an immediate involvement or engrossment in the job tasks. This lack of present-time involvement means that the work becomes primarily instrumental, a means toward future considerations rather than an end in itself. When work encourages self-estrangement, it does not express the unique abilities, potentialities, or personality of the worker. Further consequences of self-estranged work may be boredom and monotony, the absence of personal growth, and a threat to a self-approved occupational identity.

Self-estrangement is absent in two main situations: when the work activity, satisfying such felt needs as those for control, meaning, and social connection, is inherently fulfilling in itself; or when the work activity is highly integrated into the totality of an individual's social commitments. Throughout most of history, the problem of work has been dealt with in the latter manner. Adriano Tilgher, a historian of work ideologies, finds that the idea that work should be a creative fulfilment is peculiarly modern, with origins in the Renaissance. In many previous civilizations work was viewed as some kind of unpleasant burden or punishment.[17] Our modern feeling that work should be a source of direct, immediate satisfaction and express the unique potential of the individual is probably a result of its compartmentalization in industrial society. In preindustrial societies "uninteresting" work was highly integrated with other aspects of the society—with ritual, religion, family, and community or tribal relationships, for example. Therefore it could not become simply a means to life, because it was an immediate part of life's main concerns.

A number of fateful social changes have contributed to the compartmentali-

[17] Adriano Tilgher, *Work: What It Has Meant to Men through the Ages* (New York: Harcourt, Brace & Co., 1930).

zation of work. Most basic was the market economy which, in severing the organic connection between production and consumption, between effort and gratification, set the stage for the instrumental attitude toward work.[18] Second, the physical separation of household and workplace—an essential condition for the development of capitalism and bureaucratic organization, as Weber stressed—produced a hiatus between work life and family life. Third, with the secularization of modern society, the importance of the religious sanction in work motivation has declined; work and religion are now separated. Fourth, with the specialization brought about by industrial organization and the anonymity which urbanization has furthered, the average man's occupational role is not well known or understood: work is now separated from the community, as well as from the family and religion. Finally, the decline of the hours of work and the increase in living standards mean that less of life is devoted simply to problems of material existence. Time, energy, and resources are now available for other aspects of life,[19] which compete with work for emotional loyalties and commitments.

Self-estrangement is experienced as a heightened awareness of time, as a split between present activity and future considerations. Non-alienated activity consists of immersion in the present; it is involvement. Alienated activity is not free, spontaneous activity but is compulsive and driven by necessity. In non-alienated activity the rewards are in the activity itself; in alienated states they are largely extrinsic to the activity, which has become primarily a means to an end. Marx expressed these notions in his early work on alienation, the *Economic and Philosophical Manuscripts:*

> In his work, therefore, [the worker] does not affirm himself but denies himself, does not feel content but unhappy, does not develop freely his physical and mental energy but mortifies his body and ruins his mind. The worker therefore only feels himself outside his work, and in his work feels outside himself. He is at home when he is not working, and when he is working he is not at home. His labor is therefore not voluntary, but coerced; it is *forced labor*. It is therefore not the satisfaction of a need; it is merely a *means* to satisfy needs external to it. Its alien character emerges clearly in the fact that as soon as no physical or other compulsion exists, labor is shunned like the plague. External labor, labor in which man alienates himself, is a labor of self-sacrifice, of mortification.[20]

Since self-estranged activity is a means to an end rather than an end in itself, the satisfaction is in the future rather than the present, and the tone of

---

[18] Hannah Arendt emphasizes this factor as the basic precondition of alienation. See *The Human Condition* (Chicago: University of Chicago Press, 1958), especially pp. 79–174.

[19] It has been often pointed out that the reduction of hours of work is only relevant to the past century or two. In the Middle Ages as much or more leisure time existed as at the present. See Harold Wilensky, "The Uneven Distribution of Leisure: The Impact of Economic Growth on 'Free Time,' " *Social Problems*, IX (1961), 33–34.

[20] K. Marx, *op. cit.*, pp. 72–73.

feeling approaches *detachment* rather than involvement. The man on the assembly line is thinking about that beer he will have when the whistle blows; the packing-house worker at Hormel goes home from work "so he can accomplish something for that day."[21] The meaning of the job for the automobile worker is not the intrinsic activity itself but that "new car" or "little modern house," which the pay check, itself a future reward, brings closer.[22]

Lack of involvement results in a heightened time-consciousness. If it were possible to measure "clock-watching," this would be one of the best objective indicators of this mode of alienation. The "over-concern" with time is central to Fred Blum's perceptive discussion of alienation in a meat-packing plant and suggests that self-alienation is widespread in this kind of work. When Blum asked these workers whether they get bored on the job, a common response was that boredom was not a serious problem because "the time passes."

How could the passage of time possibly neutralize the monotony of the job? Whatever the answer may be, there is no doubt but that the time does, as a rule, pass fast. A large majority of workers, when asked: "When you are at work does the time generally pass slow or fast?" indicated that it usually passes quickly. Only a small minority feels that the time goes slowly. Many workers, however, intimated that sometimes the passage of time is slow and sometimes fast.[23]

On the other hand, involvement in work may come from control, from association with others, and from a sense of its purpose. A man who is controlling his immediate work process—regulating the pace, the quantity of output, the quality of the product, choosing tools or work techniques—must be relatively immersed in the work activity. For most employees, when work is carried out by close-knit work groups, especially work teams, it will be more intrinsically involving and rewarding. And involvement and self-fulfilment is heightened when the purpose of the job can be clearly connected with the final end product or the over-all goals and organization of the enterprise. On the other hand, there is no necessary causal relation between social alienation and self-alienation. A worker may be integrated in the plant community and loyal to the company and still fail to achieve a sense of involvement and self-expression in his work activity itself.

When work is not inherently involving it will be felt as monotonous.[24] The extensive industrial research on monotony[25] suggests the high degree of self-estrangement in factory employment. Unfortunately, the studies are so scattered that they do not permit an over-all assessment of the amount of felt

[21] Blum, *op. cit.*
[22] Chinoy, *op. cit.*
[23] Blum, *op. cit.*, p. 82.
[24] Of course, many people do not find monotonous work objectionable.
[25] A brilliant discussion is found in Georges Friedmann, *Industrial Society* (Glencoe, Ill.: Free Press, 1955), pp. 129–55.

monotony in the labor force. But the concern of industrial psychologists in England, France, Germany, and America with this topic, stimulated by management anxieties over dips in output, indicates that present-time involvement is a precarious thing, especially in repetitive jobs.[26]

Many industrial commentators feel that most modern jobs cannot be intrinsically involving and the best solution would be to make them so completely automatic that a worker would be free to daydream and talk to his workmates. Evidently, we are still far from this outcome, since the Roper survey, based on a representative sample of 3,000 factory workers, found that only 43 per cent could do their work and keep their minds on other things most of the time (see Table 41, Appendix B). The most unsatisfactory situation seems to be the job which is not intrinsically interesting and yet requires rather constant attention.

Still, such work does not necessarily result in intense or even mild dissatisfaction. The capacity of people to adapt to routine repetitive work is remarkable. It is quite likely that the majority of industrial workers are self-estranged in the sense that their work is not particularly involving and is seen chiefly as a means to livelihood. Yet research in job satisfaction suggests that the majority of workers, possibly from 75 to 90 per cent, are reasonably satisfied with such jobs.[27] Thus, the typical worker in modern industrial society is probably satisfied *and* self-estranged.

Self-estranged workers are dissatisfied only when they have developed *needs* for control, initiative, and meaning in work. The average manual worker and many white-collar employees may be satisfied with fairly steady jobs which are largely instrumental and non-involving, because they have not the need for responsibility and self-expression in work. They are therefore relatively content with work which is simply a means to the larger end of providing the pay checks for lives organized around leisure, family, and consumption.

One factor which is most important in influencing a man's aspirations in the work process is education. The more education a person has received, the greater the need for control and creativity. For those with little education, the need for sheer activity (working to "keep occupied") and for association are more important than control, challenge, and creativity.[28]

[26] Monotony, of course, is quite relative in the sense that minor alterations in the work routine or general situation (a new tool or a superintendent passing by) may give interest to a workday which, from an intellectual's vantage point, would appear the height of tedium.

[27] Blauner, in Galenson and Lipset, *op. cit.*

[28] Morse and Weiss, *op. cit.;* Eugene Friedmann and Robert Havighurst, *The Meaning of Work and Retirement* (Chicago: University of Chicago Press, 1954). Herzberg and his collaborators also report that those in non-manual occupations and the more educated are more concerned with intrinsic job features. (Herzberg, *et al., op. cit.,* p. 54.)

Besides education, other important factors are intelligence, personality, and occupation itself. For the most part, white-collar and professional work involves more variety, control, purpose, and responsibility than blue-collar work. It is to some degree the work itself which a person secures that instills him with specific kinds of needs to be satisfied or frustrated in the work situation. A manual worker whose work does not involve such qualities, whose education has

Finally, self-estranging work threatens a positive sense of selfhood because it fosters a damaging rather than an affirmative occupational identity. In a traditional society with little individuation, identity, the answer to the question "Who am I?" was not a problem for the masses of people. Identity, to the extent that this concept[29] was meaningful in such a society, was largely provided through the kinship system, which means that it was not a matter of choice. In a modern industrial society in which there is marked occupational, social, and geographical mobility and in which considerable freedom of choice exists among various conflicting value systems, the development of personal identity is an ongoing creative process.

An industrial society tends to break down many important past sources of loyalty, such as extended kinship, local, regional, and even ethnic attachments. In their place, occupation becomes a more important element of general social standing, since more than any other attribute it influences the income and style of life a person leads. While people construct a sense of identity by a synthesis of early childhood identifications with a large number of later commitments and loyalties,[30] occupational identity has probably become a much more significant component of total identity in modern society than in the past. In an industrial society, it is primarily occupational status which is ranked in superior and inferior grades by the spontaneous processes of stratification. The estimates of the community and other men about the jobs we hold therefore greatly affect our own estimates of self-worth.

In general, working-class jobs in the United States have lower status than white-collar and professional ones. For this reason many factory workers are ambivalent about their work and do not find that occupational identity contributes to feelings of self-esteem and self-approval. In such a situation, there is probably a tendency to de-emphasize occupation and work as important components of selfhood and to stress in their place other loyalties and statuses, such as ethnic identifications and family relations.[31] Perhaps an indication of this dissatisfaction with working-class status is the fact that 59 per cent of the factory workers in the Roper study said that they would choose *different* occupations if they were able to "start all over again at the age of 15" (see Table 37, Appendix B). In contrast, 80 or 90 per cent of those in various professional occupations would re-enter the *same* line of work if given a free choice.[32]

---

not awakened such aspirations, and whose opportunities do not include realistic alternatives, will not develop the need for intrinsically fulfilling work.

[29] Erik Erikson, "The Problem of Ego Identity," *Journal of the American Psychoanalytic Association*, Vol. IV (1956).

[30] *Ibid.*

[31] In her study of unskilled workers in a shipyard, Katherine Archibald has vividly documented their obsession with ethnic categorization. *Wartime Shipyard* (Berkeley: University of California Press, 1947), pp. 40–127. The importance of kinship relations to manual workers has been noted by many researchers.

[32] Blauner, in Galenson and Lipset, *op. cit.*, p. 343.

Self-estranging work compounds and intensifies this problem of a negative occupational identity. When work provides opportunities for control, creativity, and challenge—when, in a word, it is self-expressive and enhances an individual's unique potentialities—then it contributes to the worker's sense of self-respect and dignity and at least partially overcomes the stigma of low status. Alienated work—without control, freedom, or responsibility—on the other hand simply confirms and deepens the feeling that societal estimates of low status and little worth are valid.

The theory of alienation has been and continues to be a fruitful perspective on the world of work, but it must be pointed out that it is a limited perspective. With all its social-psychological subtleties, it does not fully comprehend the complexities and ambiguities of the inner meaning of work to the individual. As a polemic, it therefore condemns too much, and as a vision, promises too much.

Because it ignores what might be called the bipolar or two-sided ambivalence of work, alienation theory cannot totally explain the relationship between work and human happiness. For even the most alienated work is never totally unpleasant, never completely rejected by the worker. Necessity and force is never the whole story. The very worst jobs are rarely only means to exist but often become ends in themselves in some regard. Marx's conception of the function of work for man was too narrow, or perhaps too philosophical: he did not accept as essential the myriad of functions that even alienated work plays in the life-organization of human beings. Observation and research have disproved his statement that "as soon as no physical or other compulsion exist, labor is shunned like the plague." The need for sheer activity, for social intercourse, and for some status and identity in the larger society keeps even unskilled workers on the job after they are economically free to retire.[33]

Work is inherently ambivalent also at the opposite pole of freedom and non-alienation. Even in the most unalienated conditions, work is never totally pleasurable; in fact, the freest work, that of the writer or artist, usually involves long periods of virtual self-torture. Such non-alienated work is never completely an end in itself; it is never totally without the element of necessity. As Henri DeMan wrote in a profound study of the meaning of work:

Even the worker who is free in the social sense, the peasant or the handicraftsman, feels this compulsion, were it only because while he is at work, his activities are dominated and determined by the aim of his work, by the idea of a willed or necessary creation. Work inevitably signifies subordination of the worker to

[33] E. Friedman and R. Havighurst, *op. cit.* Morse and Weiss found that 80 per cent of a national sample said they would keep working if they inherited enough money to live comfortably (*op. cit.*).

remoter aims, felt to be necessary, and therefore involving a renunciation of the freedoms and enjoyments of the present for the sake of a future advantage.[34]

SUMMARY AND CONCLUSION

We have discussed four types of alienation often experienced by manual workers in industry. What do these dimensions have in common on a more general level? Basic to each one is the notion of fragmentation in man's existence and consciousness which impedes the wholeness of experience and activity. What distinguishes the separate dimensions is that they are based on different principles of division or fragmentation. Each dimension has its unique opposite, or non-alienated state, which implies a kind of organic wholeness in the quality of experience. Finally, each alienated state makes it more probable that the person (or worker) can be "used as a thing."

The split in man's existence and consciousness into subject and object underlies the idea of *powerlessness*. A person is powerless when he is an object controlled and manipulated by other persons or by an impersonal system (such as technology) and when he cannot assert himself as a subject to change or modify this domination. The non-alienated pole of the powerlessness dimension is the state of freedom and control.

Meaninglessness alienation reflects a split between the part and the whole. A person experiences alienation of this type when his individual acts seem to have no relation to a broader life-program. Meaninglessness also occurs when individual roles are not seen as fitting into the total system of goals of the organization but have become severed from any organic connection with the whole. The non-alienated state is understanding of a life-plan or of an organization's total functioning and activity which is purposeful rather than meaningless.

Isolation results from a fragmentation of the individual and social components of human behavior and motivation. Isolation suggests the idea of general societal alienation, the feeling of being in, but not of, society, a sense of remoteness from the larger social order, an absence of loyalties to intermediate collectivities. The non-alienated opposite of isolation is a sense of belonging and membership in society or in specific communities which are integrated through the sharing of a normative system.

Self-estrangement is based on a rupture in the temporal continuity of experience. When activity becomes a means to an end, rather than an end in itself, a heightened awareness of time results from a split between present engagements and future considerations. Activity which is not self-estranged, but self-expressive or self-actualizing, is characterized by involvement in the present-time context. Self-estrangement also entails a separation between work life and other concerns. When work is self-estranging, occupation does

---

[34] H. DeMan, *Joy in Work* (London: George Allen & Unwin, 1929), p. 67.

not contribute in an affirmative manner to personal identity and selfhood, but instead is damaging to self-esteem.

Thus the four modes of alienation reflect different "splits" in the organic relationship between man and his existential experience: the subject-object, the part-whole, the individual-social, and the present-future dichotomies. Each makes it more possible to use people as means rather than as ends. Since "things" rather than human beings are normally used as means, alienation tends to turn people into things: thus thingness, in addition to fragmentation, is another common denominator of the various meanings of alienation.

In sum, a person is more likely to be used as an object under these conditions: (1) when he is powerless and lacks control; (2) when his role is so specialized that he becomes a "cog" in an organization; and (3) when he is isolated from a community or network of personal relations which would inhibit impersonal treatment. The result of being a means for the ends of others is that for himself, his (own) activity becomes only a means rather than a fulfilling end.

These *fragmentations* in man's experience all seem to have resulted from basic changes in social organization brought about by the industrial revolution. That is why the alienation concept has a peculiarly modern ring. Few people in preindustrial societies seem to be alienated (the powerlessness of the masses might be the exception); in a bureaucratic mass society we are likely to regard huge numbers of people as alienated. Thus, the breadth of the alienation concept is due to the fact that it reflects the social conditions and consequences of the transition to an industrial society.[35] And conversely, when one studies the stabilization and reintegration of industrial societies in their more mature, advanced phases (a common perspective today of students of social organization), one is studying the conditions through which alienation is either overcome or rendered bearable for individuals and relatively harmless for society.

Within the world of work, the relative stabilization of an advanced industrial society has diminished some of the more glaring instances of alienation characteristic of the period of early industrialization in which Marx wrote. Yet the tendency to use people as things still persists in modern industry. And perhaps this is inevitable, since the nature of industrial organization is such that workers are productive resources and, therefore, to some degree, means to organizational goals.

But despite the common features of modern employment relations, industrial environments vary markedly in their alienating tendencies. Whether a worker approaches the state of being merely a commodity, a resource, or

[35] Note the similarity between this statement of alienation theory and the standard sociological analyses of modern industrial society (from Toennies to Parsons) which stress the predominance of instrumental over expressive orientations, of means over ends, of technology and organization over family and community.

an element of cost in the productive process depends on his concrete relation to technology, the social structure of his industry, and its economic fortunes. As stated in the first chapter, the industry a man works in is fateful because the conditions of work and existence in various industrial environments are quite different. Let us begin our attempt to support this thesis with an examination of the printing industry, a modern-day work environment with a maximum of freedom and a minimum of alienation.

3

THE PRINTER:
A FREE WORKER IN A CRAFT INDUSTRY

Printing is the oldest of the four industries compared in this study. Established before the era of the factory system and mass production, its present-day technology and social institutions still reflect these origins and traditions, despite the fact that the industry has undergone considerable change.

Printing technology is still relatively "underdeveloped," with much of the work done by hand rather than machine; the economic and social structure of the industry is more "traditional" than "bureaucratic," as employers are many, plants are relatively small and without elaborate hierarchical chains of command, and labor unions have a degree of control over the industry's labor market and plant working conditions which reminds one of the medieval guild system. As a result of these factors, printers have a non-alienated relation to their work, which again recalls the craftsmen of preindustrial times.

Printing is a craft industry with a craft technology. Other craft industries in the United States are building construction[1] and shipbuilding. Craft industries depend on the special skills of journeymen workers. The essential feature of a craft technology is the lack of standardization of the product. This inhibits the standardization, or "rationalization" of the work process, which is increasingly developed in machine, assembly-line, and automated technologies.

Because every car which rolls off an automobile assembly line is by and large the same, the extreme rationalization in automobile production is possible. In comparison, every house built by construction workers and every boat turned out in the shipyards is a relatively unique product. At the massive Boeing plant in Seattle, only eight 707 jet planes are completed a month; in the same period workers in one Ford plant will have produced seven thou-

---

[1] For an account of work relations in the building industry, see Richard R. Myers, "Interpersonal Relations in the Building Industry," in Sigmund Nosow and William H. Form (eds.), *Man, Work and Society* (New York: Basic Books, 1962), pp. 126–37.

sand Falcons. Printers turn out new editions of newspapers, new magazines, and new books every day. Since the product they work on is constantly changing, it has been more difficult to standardize the work process.[2]

Craft industries often retain a fairly primitive technology. In printing, much work is still done by hand: in 1958 hand compositors were the largest occupational group of all the printing trades.[3] Even the most important machines, linotypes and printing presses, are relatively simple, compared to such technical devices as the city-block-long Fourdrinier paper-making machine and the continuous-flow system in the chemical and oil refining industries.

A useful indicator of the level of mechanization is the ratio of total capital investment to the number of production workers. In the most highly automated industry, petroleum refining, a huge investment in technology and a small manual work force have resulted in an extremely high capital investment of more than $110,000 per individual worker. In relatively backward industries, such as garment and leather goods, a minimum investment in plant and equipment along with a large labor force has resulted in a low ratio, approximately $4,000 per production worker. Capital investment per production worker in the printing industry is $11,000, considerably below the average of $15,000 for all manufacturing industries. A similar figure, $11,700, for the other craft industry, transportation equipment (which includes the manufacture of aircraft, ships, and railroad cars, but *not* motor vehicles),[4] suggests the relatively undeveloped mechanization of craft technologies. However, both printing and transportation equipment are considerably more advanced technologically than such industries as lumber, leather, and apparel, though they are far behind the mass-production and automated industries (see Table 18, Appendix A).

The more an industry is mechanized, the more attention it must give to the maintenance and repairs of its heavy equipment. Therefore another indicator of the low level of technological development in printing is the fact

---

[2] The limits on technology imposed by the nature of the product are often neglected by those who attribute lack of rationalization largely to the vested interests of skilled craft unions. James Bright, for example, has analyzed how the enormous diversity in size, shape, and style of shoes has made the automation of this industry most unlikely. *Automation and Management* (Cambridge, Mass.: Harvard University Press, 1958), pp. 30–38.

[3] U.S. Department of Labor, *Occupational Outlook Handbook, 1959* (Bulletin No. 1255 [Washington: U.S. Government Printing Office, 1959]).

[4] Most statistics of industry classifications include the automobile or motor vehicle industry within the larger group of transportation equipment industries. For our purposes this is unfortunate, because there are important technological differences among the industries included in this category. The Roper study gives separate data for automobile workers and the employees in the other transportation equipment industries. Whenever possible I utilize industrial statistics which distinguish between the automobile and the "other" transportation equipment industries, as in the above example. In those cases when this is not possible and the category "transportation equipment" also includes motor vehicle production, this fact is indicated in a footnote.

that its payroll for maintenance purposes in 1957 was only 4 per cent of the total payroll in the industry. For all manufacturing industries, maintenance expenses were 12 per cent of expenditures, and in the automated petroleum industry, they were 44 per cent (see Table 20, Appendix A).

In Marx's view, an essential aspect of the development of factory technology was its removal of the tasks requiring intelligence and dexterity from the workman; these traits were built into the machines. Craft industries are those in which this process has not taken place. They require a high level of traditional skill, which involves the manipulation of physical materials with tools and calls for dexterity of hand and eye. Because craft technology lacks standardization, the work which calls for traditional skill is not highly subdivided and repetitive but encompasses a wide variety of operations. Often, as in the printing trades, long apprenticeships of from four to six years are required to master these skills. Traditional skill is cumulative; it increases with experience in the trade and constitutes a kind of lore which is taught and passed on through the generations.[5]

In craft industries, the majority of blue-collar workers are skilled craftsmen. This is probably the best single statistical indicator of the craft nature of the technology. Seventy per cent of the manual workers in the printing and publishing industry are skilled craftsmen and foremen; this is the highest proportion among major manufacturing industries. The transportation equipment industry is the only other manufacturing industry in which skilled workers outnumber semiskilled operatives and unskilled laborers (see Table 26, Appendix A).

Craft industries therefore have similar technological features which include a lack of standardization, a relatively low level of mechanization, and a high proportion of workers with traditional skills. However, these industries do not have common economic characteristics. The economic situation in the printing industry has unique dimensions which affect the alienation of printers but are not completely applicable to workers in other craft industries.

An industry's economic prospects depend ultimately on consumer demand for its products. With the increasing literacy, educational level, and rising standard of living of the American people, there has been and will continue to be a steadily rising demand for the products of the printed word. People are hungry for news in depressions as well as good times; the "paperback revolution" has guaranteed a rising market for book publishers for the immediate future; and the need for printed business forms seems insatiable, as

[5] Cf. Alain Touraine's discussion of phase A, craft production, in his *L'évolution du travail ouvrier aux usines Renault* (Paris: Centre National de la Recherche Scientifique, 1955). A translation of the last chapter, which summarizes the study, has recently appeared in Charles R. Walker's *Modern Technology and Civilization* (New York: McGraw-Hill Book Co., 1962), pp. 425–37.

the growing white-collar class consumes and files more and more paper in ever more bureaucratic industries. Although there are some seasonal dips in the industry, the printer, unlike the automobile and textile worker, can be relatively certain that the total number of jobs in printing will not drop, if drastic technological innovations are not introduced. Employment figures show a consistent upward movement: the number of all employees in the printing and publishing industry was 631,000 in 1940, 738,000 in 1950, and 894,000 in 1960 (see Table 24, Appendix A). And a recent Department of Labor prognosis predicts that moderate growth in employment will continue in the 1960's.[6]

JOB SECURITY IN A CRAFT LABOR MARKET

With a favorable demand situation, the printing unions' control over entrance into their trades is an effective assurance that the supply of labor will not increase to the point that there is marked job competition. Almost all manual workers in the industry are organized into craft unions, and a union-sponsored apprenticeship is still the predominant path to journeyman status.

As a result of these product-market and labor-market conditions, printers have more stability of employment than workers in most other industries. Despite some seasonal fluctuations, printers are more likely to work fifty-two weeks out of the year than other manual workers. In 1949, 67 per cent of all manufacturing employees worked more than fifty weeks, a good simple indicator of a "steady job." Among printing employees, 78 per cent worked fifty weeks or more. Of twenty-one major manufacturing industries, printing was third highest in this indicator of employment stability; only the two progressive continuous-process industries, oil refining and chemicals, had proportionately more employees working steadily (see Table 27, Appendix A). In 1960 and 1961 the industry averaged 0.8 and 1.0 layoffs for every 100 workers per month, less than half the rates of 2.4 and 2.2 layoffs found in manufacturing industry as a whole (Table 28, Appendix A). And in the years from 1958 through 1961 less than 4 per cent of all printers were unemployed, in contrast to more than 7 per cent of all factory workers (Table 29, Appendix A). None of the thirteen other manufacturing industries for which data were available had such a low proportion of jobless employees.

Printers not only have employment security based on favorable economic conditions, they also have considerable control over their conditions of employment because of union laws and union power. The laws of the International Typographical Union (ITU), the largest craft union in the industry, whose jurisdiction covers the two major printing crafts, hand composition and linotype operation, are based on the premise that "workers have a right to set the conditions under which they will work, and employers must ac-

[6] U.S. Department of Labor, *Occupational Outlook Handbook, 1959*, p. 335.

cept these conditions or face sanctions."[7] It is not that workers control the over-all policies of the enterprise:

. . . the employers' main rights concern the way in which work shall be done. *The job, however, belongs to the man rather than to the foreman or the shop.*

So strong is the workers' proprietary right to their jobs that a printer with a regular situation designates the substitute who shall take his place if he decides to take a day off or is obliged to take one off because of the need to cancel overtime. This rule that a man may designate his temporary replacement has been in existence since the turn of the century.[8]

Considering the favorable product market, the unions' control over the labor market, and the individual craftsman's job property rights, it is no surprise that printers were more optimistic about future job security than other workers in the Roper national sample. At the time of the survey, economic conditions were generally favorable, and 81 per cent of all factory workers expressed confidence that they could have their present jobs as long as they wanted them. Of the printers, 92 per cent expressed this confidence. As Table 31, Appendix B shows, employees in only one other industry, chemicals, felt a higher degree of job security (94 per cent confident); petroleum refining, a second automated continuous-process industry, had the same proportion of "secure" workers as printing.

Similarly, only 3 per cent of the printing workers, compared to 11 per cent of all factory workers, expressed the fear that they were "likely to be laid off temporarily at any time during the next six months." Again only the two continuous-process industries, chemicals and petroleum, had slightly fewer workers who were anxious about a possible layoff. On the other hand, 29 per cent of the automobile workers expected this contingency (Table 32, Appendix B).[9]

Compared to workers in other industries, the skilled printer suffers little

[7] Seymour Martin Lipset, Martin Trow, and James S. Coleman, *Union Democracy* (Glencoe, Ill.: Free Press, 1956), p. 24.

[8] *Ibid.*, p. 24. (My emphasis.) See also A. R. Porter, Jr., *Job Property Rights; A Study of the Job Controls of the International Typographical Union* (New York: Columbia University Press, 1954).

[9] These findings are supported by Lipset and his collaborators' study of the ITU printers. Of the five hundred printers interviewed, only 5 per cent had been without work for a period of more than a week in the six months preceding the study. Ninety-five per cent had had less than one week's enforced layoff. The same study also confirms the printer's satisfaction with his employment security. Thirty-five per cent rated job security in the printing trades as excellent, and 43 per cent rated it good. Twenty per cent rated the security fair; only 3 per cent felt it was poor. On the whole, security was rated significantly higher than pay (only 22 per cent said excellent); however, prestige of printing was rated somewhat higher (41 per cent said excellent). Forty-one per cent of the printers working for newspapers rated their employment security excellent, compared to 30 per cent of those in book-and-job shops, however, newspaper printers were somewhat more likely also to rate security fair and poor. As would be expected, the older workers were more likely to be highly satisfied with job security than younger workers, since their positions were more protected.

from insecurity. Instead of being powerless in the face of his conditions of employment, he has a remarkable degree of control over them, owing to the economic position of the industry, the unions' labor-market monopoly of craft skills, and those unique social institutions of the industry which have given him a recognized property right to his job.

Yet fears of unemployment still persist among many printers. Of ITU members in New York, 46 per cent had been without steady situations for as long as a year during their work careers.[10] In the past, such technological innovations as stereotyping and linotype machines eliminated many jobs: the fear exists that future technological changes may also threaten the present job security in the industry. Such presentiments are the principal reason why the ITU retains the notorious "bogus" or reproduction clause in union contracts, a rule which gives printers the right to "make work" by breaking down perfect usable matrices of type, in order that they may be reset.[11]

CRAFT TECHNOLOGY AND WORKER CONTROL:
THE PRINTER'S FREEDOM

If printers have such impressive control over their conditions of employment, do they exercise a parallel control over the immediate work process? Before considering the extent of the printers' freedom in this area we must briefly examine the nature of their work.

Of the 320,000 printing craftsmen employed in the United States in 1958, about 200,000 were hand compositors, linotype operators, and printing pressmen—the three main printing occupations. The work of these trades therefore gives a fairly representative picture of work in the industry.[12]

Hand compositors are members of the oldest and largest occupational group in printing. They set type by hand for the printing of advertisements and other small jobs that are impractical to set by machine. In setting type by hand, the hand compositor, reading from the manuscript copy, sets each line of type in a "composing stick," a device which holds type in place, letter by letter and line by line. When this stick is full, he slides the completed lines onto a shallow metal tray called a "galley." The next step is the major function of the hand compositor—to assemble all the materials necessary to complete the job by arranging the machine- and the hand-set type and any needed engravings into pages. He then locks the completed pages into forms

---

[10] Data from files of the ITU study.

[11] Surveys of the situation show that this kind of "unwork," as Paul Jacobs has termed it, is disliked by craft-minded printers and is therefore only rarely practiced. However rationalization of union law is resisted because of the possibility that in a future situation, this right may mean the difference between some work and no work at all for many printers. See Paul Jacobs, *Dead Horse and the Featherbird: A Report To the Center for the Study of Democratic Institutions* (Santa Barbara, Calif.: Fund for the Republic, 1962).

[12] The following pages are based largely on the job descriptions in the U.S. Department of Labor, *Occupational Outlook Handbook, 1959*, pp. 338–45.

before sending them to the pressroom or the plate-making departments. After the final printing on the presses, the hand compositor also breaks down the type forms and distributes the foundry type to the proper storage compartments for re-use (see Plate 1*a*).

Not only is a high degree of manual dexterity necessary for such work, the compositor must also know type faces of various sizes and styles and be familiar with a great number of printing processes. "Each item has its own design and execution problems, requiring the personal supervision of the craftsman. For many tasks, artistic ability of a fairly high order is needed." [13]

There are more than 75,000 *linotype operators* in printing establishments; this is the second largest trade in the industry. The semiautomatic linotype machines set type much more rapidly than can be done by hand composition. Nearly all newspaper plants or large commercial shops which need large amounts of type composition use linotype machines. Although it is a highly skilled trade, it does not involve such varied craft skills as that of the compositor. In setting type, the operator, reading from copy clipped to the machine's copy board, selects the letters and other characters by operating a keyboard (somewhat similar to that on a typewriter) which has ninety keys. As he presses the keys, the letters, in the form of metal molds or "matrices," are assembled into words and lines. After he completes each line, the operator works a lever and the machine automatically casts the line of type into a solid strip of metal called a "slug." The slugs are then deposited in a galley and are later assembled into type forms from which either the printing impressions or plates are made. In the smaller plants, the linotype operator maintains and repairs his own machines; in larger shops maintenance machinists make all but minor adjustments.

After the type forms from the composing room, the press plates from the electrotyping and stereotyping department, and the gravure and the lithographic plates have been brought together, they are made ready for final printing by the *printing pressman*. Approximately 40,000 work in this craft. Their basic duties are to "make ready" and then tend the presses while they are in operation.

The object of the make-ready, which is one of the most delicate and difficult parts of the pressman's work, is to insure printing impressions that are distinct and uniform (see Plate 1*b*). This is accomplished by such means as placing pieces of paper of exactly the right thickness underneath low areas of the press plates to level them and attaching pieces of tissue paper to the surface of the cylinder or flat platen which makes the impression. Pressmen also have to make many other adjustments—for example, those needed to control the margins and the flow of ink to the inking roller. In some shops,

[13] Eugene Friedmann, "The Meanings of Work for Skilled Craftsmen," in Eugene Friedmann and Robert Havighurst, *The Meaning of Work and Retirement* (Chicago: University of Chicago Press, 1954), p. 132.

they are responsible not only for tending the presses but also for oiling and cleaning them and making some minor repairs. On the larger presses, they have assistants and helpers.[14]

Control over the immediate work process.—By its very nature, traditional skill, the main job requirement in the occupations described, implies a large degree of control over the technical environment. In fact, craft skill can even be defined as direct control over the technological environment by means of the manipulation of tools and materials. It cannot be performed when machines or assembly lines set the pace, nor can it be done under great pressure.

In a craft technology, the worker sets his own pace of work, because he must be able to take special pains when the process requires it. Since operations aren't standardized and craftsmen are responsible for a high quality product, they need time to "putter" and to perfect their work. When hand compositors are working up a page form, they must insert an unspecified number of empty metal lines or spaces on various columns of the page so that the lines of type are spaced evenly (see Plate 1a). And when pressmen make-ready the presses and page forms for final printing, they must make a large number of elaborate and unpredictable adjustments.

Clearly these kinds of operations cannot be done under pressure. A printing craftsman not only sets his own work rhythm, he is free from pressure on the job. In addition to the nature of the work itself, the printer is aided in his struggle against job pressure by his craftsman's sense of dignity; his craft consciousness and pride; and his strong union organizations, which monopolize control over rare skills.[15]

Twenty-four per cent of all factory workers in the Roper survey reported that their jobs made them work too fast most of the time. Only 10 per cent of the printers made this complaint about work pressure. As Table 33, Appendix B shows, printing was the second most "pressure-free" industry; only petroleum refining had a smaller proportion of workers who felt they had to work too fast. Only 11 per cent of the transportation equipment workers reported excessive pressure, which gives further support to the notion that a craft technology implies the worker's control over the immediate work process.

Fatigue in work results from many different factors. Heavy physical demands, pressure, and monotony—all increase feelings of tiredness. Most printing jobs are relatively light, free from pressure, and intrinsically interesting. For these reasons, it is not surprising that fewer printers report that their jobs make them too tired most of the time than workers in any other industry. Only 12 per cent of the printers, compared to 30 per cent of

---

[14] U.S. Department of Labor, *Occupational Outlook Handbook, 1959,* p. 345.

[15] "Printers have demanded and won the right to be treated as independent craftsmen who control their own work and maintain and enforce their own standards of workmanship" (Lipset, Trow, and Coleman, *op. cit.,* p. 29).

all factory workers, complain of excessive fatigue. In the other craft industry, transportation equipment, only 20 per cent of the workers get too tired, the fourth lowest industrial figure (Table 34, Appendix B).

The freedom to determine techniques of work, to choose one's tools, and to vary the sequence of operations, is part of the nature and traditions of craftsmanship. Because each job is somewhat different from previous jobs, problems continually arise which require a craftsman to make decisions. Traditional skill thus involves the frequent use of judgment and initiative, aspects of a job which give the worker a feeling of control over his environment.

Although fewer than half (49 per cent) of all factory workers in the Roper study said that they were able to try out their own ideas on the job, more than three-quarters of the printers reported this important work freedom. As Table 35, Appendix B, shows, no other industry even approaches this. Again it is significant, however, that the third highest frequency of opportunity for work initiative occurs in the other craft industry, transportation equipment.

Craftsmen generally have considerable freedom of physical movement, too, since they do not work on conveyer belts or other machines which control their pace. Printers usually can walk anywhere they want, not only on the shop floor but also to editorial offices and other parts of the plant. One question in the Roper survey gives some indication of freedom of physical movement: "Is yours the kind of job on which someone would have to take your place if you had to leave your work for a half hour or so, or could you let your work go for a half an hour and catch up on it later?" About two-thirds of the entire sample reported the ability to leave their work for thirty minutes; four-fifths of the printers, however, enjoy this freedom.[16]

The craftsman's high degree of personal control implies a complementary freedom from external supervisory control. Craftsmen, with their strong sense of independence and dignity, resent close supervision and are likely to resist it more militantly and successfully than other manual workers. They have little need for external controls, since they have internalized standards of responsibility, output, and workmanship. Their discipline is self-discipline, supported by the group discipline of the professional craft, which enforces collective standards of excellence and behavior. Craftsmen generally consider themselves as good as their supervisors in social status as well as professional competence. In craft industries, the foreman is often the oldest and most experienced journeyman. He may be more respected, but he is not basically different from the others.[17]

[16] In two other industries—stone, clay, and glass; and leather—even higher proportions of employees are free to leave their work (Table 36, Appendix B).

It would be interesting to know which printing occupations have less freedom of movement. The Roper survey analysts unfortunately did not code occupational categories within industries.

[17] Touraine, *op. cit.*, p. 179.

Printers have extended the freedom from supervision natural to craft production to a point perhaps unrivaled in modern industry. Foremen are required to be union members, and thus their actions may be controlled by the workers themselves, who can invoke union rules to check them. In addition, the ITU, which represents compositors, linotypists, and layout men but not pressmen, has a rule, accepted by employers, which forbids the physical presence of non-union members on the shop floor during working hours. Although rarely enforced, it symbolizes the unusual job control enjoyed by printers, particularly in those areas which are the prerogatives of management in most other industries.[18]

The typographical union has "the most complete control over job conditions of any union in the world," according to Selig Perlman and Philip Taft, leading authorities on American trade unionism.[19] Supporting this generalization, Lipset, Trow, and Coleman add, "To a considerable extent the workers run the composing room." [20]

The case of the printing industry illustrates how a craft technology encourages a high degree of worker control over the immediate job process. In craft industries, the alienation of powerlessness is rare indeed. Especially the numerically dominant skilled craftsmen, but even the minority of less-skilled workmen, enjoy important freedoms on the job. They control the pace of their work and are free from excessive pressure. They have some control over the methods and techniques involved in craft production and have considerable freedom of movement. They control the quality of their product, which must maintain craft standards, and to an important degree can also control the quantity of output. The Roper survey indicates that the situation of printers is indeed superior to that of other factory workers on a number of questions which pertain to these job freedoms. Of the four indicators of immediate job control so far mentioned, printers were first in rank among the sixteen factory industries on two items, second in rank on a third item, and third in rank on the fourth.

Although the printer's freedom and control is largely due to the nature of craft technology, it is reinforced and strengthened by special economic conditions and by social institutions of the industry which have a long history. The unusual power of the union and the reduced authority of supervisors are two such unique features of the industry. In considering further

---

[18] Lipset, Trow, and Coleman, *op. cit.*, pp. 24–25.

[19] Selig Perlman and Philip Taft, *History of Labor in the United States* (New York: Macmillan Co., 1935), p. 51. Cited in Lipset, Trow, and Coleman, *op. cit.*, p. 23.

[20] Lipset, Trow, and Coleman, *op. cit.*, p. 24. William Foote Whyte has described a similar case of freedom from supervision among craft workers in the glass-blowing industry. When glass-blowers encounter unusual difficulties in their highly skilled and responsible work, they are free to walk off the job, abandoning it for the remainder of the day without penalty. Management realizes that interference with this freedom would only result in bad work and imperfect products. William Foote Whyte, *Men at Work* (Homewood, Ill.: Dorsey Press and Richard D. Irwin, 1961), p. 177.

dimensions of alienation, the special conditions of the printing trades are even more important.

CRAFT DIVISION OF LABOR:
WORK WITH MEANING AND PURPOSE

The alienation of meaningless work, which reduces understanding of the total operation and dilutes a worker's feeling of purpose, increases generally with the division of labor and the fractionization of individual tasks. By definition, a craft technology does not imply the elaborate subdivision of work characteristic of mass production. A craftsman may no longer be a "jack-of-all-trades" who makes an entire product himself; still, his work is always quite varied, and he continues to work on a large segment of the product. His craft training is often very broad, rather than narrowly specialized, and the responsibility inherent in the work disposes him to think in terms of a broad productive process.

In the printing industry, the degree of specialization varies according to the individual craft, the type of printing establishment, and the size of the print shop. Among the three major crafts considered, the hand compositor's work has probably most resisted the fractionization involved in the division of labor. Compositors in a newspaper plant may work on several pages of the issue at once, and their job involves much variety.

There is probably somewhat less variety in the work of the pressman, who must spend a good deal of his time simply tending the operation of the press. But preparing the pages for printing (the make-ready) requires understanding of many other crafts besides his own, and the pressman even more than the compositor handles a large proportion of, if not all of, the product in process.

Linotype machine operators, however, though highly skilled, have a much narrower range of tasks. They are also more tied down to their individual machines, which gives them fewer opportunities each day to experience the print shop as a whole. Yet because of the nature of craft technology, which implies a unique and changing product rather than a standardized one, linotype operators can still recognize their own distinctive contribution to the finished product. Linotypist Smith can read a news article on page 14 of the morning *Times* and know that he, and only he, set the type for that article. A Ford worker can never be sure that it was he, rather than a man on another shift or in another plant, who put the right rear hubcap on the vehicle he passes in the street. Thus the individuality of the products of a craft technology preserves the organic integration of part and whole, even when the work itself becomes subdivided.[21]

---

[21] Although each issue of a magazine or newspaper and each book published is unique, they may of course be printed in hundreds of thousands, or even millions of copies. In a sense the craft uniqueness is expressed in the composing room and the mass-production run takes place in the pressroom.

Also contributing to the relative lack of specialization in printing is the small size of the typical shop in the industry. Of the twenty major manufacturing industries, only the lumber industry has smaller plants, on the average, than printing. The average printing establishment in 1955 had 25 employees, compared to 69 employees in chemicals, 134 in textiles, and 334 in automobile manufacturing (see Table 22, Appendix A).[22] And 42 per cent of all printers work in shops with fewer than 100 employees, compared to 26 per cent of all factory workers and to 23, 15, and 4 per cent, respectively, of chemical, textile, and transportation equipment workers (Table 23, Appendix A).

In the small or middle-sized plants characteristic of the industry, there is much less of the functional rationality which Karl Mannheim feels leads to the substantial irrationality of the worker: the individual printer, therefore, can quite easily get a picture of the company's organization and goals and recognize where his own tasks fit into the whole.

Within the printing industry, division of labor is naturally less in the smaller plants. Here craft jurisdictions are less carefully controlled, and men will sometimes work as all-round printers, setting type, running presses, and doing other jobs as well. In the ITU study, 38 per cent of all printers mentioned variety and lack of monotony as a principal reason for liking printing; in the smallest shops (fewer than fifteen workers), 52 per cent offered this reason. And the greater specialization of the linotypist's trade is suggested by the fact that only 26 per cent of the linotype operators mentioned variety and lack of monotony, as compared to 48 per cent of the hand compositors.[23]

The printer's rational understanding of his work environment is enhanced by the long apprenticeship period. The training is broad and relatively unspecialized. Printers are required to learn all the skills of printing, even when they may never use many of these skills.[24] Thus, the specialized linotype operator knows the job of the hand compositor; he also understands the work of the pressroom. The apprenticeship also instills a technical orientation, and craft printers retain an interest in the technological developments within their industry, often reading books and trade magazines which describe new machines and processes.

There is a unique aspect of the printer's work which confers a dimension of meaning not found in other factory industries. The printer manufactures the printed word; he is therefore a link in the chain through which news, knowledge, and culture are transmitted. Traditionally he has been the most literate, the most highly educated, and reputedly the most intelligent of manual workers. Whether this is still true or not, many printers are exposed

---

[22] No separate figures are available for the automobile industry, and the statistic given above is based on data for the transportation industry as a whole, including motor vehicles. The average automobile plant probably employs even more than 334 workers.

[23] My calculations from ITU data.

[24] Lipset, Trow, and Coleman, *op. cit.*, p. 31.

to intellectual stimulation in the course of their work, and many printers take a lively interest in the content of the materials they print.[25]

INTEGRATION AND MEMBERSHIP IN AN OCCUPATIONAL COMMUNITY

The craft worker experiences little social alienation in work, since his strong identification with his craft gives him a personal identity in an occupational role which carries respect and high status in the work place and community. Craft loyalty stems from the fact that members of the same craft share a common kind of work, a common relationship to the labor market, and therefore a common fate. Because of this shared work situation, common technical, economic, and social problems arise for which crafts develop solutions. These solutions are the technical "tricks of the trade" and the economic and social institutions which make up an occupational culture. The printing industry has a particularly well-developed craft culture because of its venerable age and historic traditions.

Craft identification, a product of socialization, sometimes begins early in life, since there is a strong tendency for sons to follow fathers or other relatives into the same skilled trade. The long apprenticeship period is the formal process through which a craftsman learns occupational norms as well as proficiency in work. Craft identification and loyalty is further reinforced through membership in craft unions.

The commitment of printers and other craftsmen to their roles as producers is based more on the internalization of professional standards of the craft, such as norms of a fair day's work and quality workmanship, than on acceptance of the goals of the employer and the work organization. In other words, the loyalty of the skilled worker tends to be to the craft and occupation rather than to the company. This fact does not necessarily imply any lack of acceptance of employer goals or active disloyalty; on the contrary, craft commitment and loyalty may further integration with the company.

The survey data demonstrate that the pull of the occupation is more persuasive than that of the company. Fifty-nine per cent of the entire Roper sample said they would prefer different occupations if they could be free to begin their careers over again at the age of fifteen. But only 36 per cent of the printers would have wanted different kinds of work; this industry thus ranked first in positive identification with the occupation (see Table 37, Appendix B).

However, on indicators of loyalty to the company, printers were very close to the sample norm. Seventy-eight per cent of the printers, compared to 73 per cent of the sample, agreed that their company was about as good a place as any to work (see Table 38, Appendix B). And similarly, the proportion of printers who felt that their jobs were "really essential to the success of

[25] *Ibid.*, pp. 123–24.

the company," though very high, was less than the average for all factory workers (Table 39, Appendix B).

Although printers, like other craftsmen, are more oriented toward their occupational group and less oriented toward their employers than workers in most other industries, the balance of these allegiances varies with the social structure of the printing establishment. Most important is the size of the print shop a man works in. In the large shops men are more highly involved in the union and other activities of the occupational community; in the small shops printers are more identified with the company and view printing as a business which they hope to enter some day. Lipset and his collaborators asked ITU printers in New York whether they would prefer to be union officers or foremen: this question to some degree measures orientation toward the occupational as opposed to the organizational collectivity. In the larger shops (those with more than thirty workers), 35 per cent preferred union offices, 31 per cent the jobs of foremen, and 34 per cent responded "neither." In the small shops (fewer than thirty men), 27 per cent preferred union jobs, 52 per cent those of foremen, and 21 per cent responded "neither." [26] In the very smallest shops (fewer than six workers), 70 per cent wanted to be foremen; in the largest shops (more than two hundred workers), only 24 per cent wanted to be foremen. [27]

Since company loyalty is greater in small shops, the high degree of occupational identification in printing is all the more remarkable because printing is essentially a small-firm industry. This tendency toward company loyalty that the small shop furthers is counteracted, however, by the high degree of interfirm mobility. The large number of firms in this competitive industry gives many alternative sources of employment to the printer, whose skills are scarce resources and in great demand. Because he can and does change jobs frequently, the skilled printer is not as likely to develop a strong attachment to one employer as is a semiskilled worker in a mass-production industry, who works for a large company and has fewer alternative employment possibilities. In the Roper study, printing, along with the furniture industry, had the lowest percentage of workers who had been with their employers more than five years. Only 35 per cent of the printers had worked this long for their employer, compared to 48 per cent of the entire sample (see Table 40, Appendix B). The job mobility of printers is part of the craft's traditions: the itinerant printer who moved from city to city constantly finding new employment on the strength of his union card was a notable figure in American history.

Unlike some other workers, printers do not seem to be particularly cynical toward the system of distributive justice in their industry. Their relative

---

[26] My calculations from Table 30, *Ibid.*, p. 156.
[27] There were 46 printers in the very smallest shops and 170 in the largest shops (my calculations from ITU data).

The Hand Compositor
and the Pressman

a) A hand compositor inserts an empty line by means of a small metal tool, as he makes up a newspaper page. Note the rack of different sized slugs behind his head.

b) Pressman inserts the completed page form into his press before running it off. The numerous small devices on the top and side of the press suggest the many minor adjustments this skilled craftsman must make to insure a perfect impression. (Courtesy of the International Typographical Union.)

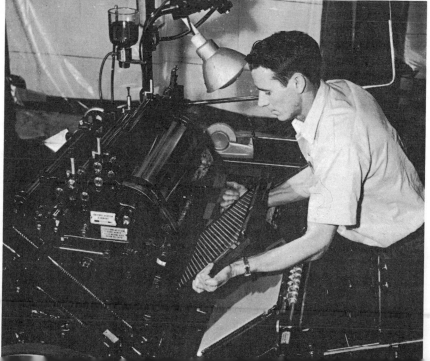

a) Closeup of traditional skill in action. Hand compositor inserting last-minute story on the front page. The basis of traditional skill is the unique product manufactured by craft technologies, in this case, the newspaper with its changing daily contents. (Courtesy of the International Typographical Union.)

b) When the product is standardized, as in the textile industry, machines can be built to perform most operations. The work of the spooler is unskilled and routine; when a bobbin of yarn has been used up by the machine, she "doffs" it and replaces it with a full one. (Courtesy of the American Textile Manufacturers' Institute, Inc.)

satisfaction with the standards and practices of advancement suggests that they are not alienated from the normative order. Perhaps the best evidence for this statement is the printers' responses to the question, "What do you believe gives a person the best chance to advance in the plant where you work?" Compared to 56 per cent of the whole sample, 64 per cent of the printers said that "the quality of his work" was very important in getting ahead—this, of course, is particularly a craft standard. Forty-eight per cent of the printers said that a man's "energy and willingness to work" was a viable factor; this was virtually the same proportion as among all factory workers. These two integrative responses predominated. Fewer printers (30 per cent) than other factory workers (39 per cent) offered one of the cynical responses which suggest alienation from the standards of distributive justice; "how well he gets on personally with his immediate bosses"; "how good a politician he is"; and, "whether he is a friend or relative of a high official or foreman" (see Table 46, Appendix B).

Again, there is more normative integration in the small print shops. In the larger establishments, cynicism increases as the social distance between workers and management widens. In shops with more than fifty printers, cynical responses were 46 per cent of the total; in the small shops with fewer than fifty men only 20 per cent of the responses were cynical. Instead, in the smaller shops, 73 per cent said "quality of work" was most important, and 54 per cent said "energy and willingness to work." In the larger shops only 53 per cent and 39 per cent, respectively, gave these two integrative responses. Table 1 gives more complete statistics on the factors printers view as important.

TABLE 1

FACTORS MALE PRINTERS VIEW AS MOST IMPORTANT IN ADVANCEMENT, BY SIZE OF PRINT SHOP*

FACTORS	SIZE OF PRINT SHOP (Number of Employees)				TOTAL: ALL MALE PRINTERS	TOTAL: ALL FACTORY WORKERS
	1–20	21–50	51–250	251 and over		
Quality of work............	81%	60%	54%	50%	63%	56%
Energy and willingness to work....................	56	50	29	50	47	50
Cynical responses†..........	19	20	50	41	30	39
Seniority..................	19%	30%	42%	9%	24%	25%
Number of respondents....	(36)	(20)	(24)	(22)	(102)	(2,940)

* Totals do not add up to 100 per cent because respondents mentioned more than one factor.
† Cynical responses include "how well he gets along personally with the boss"; "whether he is a friend or relative of the boss"; and "how good a politician he is."

In examining integration in the printing industry, I have emphasized the norms of the craft community and the consensus between workers and employers on standards of performance and advancement. The social alienation of printers is also counteracted by membership in meaningful social groups, both on and off the job.

The printer's freedom from job pressure, his relative ease of movement, and his light supervision make it possible to talk with other craftsmen in the course of his work. Many printers work night shifts, and night work generally increases opportunities for socializing. Some printing trades, e.g. pressmen, usually carry out their work in teams made up of a journeyman aided by helpers and apprentices. Whether or not they work in teams, the strong occupational identity and concern with competence that printers share with other craftsmen and with professionals make it essential that they have colleagues to talk shop with. Thus, in the Roper study, the printing industry had by far the highest proportion of workers who felt that "pleasant personal contacts" made their work place better than others.[28]

More than most industrial workers, printers have a sense of membership in their industry. An important factor which contributes to this is the highly developed off-the-job occupational community.[29] The printer's leisure life is full of voluntary associations made up of fellow printers: social clubs, fraternal orders, ethnic lodges, veteran's groups, technical clubs, discussion groups, bowling societies, and other sports teams. These associations provide an organized independent group life which is unusual for factory workers in modern American industry.

All printers are not equally involved in the occupational community.[30] As we shall see in the next section, those categories of printers who are most active in occupational clubs—newspaper employees, men in large plants, linotypists—are also those whose satisfactions with their trades tend to be more extrinsic and less based on craft gratifications. Those printers who are oriented toward intrinsic craft rewards, men in small shops and hand compositors, are much less likely to be active in leisure time pursuits. This suggests the possibility that activity in those clubs which make up the printer's occupational community may be a substitute for, rather than a spontaneous

---

[28] Lipset, Trow, and Coleman (*op. cit.*, pp. 157–63) found that printers in large shops had more opportunities to develop close friendships on the job than printers in small shops. This was due to the greater freedom from supervision, the recurrence of slack periods, the larger pool for voluntary friendship choices, and the characteristically longer seniority in the large print shops.

[29] The causes of this occupational community and its consequences for the internal political life of the ITU have been brilliantly analyzed by Lipset, Trow, and Coleman (*op. cit.*).

[30] Sixty-four per cent of those employed in newspaper plants had at one time or another been members of such off-work associations; only 32 per cent of printers in the book-and-job branch of the industry had been in such clubs. Newspapers, particularly in New York where the study was made, are large employers; most book-and-job shops are small. Thus, in the very largest print shops (more than two hundred employees), 65 per cent had been club members; in the smallest shops (fewer than fifteen employees), only 22 per cent had been active. Activity in the intermediate-sized plants, from fifteen to two hundred printers, fell in between with 45 per cent membership. And there was also a tendency for linotype operators to be more active in the occupational community than hand compositors (53 per cent, compared to 38 per cent active). These figures are based on my calculations from ITU data.

consequence of, the satisfactions of craftsmanship. Whatever the factors involved, social alienation is rare among printers, who have a strong sense of membership in an industrial community organized around their crafts and unions.

INVOLVEMENT, SELF-EXPRESSION, AND SELF-ESTEEM:
THE CRAFTSMAN'S DIGNITY

The craft technology and the social and economic structure of the printing industry mitigate many of the alienating tendencies which arise in large-scale mass-production industries. Printers therefore exercise considerable freedom and control in the immediate work process, wield understanding and purpose in carrying out meaningful jobs, and develop commitment to their work role and loyalty to their craft. According to the hypothesis stated in the last chapter, there should be little self-estrangement in this industry. When the work situation encourages control, commitment, and meaning, work will be instead self-actualizing and self-expressive.

More specifically, we would expect that the work of printers (1) will be intrinsically involving and interesting rather than monotonous; (2) will give opportunities for the expression of both present resources and skills and the development of new potentialities; (3) will be viewed chiefly as an end in itself with rewards in the actual activity, rather than as a means to satisfy future ends; (4) and will become an important and approved element of their total personal identity.

The data available give considerable support to these propositions. Present-time involvement is generally characteristic of craft work, because the high degree of precision required, the inherent variety, and the occurrence of problems to be solved are all conditions which demand more or less constant attention. In the Roper survey 43 per cent of the factory workers reported that they could do the work on their jobs and keep their minds on other things most of the time. Only 27 per cent of the printers gave this response—this was the lowest industrial figure. In the other craft industry, transportation equipment, only one-third of the workers could take their minds off the work (Table 41, Appendix B).

Only 4 per cent of the printers, compared to 20 per cent of the Roper sample, found their jobs dull or monotonous. This is by far the lowest industrial figure (Table 42, Appendix B). In every other industry except printing there were some workers who found their jobs always dull; no printers gave this response. In addition, printing had the highest proportion of workers who found their jobs interesting nearly all the time rather than simply interesting most of the time.[31]

[31] Although it is a craft industry, 23 per cent of the workers in transportation equipment found their jobs dull most of the time, a degree of monotony somewhat above the Roper sample

Non-alienated work in craft industries permits the expression of present capacities and the development of innate potentialities: it is therefore self-actualizing. As we have seen earlier, the printer's work contains constant opportunities to solve technical problems and to learn new craft skills, including those of other trades in the same industry. Thus, 79 per cent of the printers, compared to 49 per cent of all factory workers, feel that their jobs give them a chance to try out their own ideas. No other industry even approaches this figure, although the other craft industry, transportation equipment, is third in rank, with 63 per cent reporting the opportunity for such independent initiative (Table 35, Appendix B).

In addition, only 16 per cent of the printers, compared to 25 per cent of the Roper sample as a whole, felt that their jobs were "too simple to bring out [their] best abilities." Only one industry, paper manufacturing, had fewer workers who felt frustrated in the expression of their talents (Table 43, Appendix B). Since a worker's aspiration for challenging jobs increases with education, the printer's satisfaction is especially impressive, since 76 per cent of them had at least high-school educations, compared to 50 per cent of all factory workers in the Roper study.[32]

In many industries, the development of a worker's potentiality is contingent on advancement to work in which the level of skill and responsibility provides more challenge than the more numerous production jobs. In printing, however, opportunities for growth are present in journeyman status. Advancement seems less important. In fact, the typical skilled printer is in an ambiguous position with respect to advancement. On the one hand, he has already achieved considerable mobility, either through a formal apprenticeship or through on-the-job promotions. And while supervisory positions, self-employment, or a career in the union are available for a few, for most manual workers promotion means the upgrading of skill, status, job grade, and wages within the ranks of blue-collar work.[33]

---

norm. Two factors probably explain the difference between this industry and printing on this question. The skill level in transportation equipment, where 39 per cent of the sample had jobs requiring more than two years' of training, was considerably lower than in printing, where 70 per cent had high-skilled jobs. In addition, transportation equipment workers were concentrated in large plants, chiefly aircraft factories. Half of the transportation equipment employees were in plants with more than five thousand workers; none of the printers worked in such large establishments.

[32] See Table 44, Appendix B, for the educational distribution of the Roper sample. The high degree of over-all satisfaction (25 per cent dissatisfied) on this question is perhaps a little surprising, considering our image of modern factory work. While such results should spur us to question conventional stereotypes, the high level of contentment on this item probably reflects more a generally low level of aspiration rather than the challenging nature of most industrial jobs.

[33] Promotion to foreman is possible for a small number of printers because they, unlike most blue-collar workers, possess the necessary technical and social skills. Many skilled craftsmen, however, do not see any advantage in "rising" into supervision: their work, pay, and status are already sufficiently rewarding. Self-employment is also a realistic avenue for many printers. Because there is room in the industry for a large number of small shops which require little

With 70 per cent of the blue-collar workers in the industry skilled crafts-men or foremen, most printers are already at the top, where there is no higher to go. This is probably the reason why in the Roper survey only 48 per cent of the printers said that their jobs lead to promotions if they do them well. This proportion is almost identical with the general sample norm for all factory workers (Table 45, Appendix B).

Advancement to more skilled and responsible work is not therefore as important an element in the development of the printer's potentialities as it is for a semiskilled worker. The skilled printer feels that he has already made it to the pinnacle of the working-class world; and with his strong craft consciousness and satisfying work, the lack of further formal advance-ment is not felt as depriving. Because his experience and knowledge ac-cumulates, the old printer at the end of his career maintains his usefulness and is often the most respected man in the shop,[34] unlike the old automobile worker, who may skid to the lowest job in the plant hierarchy.

When work provides opportunities for control, meaning, and self-expres-sion, it becomes an end in itself, rather than simply a means to live. For printers, the job means much more than a weekly pay check. Their satisfac-tions are largely intrinsic, related to the nature of the work itself, rather than extrinsic, or concerned with aspects of the job beyond the actual work. In the ITU study, only 11 per cent gave wages, security, or working condi-tions as their sole reason for liking printing.[35] In contrast, a study of auto-mobile workers found that such extrinsic concerns as wages and job security were seen as the predominant positive aspects of the job, rather than the nature of the work.[36]

When ITU printers were asked what they liked most about printing, the average respondent offered two reasons. The most frequent response, men-tioned by 38 per cent, was that the work was varied and lacked monotony. Almost as many printers, 37 per cent, said that they liked the creativity and challenge of their work. These two intrinsic motivations were followed by an external response, wages and security, mentioned by 29 per cent. Another intrinsic reason, the educational character of the work, was offered by 21 per cent. In addition, 21 per cent were concerned with working conditions and 6 per cent with the prestige of the occupation. Even when the last two,

---

capital, a printer, like a building-trades craftsman, is quite likely to start his own business at some time during his career. If the shop fails or turns out to be "more trouble than it's worth," he slips back into the status of an employed journeyman printer without great difficulty. A union office is another possibility. Printers are more likely to be interested in a union career than workers in other industries for a number of reasons: their literacy and social confidence, their high level of participation and interest in the affairs of their local chapel, and the fluid leadership structure in the union itself.

[34] E. Friedmann, in E. Friedmann and R. Havighurst, *op. cit.*, p. 133.

[35] Lipset, Trow, and Coleman, *op. cit.*, p. 123.

[36] Charles R. Walker and Robert Guest, *Man on the Assembly Line* (Cambridge, Mass.: Harvard University Press, 1952), pp. 62–64.

somewhat borderline, responses are classed as extrinsic motivations, the ratio of all intrinsic reasons given to all extrinsic reasons was 171 to 100.

As would be expected, hand compositors, whose work most exemplifies the craft nature of the industry, are shown by their greater emphasis on the intrinsic quality of work as an activity to be relatively less self-estranged than linotype operators, whose work partakes more of mass-production characteristics. For linotypists, intrinsic satisfactions predominated over external rewards, but the ratio was relatively small, 135 to 100. For compositors, intrinsic rewards overshadowed extrinsic gratifications by a ratio of 207 to 100.[37]

Another factor which influences the balance of self-actualization and self-estrangement within the printing industry is the size of the plant. In the smallest shops, workers seem to be relatively unconcerned with the instrumental aspects of their work, and work is almost totally an end in itself. Intrinsic factors were mentioned more than three times as frequently as extrinsic reasons. In the larger shops, intrinsic craft motivations still predominate, but external rewards are considerably more important than in the smaller shops. Table 2 gives the relation between intrinsic and extrinsic reasons for liking printing for men in shops of four different sizes.

TABLE 2

RATIO OF INTRINSIC TO EXTRINSIC REASONS FOR LIKING PRINTING,
BY SIZE OF PRINT SHOP*

SIZE OF PRINT SHOP (Number of Employees)	RATIO: INTRINSIC/EXTRINSIC REASONS	NUMBER OF RESPONDENTS
1–15.....................	305	111
16–40.....................	198	125
41–199.....................	133	94
200 and over.................	140	170
Total: all shop sizes.........	171	500

* Source: My calculations from ITU data. Intrinsic reasons include lack of monotony and variety, educational nature, creativity, and challenge of the job; extrinsic reasons include pay and security, working conditions, and prestige.

A study which compared the meaning of work and retirement in five occupational groups also confirms the lack of self-estrangement among printers. The intrinsic aspects of work, "purposeful activity, self-expression, and new experience," were more important to printers than to steel workers, coal miners, sales clerks, and even doctors.[38]

In such a situation it is no surprise that printers, in contrast to most manual workers, are able to make their occupation an approved and important aspect of their total personal identity. Besides the factors already discussed, the traditionally high status of the craft is another reason why this is possible.

[37] My calculations from ITU data.
[38] E. Friedmann and R. Havighurst, op. cit., p. 173.

The printers' status has been historically—and remains today—higher than that of other manual workers: Lipset and his collaborators have characterized it as marginal between the working class and the middle class. In his study of skilled printers, Eugene Friedmann found that they were "characterized by a very high degree of emphasis on work as a source of self-respect and the respect of others," referring to the status accorded a skilled craftsman in the community, as well as the recognition received in the work group and family.[39] The importance of prestige to the printer is expressed by an officer of the ITU:

Anytime you mention printer to a salesman, on the corner, a garageman, etc. they say "you guys make plenty of money." They regard you differently. They still hold the printing industry in high esteem. I would say the prestige is between good and excellent. In the past it wasn't different. There's a certain amount of ego we printers carry.[40]

This sense of well-being or even superiority ("There's a certain amount of ego we printers carry") that printers derive from their occupational identity is more typical of the attitudes of craftsmen in the preindustrial society, as Thorstein Veblen, in an interesting passage, has described it:

Craftsmanship ran within a class, and so had the benefit of that accentuated sentiment of self-complacency that comes of class consciousness. Whether their conceit is wholly a naive self-complacency or partly a product of affectation, the sentiment is well in evidence and marks the attitude of the handicraft community with a characteristic bias. The craftsmen habitually rate themselves as serviceable members of the community and contrast themselves in this respect with the other orders of society who are not occupied with the production of things serviceable for human use. *To the creative workman who makes things with his hands belongs an efficiency and a merit of a peculiarly substantial and definitive kind, he is the type and embodiment of efficiency and serviceability.* The other orders of society and other employments of time and effort may of course be well enough in their way, but they lack that substantial ground of finality which the craftsman in his genial conceit arrogates to himself and his work. And so good a case does the craftsman make out on this head, and so convincingly evident is the efficiency of the skilled workman, and so patent is his primacy in the industrial community, that by the close of the era much the same view has been accepted by all orders of society.[41]

[39] *Ibid.*, p. 176–77.

[40] From the files of the ITU study. In this study, 41 per cent rated the prestige of printing excellent, 46 per cent good, only 10 per cent fair, and 1 per cent poor. Ratings for prestige were higher than for pay and security.

[41] Thorstein Veblen, *The Instinct of Workmanship* (New York: Macmillan Co., 1914), p. 243. (My emphasis.)

That the printer still retains a satisfaction with his occupational status is confirmed by the fact that only 36 per cent of the printing workers in the Roper study would have considered other occupations if they were beginning their careers anew, in contrast to 59 per cent of all factory workers. There was no other industry in which such a high proportion of workers approved, in this way, their own occupational identity (see Table 37, Appendix B).[42] On this point, the printer is marginal between the mass of more alienated factory workers and the highly committed professional employee. Studies of the latter suggest that only 15 per cent would change their occupations.[43]

Similarly, 73 per cent of the ITU printers liked their occupations very much; 23 per cent liked them fairly well; only 4 per cent disliked or felt indifferent to their occupations.[44] And a study of work and retirement found that printers were more likely to want to continue working past retirement age than steel workers and coal miners.[45] When an occupational identity makes a regular daily contribution of self-esteem and self-approval, it is naturally somewhat difficult to give it up.

Printers do not own the shops in which they work; nor do they have any claim to the finished products of their work. But this is virtually all they have in common with the most alienated of modern factory workers. In some ways, the printer is almost an anachronism in the age of large-scale industrial organizations. His relation to his work is reminiscent of our picture of the independent craftsman of preindustrial times. Craft technology, favorable economic conditions, and powerful work organizations and traditions result in the highest level of freedom and control in the work process among all industrial workers today. Because printers work in relatively small plants, their work is not as subdivided as work in most industries. They are meaningfully related to the total organization of work, and they are less dominated by the hierarchic authority structure characteristic of modern industrial organization. Because of the strength of their economic position and craft unions, they are not subject to the discipline that falls on the average factory worker. Their control over the process of work extends into the social relations of production, since their property rights to their jobs give them a unique kind of control over their conditions of employment.

Work for craft printers is a source of involvement and commitment. It is not chiefly a means to life, but an expression of their selfhood and identity. For craftsmen, work is almost the expression of an inner need, rather than the grudging payment of a debt imposed by external sources. Since the

[42] In the transportation equipment industry, only 48 per cent wanted different occupations. This craft industry was third in satisfaction with occupational identity, the paper industry falling between it and printing.

[43] Blauner, in Galenson and Lipset, *op. cit.,* p. 343.

[44] Lipset, Trow, and Coleman, *op. cit.,* p. 122.

[45] E. Friedmann and R. Havighurst, *op. cit.,* p. 173.

printer is almost the prototype of the non-alienated worker in modern industry, he can provide a useful reference point with which to compare the situation of workers in a number of different industrial settings.

Yet, it is not certain how long printers can maintain this position, for technological innovations and economic developments threaten to eliminate not only the typesetter's control but the job itself. The newspaper industry has developed a process by which printed type can be set automatically by a columnist or reporter as he writes out his copy on the typewriter. The craft unions may remain strong enough to resist this and other similar technological developments, but if they do not, printing may change rapidly from a craft to an automated industry, and this chapter will retain only historical interest.

4

THE TEXTILE WORKER:
INTEGRATION WITHOUT FREEDOM
IN A TRADITIONAL COMMUNITY

In the same sense that printing represents the workshop of the preindustrial era, textiles can be considered the prototypal industry of early industrialism. For many countries it has been the most important manufacturing industry in the early stages of industrialization. The classic critiques of capitalism and the new industrial order[1] were based largely on conditions in cotton mills and cotton towns. Particularly in eighteenth-century England and nineteenth-century America, this industry epitomized all the worst evils of early, rapid industrialization—the fourteen-hour day, subsistence wages, inhuman discipline, company towns, and the exploitation of women and children.

In such glaring form these conditions no longer exist. Yet the textile industry in the United States still remains a social-problem industry, and its unique characteristics have been studied by many social scientists and social reformers. In the textile employee's rather complicated relationship to his work process and industrial community, five factors stand out as basic: a machine-tending technology, a low skill level and large numbers of women workers, a traditional social structure, location in small southern communities, and economic sickness. Technology and economics contain strong alienating tendencies, but there are important features of the industry that further social integration and counter self-estrangement.

Textiles is a machine industry rather than a craft industry like printing. Its products are standardized, and the hand work which once existed has long since been eliminated. Highly mechanized power machinery, particu-

[1] For example, F. Engels, *The Condition of the Working Class in England* (London: George Allen & Unwin, 1892); K. Marx, *Capital* (New York: International Publishers, 1939); and J. L. and Barbara Hammond, *The Skilled Labourer: 1760–1832* (London: Longmans, Green & Co., 1920) and *The Town Labourer: 1760–1832* (London: Longmans, Green & Co., 1932).

larly semiautomatic spinning frames and automatic looms, carries out the basic production processes. The job of the typical worker is to mind or tend a large number of spinning frames, looms, or similar machines. He may feed yarn to, and remove yarn from, the machines when necessary and watch out for and repair breaks in the yarn when they occur. He does not operate an individual machine, as is characteristic in the garment and the shoe industries. Instead he minds or tends dozens of identical machines lined up in rows in the carding, spinning, weaving, and other rooms of the textile mill.

In a machine-tending technology, the traditional manual skills which workers in a craft technology command have been built into the machine system. In contrast to printing, where 70 per cent of the blue-collar workers are skilled craftsmen, only 12 per cent of the manual workers in textiles are skilled. Although classified officially as semiskilled, the basic production operations do not require a moderate, rather than a large, amount of skill.[2] Most textile jobs are actually unskilled, since they require little knowledge, training, and experience. The basic tasks are learned in a few weeks, although a considerably longer period of practice may be required to reach the necessary level of speed and dexterity.

Work that requires little training and is also physically light is highly suitable for women in our society. Since the days of the home spinning wheel, many of the operations in the production of cloth have traditionally been defined as women's work. In 1960 more than 40 per cent of all employees in the textile industry were female. Other light-machine industries with low-skilled work forces also have large proportions of women. In apparel, women constituted 80 per cent of all employees, and in the leather (chiefly the shoe) industry, 51 per cent are women. (see Table 25, Appendix A).

In these generally low-skilled industries, women tend to be concentrated more than men in the lowest-skilled jobs. In textiles only 1 per cent of the women are skilled, compared to 17 per cent of the men.[3] As I argue later, the sex division of labor significantly affects the alienation process in the industry. Objectively alienating conditions are more pronounced in women's jobs. Yet women are more protected from the self-estranging consequences of alienation because of their more traditional attitudes, their alternative roles, and their secondary commitment to the labor force.

Textiles is an old industry which originated in the period of small-scale entrepreneurial manufacturing. For this reason its economic and social structure has been traditional. Unlike modern bureaucratic industries, which tend

---

[2] All jobs operating or tending machines or mechanized processes in factories are classified by the Census Bureau as semiskilled. The unskilled laborer category is reserved for unmechanized physical labor such as the work involved in lifting heavy objects.

[3] Calculated from U.S. Department of Commerce, Bureau of the Census, *Occupation by Industry* (Washington, U.S. Government Printing Office, 1955), p. 33.

to be oligopolies dominated by a few huge firms, it has been made up of many relatively small firms, highly competitive with one another. The typical plant in the industry has not been large. However, in recent years there have been increasing tendencies toward economic concentration, larger plants, and bureaucratization. But traditional organizational practices still predominate in much of the industry and have limited its ability to adapt to modern circumstances.

Although many mergers have taken place in the past two decades, the textile industry is still less concentrated than most modern mass-production industries. Its concentration ratio of 11.9 is higher than that of the highly decentralized printing industry (2.3), but it is far less than the concentration indexes in the automobile industry (96.3) and the chemical industry (59.4) (see Table 21, Appendix A, for explanation of this ratio). Rationalization is most advanced in the basic textile industry, where thirty-six large and middle-sized companies now account for 58 per cent of the total employment. The three largest firms, Burlington Industries, J. P. Stevens, and Cannon Mills, employ almost a third of all workers in basic textiles.[4] Though this concentration is impressive, it is on a much smaller scale than in the automobile industry where the "Big Three" hire more than 90 per cent of the workers assembling motor vehicles. And some branches of the textile industry—hosiery-knitting, carpets and rugs, and synthetics—are much less concentrated than the basic spinning and weaving operations.

The typical plant in the textile industry is neither large nor small, but a middle-sized operation. Textile mills average 134 employees per establishment, in contrast to print shops, which average 25 workers, and plants in the transportation equipment industry, which average 334 (Table 22, Appendix A). Only 15 per cent of all textile workers are employed in mills with fewer than 100 men, as compared to 26 per cent of all factory workers. And although the bigger companies in the textile industry tend to have a fairly sizable number of quite large mills, only 25 per cent of the textile employees work in plants which have more than 1,000 men, as compared with 34 per cent of the entire manufacturing labor force. Thus textile workers are more bunched up than average in middle-sized mills, which hire between 100 and 1,000 employees (Table 23, Appendix A).

In recent years the industry has lost many of its markets. As the population prospers in the affluent stage of industrialism, people spend less of their income on clothing. Nations which have industrialized late and have the advantage of low labor costs have developed textile industries which have taken over many of the foreign markets and some of the American domestic market. And other domestic industries which are newer and more dynamic have developed products which compete successfully with textile products.

⁴ Textile Workers Union of America, Research Department, "Major Textile Interests in the United States," 1-#75 (New York, 1961, mimeographed).

Facing declining demand, the textile industry has been inhibited by its economic and social structure from responding in ways which could overcome its crisis. The majority of small and economically marginal firms have lacked the financial and personnel resources to introduce major innovations. And even the larger firms, affected by the long-term traditionalism of the industry, have not emphasized the research for new products and processes which might bring new markets. The proportion of its income which the textile industry expends on research is about one-twentieth the level of all industries.[5] The organizational backwardness of the industry is further indicated by its relative neglect of market research and sales-engineering.[6]

One of the industry's most important responses to competitive pressures has been migration from New England to the South. The process is most complete in cotton textiles, more than 90 per cent of whose workers are now in the southern states. Only a few mills remain in New England, the center of the industry at the turn of the century. The wool industry has remained longer in the Northeast, but its movement has progressed so rapidly that more than half of wool production is also in the South. The larger companies took the lead in the southern movement, and most of the remaining northern plants are small and marginal.

The attraction of the South is both the community atmosphere and the labor force. Southern towns often underwrite some of the costs of plant development because of their desire to attract new industry. And there is an abundant supply of labor largely resistant to the appeals of union organizers and content to work for relatively low wages, since other opportunities are usually absent. Like its high proportion of women workers, the location of the industry in the small towns and villages of the South also affects workers' alienation. The integrated community atmosphere and the traditional orientation of the labor force counteract the tendencies toward self-estrangement in the work process.

The move southward took place in the context of the industry's economic sickness. In the period of "postwar prosperity," between 1947 and 1957, the volume of industrial production for all manufacturing increased from an index level of 100 to 145. In the same period, production in the textile industry declined from 100 to 98.[7] While the total number of employees in all manufacturing industries was increasing from 15.3 to 16.8 million in the same ten-year period, employment in textiles dropped from 1,335,000 to

[5] "All industry spends about 2 per cent of gross sales annually on research. . . . The best estimate for the textile industry is 0.1 per cent." Statement by Malcolm Campbell, Dean of School of Textiles, North Carolina State College, cited by Solomon Barkin in U.S. Senate, *Hearings, Problems of the Domestic Textile Industry,* 85th Cong., 2nd sess. (Washington: U.S. Government Printing Office, 1958), I, 307.

[6] In 1955, Solomon Barkin, the research director of the major textile union, The Textile Workers Union of America (TWUA), reported that there were no economists employed by any of the textile corporations. *Ibid.,* p. 289, pp. 306 ff.

[7] *Ibid.,* p. 51.

1,000,000—a loss of more than 300,000 jobs.[8] The decline has continued, and in 1960 there were only 946,000 employees in the industry (Table 24, Appendix A).

Even the older worker with years of seniority cannot feel secure unless he is an employee of one of the few large and prosperous firms. Because a small-firm competitive structure has prevailed in much of the industry, many marginal mills have shut down permanently, and older workers have been hit harder than younger ones.[9] Economic insecurity has affected textile workers more severely than many other factory workers because they lack the welfare benefits common in many other industries. And because of the low wage levels (in 1960 the average weekly wage for production workers in textiles was $64.00 in comparison to an average of $91.00 for all manufacturing),[10] it is difficult to save money for periods of unemployment.[11]

In such an economic and social context, the textile worker has relatively little control over his employment. He suffers from considerable insecurity. Unlike the printer, he possesses no skill in special demand to give him bargaining power, and therefore he tends to be an interchangeable commodity in the productive process. Since less than 25 per cent of the industry is organized by unions, the textile worker rarely has this source of protection, which contributes greatly to the security of printers and automobile workers.

As we shall see, the economic depression and lack of union protection result not only in a lack of control over employment conditions but also contribute to the textile worker's powerlessness over his immediate work process.

TECHNOLOGY AND WORK ORGANIZATION:
INSIDE AN INTEGRATED COTTON MILL[12]

The two basic processes in the cotton-textile industry are spinning and weaving. In the spinning room, spindles convert cotton fiber into threads

[8] *Ibid.,* p. 55

[9] In contrast, economic problems in large-scale industries, such as automobiles, are reflected in periodic reductions of force, rather than total shutdowns, which discard the younger, low-seniority employees and tend to protect, relatively, the older workers.

[10] U.S. Department of Commerce, *Statistical Abstracts of the United States, 1961* (Washington: U.S. Government Printing Office, 1961), p. 220.

[11] Severe economic decline in textiles began in 1949; the 1947 Roper study therefore does not illustrate the special insecurity of textile workers. Only 14 per cent of the textile workers and 14 per cent of all workers expected to be laid off in the next six months. Eighty-four per cent of the textile employees and 81 per cent of all employees felt they could have their jobs as long as they wanted (see tables 32 and 31, Appendix B). However, more security was present in the southern industry, where plants were newer and more profitable. Rumors of southern migration must have been quite pronounced in the northern mills. Among southern textile workers only 7 per cent expected to be laid off; 7 per cent were unsure ("don't know" responses); while 86 per cent felt secure. Among northern employees 19 per cent expected a layoff; an additional 18 per cent were unsure; only 63 per cent voiced attitudes of confidence.

[12] I am grateful to Harriet Herring of the University of North Carolina for help in the writing of this section.

or yarn. In the weaving room, looms weave the yarn into cloth. Plants vary in the number of processes carried out. An increasing number of mills, especially the largest ones, carry out every process from the cleaning of the cotton bale to the packaging of finished articles ready for the consumer. At the other extreme, some plants process the cotton only through the spinning stage and sell the yarn to knitting or weaving mills to be made into fabrics. The majority of textile employees work in plants which combine spinning and weaving.[13]

For a closer look at the range of jobs which result from the technology and organization of work in textiles, I shall describe a totally integrated cotton mill which carries out all the processes in the manufacture of sheets and pillow cases. Such a fully integrated mill requires a large plant and at least several hundred workers. There are more than a dozen rooms through which the product moves, in each of which different machinery carries out a particular phase of the manufacturing process.

In the first, the breaker room, three things take place. The cotton, which has been tightly packed into bales at the gin, is loosened. A great deal of the dirt and trash which has accumulated is shaken out. And cotton from dozens of bales is mixed, in order to begin averaging out the differences in the fiber caused by variations in soil and growing conditions. Only a few workers are required on these machines; their work handling the bales is heavy, dirty, and unskilled.

From the breaking room, a mechanical conveyer moves the loose cotton to the picking room, where machines further clean it, form it into sheets, and roll these into "laps" for carding. The work of handling the laps is also heavy and dirty, though less so than the jobs in the breaking room. It requires somewhat higher skill, since it involves the operation of more elaborate machines and controls.

The tasks more characteristic of textile technology and work operations start in the carding room, where the process of straightening the fibers begins. On the carding machine, the lap from the picker is passed over a surface thickly set with bent wires, which comb it, removing noils and aligning the fibers into a sheer, fragile sheet; gather the sheet into a soft roll; and coil it into a deep container or can. Only a few workers are needed to attend many carding machines. The operator feeds the lap into the machine, or, more commonly, joins a new one to the old just before it is exhausted. Besides keeping the card supplied with material, he removes or "doffs" the filled cans. He must also patrol all the machines assigned to him, watching for malfunction. If something goes wrong with the mechanism for gathering and coiling the delicate veil-like sheet of cotton, it spills off the card like a heavy snowfall. The carder and especially the card-grinder, who

---

[13] Many of these mills, however, do not do their own finishing but sell their cloth as "gray goods" to other plants which prepare it for the apparel industry or for the retail trade by bleaching, dyeing, printing, and other processes.

sharpens and keeps the mechanism in working order, are among the most valued machine operatives in a mill, since their process is the basic preparation for spinning.[14]

In the spinning room, fibers are spun into thread through a twisting process which increases their strength. Here, row on row of spinning frames containing thousands of spindles move incessantly up and down, filling the air with a droning hum. These machines are largely automatic. The spinner starts the process by attaching the roving between rollers which attenuate it to a narrow, filmy sliver and deliver it to the fast-turning spindle. The spindle twists the sliver into yarn and winds the yarn onto a bobbin. When this automatic process fails, slivers of cotton accumulate on a waste roll and are visible up and down the alleys between the spinning frames. Reacting to this signal that an "end is down," the spinner hurries to the trouble spot, unwinds a bit of yarn from the bobbin, and "pieces it up," touching the yarn to the sliver to restore the twisting (see Plate 3). She then clears the accumulated cotton from the waste roll. A spinner tends many long frames and must keep on the move, looking for such breaks and stoppages. The work is light and requires only a quick, facile movement in the piecing-up, which is readily learned. In spinning, the work has been more subdivided than in carding, for spinners do not "doff" their own machines. When the bobbins are full, the frames stop automatically, and a doffer, always a male worker, exchanges empty bobbins for the full ones and starts up the machine again. The spinning itself is done exclusively by women. Spinning and weaving are numerically the two largest occupations in the textile industry.[15]

In the weaving room, hundreds or thousands of identical automatic looms weave the yarn into cloth. This is the largest and the noisiest place in a cotton mill. The atmosphere is almost bizarre: the constant back-and-forth motion of the shuttles creates a considerable din, and the striking red and green colors of the looms contrast with the whiteness of the lint settling on everything with a light film.

Although in the past highly skilled weavers performed virtually all the operations in making cloth themselves, the work organization in the weaving room is now extremely subdivided. The most skilled and prestigeful job is that of loom-fixer, who does all the maintenance and repair work.[16] Weaving

[14] There are a number of minor machine processes between carding and spinning which continue the work of straightening the fibers and reducing them into fine "roving" for the spinning frames.

[15] Before the spun yarn is ready to be woven into cloth, several intermediate processes are necessary. Spooling and warping combine yarn from the relatively small bobbins of the spinning frame into larger "packages" for use on the loom (see Plate 2b). These processes are carried out by semiautomatic machines which stop when a thread breaks. The jobs are light, low skilled, and monotonous. The warps, thousands of threads wound parallel on huge spools or beams, then go to the slasher room, where men feed them into a large machine for sizing and starching.

[16] All loom-fixers are men, but there are now as many female as male weavers.

itself is a relatively high-paying job, but the weaver does little except tie together threads which have broken, look for imperfections in the cloth, and start up the machines when necessary. Like the carder, the spinner, the spooler, and the doffer, the weaver is responsible for a large number of machines and must patrol a wide area to keep them from standing idle[17] (see Plate 4).

The remaining processes are finishing operations. From weaving, the woven cloth goes downstairs into a bleaching room, where immersion in huge kettles makes it whiter and cleaner. After bleaching, the cloth moves into an inspection room. Here women inspect the cloth as it is unrolled by a large machine, marking off imperfections with a heavy pencil and rubbing out dirty spots with cleaning fluid. Nearby, male workers operate shearing machines which cut off the frayed ends of the cloth. In the next work area, employees use relatively simple machines to cut cloth into the appropriate sizes for the final products, pillow cases and bedsheets. These jobs are cleaner and lighter than the basic spinning and weaving operations, but they are even more repetitive and routinized, since the worker performs the same operation, standing or sitting in the same place, all day long. These jobs include cutting cloth with a hand cutter, stacking pieces of cloth into neat piles, turning pillow cases "inside out," and operating folding and automatic cutting machines. After these operations the sheets and pillow cases are completed except for the sewing of hems, contour corners, or in a few cases such fancy finishing as scalloped edges. This takes place in the sewing room, where dozens of women operate sewing machines. Next to the sewing room are the packaging machines, where the finished products are wrapped, labeled, and packed in boxes for shipping.

The majority of textile mills do not contain such a wide gamut of processes and jobs. But in their own specialties they still utilize the same kinds of machines and similar principles of work organization. This intensive rationalization means that except for such jobs as loom-fixing, card-grinding, and other maintenance operations, most textile jobs require deftness and alertness rather than skill and can be learned in a few days or at most a few weeks. They become largely automatic and require no refined judgment. John Kenneth Morland, referring to the consequences of this highly developed technology and work organization, writes that textile workers "tend to be interchangeable parts in a machine process." [18]

[17] Other jobs in the weaving room, now done by helpers, are those of doffing, filling batteries, and cleaning looms. Doffers remove rolls of woven cloth; the battery hands keep the magazines on the looms filled with bobbins of yarn which the automatic mechanism inserts into the shuttle as needed; loom-cleaners move along the rows of machines with air hoses and blow lint away from the looms.

[18] John K. Morland, *Millways of Kent* (Chapel Hill: University of North Carolina Press, 1958), p. 30.

THE TEXTILE WORKER'S POWERLESSNESS

The technology and division of labor in textile production reduces the typical worker's control over the immediate work process to a minimum. The textile worker's powerlessness is expressed in a constant work pressure, an inability to control the pace and rhythm of his work activity, a lack of choice of work techniques, and the absence of free physical movement. In his lack of freedom and control, the textile hand's situation is virtually the polar opposite of that of the free craftsman in the printing industry.

In most mills, there is a great deal of work pressure. Each operative has a large number of machines to tend, and there has been a long-run tendency to increase the number that he must look after. In the integrated mill described above, the number of looms each weaver tends was increased from forty-two to sixty in a few years; the workers half-jestingly speak of tending looms "by the acre." The colorful term "stretchout" is the distinctive textile industry word which captures the psychological and bodily strain and stress involved when a worker is given responsibility for more machines than he feels he can comfortably handle.[19] It is analogous to the automobile worker's term for increased work pressure, "speedup." The difference in the two expressions suggests the fact that automobile workers are relatively stationary with respect to the moving conveyer belt which brings them their work load, while textile workers move around and patrol stationary machines. Solomon Barkin describes the textile hand's mixed feelings to the stretchout as a long-standing hatred of this policy, coupled with a persistent anxiety that he will not be able to keep up:

Most moves to increase the number of machines tended by operators create new fears, anxieties and pressures—the cumulative effects of which have bred the historic hatred of the "stretchout." Tension increases among workers as they face both new work patterns and the larger machine assignments with the fear that they may not be able to handle the new job. . . . The worker's greatest fear is that machines will stand idle waiting for him. Not to be 'on top' of the job is a mark, to his peers, of inferior performance as well as an invitation for criticism and reprimand by his superiors. This constant state of alertness to breaks and stops creates a high degree of stress for the textile worker and contributes to his highly emotional responses.[20]

In industries with progressive policies or labor unions which protect the interests of employees, work pressure is relieved by regular rest periods. In some especially arduous steel and longshore jobs, for example, workers

---

[19] Richard C. Nyman, *Union-Management Cooperation in the "Stretch-out"* (New Haven: Yale University Press, 1934).

[20] Solomon Barkin, "The Personality Profile of Southern Textile Workers," *Labor Law Journal*, II (1960), 5.

punctuate every hour of labor with an hour of rest. But there was only one fifteen-minute smoking break per eight-hour shift in the southern mill studied by Morland.[21] Many workers were kept under so much pressure that they could not stop for a drink of water.[22] Sometimes there are not even lunch periods. Workers either eat when they "have caught up to their machines" or continue working while eating.[23] Such extreme conditions are probably more common in the smaller mills. The larger plants are more likely to be unionized and to provide such amenities.

The pressure in the mills prevents most textile workers from controlling the pace at which they work. Only a few workers, e.g., cloth-inspectors, operate machines whose speed they are able to control. The predominant occupations—weavers, spinners, winders and doffers—mind large numbers of machines and must adapt their activities and movements to the technical process. When breaks occur in the yarn which stop a machine or cause material waste, the worker must respond immediately, or he will fall behind in his production quota. There is a constant strain and necessity to keep on the move. It is therefore no surprise that relatively large numbers of textile workers complain of working too fast and getting too tired at the end of a day.

In the Roper study, more textile workers said their jobs made them work too fast than workers in any other industry except automobile manufacturing. Thirty-two per cent complained of pressure, in contrast to 24 per cent of all factory employees (see Table 33, Appendix B). And 38 per cent of the textile workers reported that their jobs leave them "too tired at the end of the day." This was the highest proportion in all sixteen industries except the apparel industry, where a similar percentage is found. The sample norm was 30 per cent. Physical tiredness in the textile industry is not only due to pressure but also stems from the nature of the work, which requires operators to walk around all day, in contrast to printers, who can alternate sitting and standing. Only 12 per cent of the printers report excessive fatigue (see Table 34, Appendix B).

The textile industry is unusual in that job pressure is not limited to the low-skilled jobs. A sizable proportion of skilled workers must also work too fast. Table 3 shows that at each skill level about one-fourth of the male textile workers complain of work pressure, while in the automobile industry, another high-pressure industry, work pressure decreases as the skill level rises.[24]

[21] Morland, *Millways of Kent*, p. 33.
[22] *Ibid.* "Rare is the mill which maintains specified rest periods," according to Barkin (*op. cit.*).
[23] Morland, *Millways of Kent*, p. 33.
[24] I have divided the Roper sample into four skill levels based on the respondents' answers to the question, "How long does a person have to spend in training or experience to be able to handle a job like yours?" In the tables and textual discussions of skill differences in

Because they have little control over their work pace, textile workers do not have as much ability to control the quantity of output as do machinists, sewing-machine operators in the garment industry, or bench workers in light-assembly industries. Since the speed of the carding machines, spinning

TABLE 3

PROPORTION OF MALE TEXTILE, AUTOMOBILE, AND ALL FACTORY WORKERS WHO MUST WORK TOO FAST, BY SKILL LEVEL

INDUSTRY	UNSKILLED (Less than 30 days' training)		LOW SKILLED (1 to 3 months)		MEDIUM SKILLED (3 months to 2 years)		SKILLED (More than 2 years)		TOTAL	
	Per Cent	Number	Per Cent	Number	Per Cent	Number	Per Cent	Number	Per Cent	Number
Textile..........	26	69	24	38	24	62	26	50	25	219
Automobile......	48	73	26	23	24	33	10	29	32	158
All male workers	26	606	23	259	22	581	18	810	22	2,256

frames, and automatic looms is known, it is possible to figure the maximum potential production. By repairing breaks rapidly and keeping machines fed with supply packages, the tender can achieve a higher rather than a lower proportion of that potential. In order to encourage such productivity, incentive pay plans are common in the textile industry, covering about 40 per cent of all workers.[25] Bonus pay for achieving a certain percentage of maximum production encourages the weaver to move rapidly among his looms to see if any have stopped and get them started again. But the textile worker determines output only by default, not by active participation, as does a worker who controls his machine or uses tools.[26]

In contrast to craft industries, workers in machine-tending industries have comparatively little freedom to determine techniques of work, to select tools, and to vary the sequence of operations which make up their jobs. For the

this and in the following chapters the workers with less than thirty days' training are referred to as *unskilled;* those with between one and three months' training, *low skilled;* those with between three months' and two years' training, *medium skilled;* and those with more than two years' training, *skilled.*

[25] U.S. Department of Labor, *Wage Structure: Cotton Textiles* (Bureau of Labor Statistics Report No. 82 [Washington: U.S. Government Printing Office, 1954]), p. 2.

[26] Solomon Barkin, personal communication to the writer. In those situations where workers can control their own pace, piecework may reduce alienation, since it gives the employee more responsibility for the volume of his production. Often piecework reduces the necessity for close supervision over work pace, since financial incentives for high output lessen the importance of external controls. (On the other hand, piecework systems may increase the amount of supervision of quality control and also require more accounting and bookkeeping work.) Piecework often adds to the interest of the job, since the worker measures his output against standards and goals which he has set for himself. It is questionable whether incentive pay plans have had such salutary effects in the textile industry, where companies have tended to increase work loads and cut piece rates whenever mechanical improvements have made this technically feasible and economic pressures have made it necessary. Labor unions have long emphasized these negative consequences of incentive pay plans and usually have worked to eliminate them.

majority of jobs in these industries, which are semiskilled and unskilled, these decisions are incorporated into the machine process, or the work design, or relegated to the supervisor. Judgment and initiative, essential components of traditional skill, are necessary only for a small minority of workers. The mass of operatives in machine-tending industries do repetitive tasks on a fairly standardized product; there is then no technical necessity for decision-making. Even the work of repairing yarn breakages is routine.[27] Whereas 79 per cent of the workers in the printing industry said they could try out their own ideas on the job, the Roper study showed that less than half as many textile workers, 38 per cent, possessed this freedom. Only in leather manufacturing, another machine industry, were there fewer workers with opportunity for initiative. Among all factory workers, 49 per cent could try out their own ideas (see Table 35, Appendix B).

Some industrial workers, like bench assemblers, are restricted to one work station and thus have no physical mobility on the job. Textile workers are also restricted to their work area, but within their stations they are quite mobile. They are constantly moving to keep up with their machines. Yet they have little real freedom of physical movement because they can rarely decide themselves where to go in the department or mill. The constant pressure does not give them the possibility of leaving their work area that the skilled printer, who moves freely about his shop, enjoys. Of the sixteen industries in the Roper study, textiles was one of two in which a majority of workers said they could not leave their work for thirty minutes without someone taking their place (see Table 36, Appendix B).

Lack of free movement is made even more oppressive by the unpleasant atmosphere of the mills. During the summer, humidity is unusually high, and the temperature is often above 100 degrees. In addition, the air in many rooms becomes saturated with lint. Faintness and physical weakness are common,[28] particularly among women who often have full household responsibilities in addition to their employment. Only a few companies have installed air conditioning. Because of the physical atmosphere and the lack of freedom, mill hands refer to the mill as the "prison"; they also call it the "sweatshop" and the "death hole."[29]

A further element of powerlessness in textiles is the fact that the unorganized worker is at the mercy of both major and minor supervisors.[30] In most modern industries, the bureaucratization process has transferred much of the foreman's past power to the personnel office. In this traditional industry, many foremen still have the power to discharge workers and to decide which employees are to be retained in the event of layoffs. They can violate seniority

---

[27] Elliot D. Smith, *Technology and Labor* (New Haven: Yale University Press, 1939), p. 18.
[28] Barkin, *op. cit.*, p. 7.
[29] Morland, *Millways of Kent*, p. 34.
[30] Barkin, *op. cit.*, p. 6.

provisions and give preference to their own favorites. Thus, the worker is always on guard with his superiors and develops a characteristic subservience.[31]

Why have past patterns of close and arbitrary supervision persisted in textile production and not in most other industries today? One explanatory factor is technology. Unlike the automobile assembly line described in the following chapter, a machine technology does not fully control the actions of the worker. When workers are given more machines to tend, supervisors have to make sure that increased work loads are carried out. Their function is to police and enforce. A second factor is economic. The market situation in a declining industry made up principally of small firms, many of which face the threat of bankruptcy, does not permit the kind of relaxed work atmosphere which exists in the economically prosperous chemical industry described in chapters 6 and 7. The social backwardness of the industry is another factor. Sociologically, the textile industry is still in the stage of early industrialism and has not yet been greatly affected by concepts of human relations, modern personnel organization, and other trends that have democratized and bureaucratized relations between workers and employers. Therefore, textile mills often react to the need for greater production by driving workers. And they are able to do this largely because of the absence of unions which could stand as a countervailing power between the workers and arbitrary actions of management.[32]

SOUTHERN MILLS AND WOMEN WORKERS: THE STATISTICS OF A SOCIAL PROBLEM

Objective powerlessness is greater for women textile workers than it is for men and southern employees are less likely to have control over their work process than northern workers. In a sense regional variations in alienation are chiefly of historical interest, since virtually the entire industry is now located in the South. But in 1947, when Roper made his survey, the North-South division was a basic factor in textiles, and his sample was almost evenly divided between workers from the two regions. And if the more mechanized southern industry with its higher levels of powerlessness is now *the* textile industry, then our previous data probably have underemphasized the degree of objective alienation in textiles, compared to other factory work environments. What stands out most strikingly in the regional and sex

---

[31] *Ibid.*

[32] Unions are, in fact, the principal force for modernizing the industry. Union research departments have gathered more facts on the industry and its problems and have a considerably more sophisticated program for its revival than have the companies and their associations. This is made evident by a comparison of union and management analyses and proposals at the U.S. Senate hearings on *Problems of the Domestic Textile Industry* (see n. 5 above).

variations is the especially unfree situation of the women workers in the southern mills.

In textiles, sex is the most important principle of occupational assignment. The very top jobs in skill and pay, for example those of loom-fixer and maintenance machinist, are exclusively male jobs. Women are concentrated in such unskilled occupations as spinners, spool-winders, and battery hands.[33] But the association between sex and skill is not perfect: some routine machine-tending, doffing, and carding-machine operations are performed chiefly by men, and there are as many women as men in weaving, a fairly high-paying and prestigeful occupation in the mill.[34]

Despite this overlap, male textile workers are more likely to be in occupations which give them some degree of control over their work process. Only 24 per cent of the male employees complained that their jobs made them work too fast, compared to 42 per cent of the female employees in the Roper study. Marked work pressure not only characterized women's jobs, it was also more prevalent in the South. Thirty-seven per cent of the southern mill hands compared to 27 per cent of the northerners, said they had to work too fast.[35] And the sex differential is greatest in the South, where 49 per cent of the women complain of excessive pressure in contrast to only 27 per cent of the men (Table 4).

TABLE 4

PROPORTION OF TEXTILE WORKERS WHO MUST WORK TOO FAST, BY REGION AND SEX

REGION	MEN		WOMEN		TOTAL	
	Per Cent	Number	Per Cent	Number	Per Cent	Number
North.........	22	149	35	83	27	232
South.........	27	99	49	75	37	174
Total........	24	248	42	158	31	406

Since women have, on the average, less physical stamina than men, and working women often double as housewives and mothers, it is to be expected that they would be more fatigued by their work. Thus, 49 per cent of the female textile workers are too tired at the end of the workday, compared to 29 per cent of the males. Again, levels of fatigue are higher in the South; 35 per cent of southern men get too tired, as compared to 26 per cent of northern men. For women, the regional differential is dramatic. In the

[33] The low-skilled and low-paying jobs which require heavy lifting and materials-handling, those of bale-handlers, janitors, and hand-truckers, are held down by Negro men in the South.

[34] U.S. Department of Labor, *Wage Structure: Cotton Textiles*, pp. 16 ff.

[35] The stretchout in the southern textile industry was a major cause of the unrest and the strike movements of the 1920's and 1930's. Cf. Liston Pope, *Millhands and Preachers* (New Haven: Yale University Press, 1942).

North 37 per cent of the female employees complained of fatigue; in the
South 61 per cent said that their jobs made them too tired.

TABLE 5

PROPORTION OF TEXTILE WORKERS WHO GET TOO TIRED, BY REGION AND SEX

REGION	MEN		WOMEN		TOTAL	
	Per Cent	Number	Per Cent	Number	Per Cent	Number
North..............	26	149	37	83	30	232
South..............	35	95	61	75	47	170
All textile workers.....	29	244	49	158	37	402
All factory workers....	29	2,196	33	695	30	2,891

One consequence of women's participation in the industrial labor force
is rarely discussed: the upgrading of men's work which results when women
perform most of the unrewarding jobs.[36] Because only one out of five female
textile workers had a job which allowed her to try out her own ideas, it was
possible for almost one out of two male workers to have work permitting
such initiative. Equally large and even larger sex differences in opportunities
for job initiative appear in all other industries with sizable numbers of
female employees, as Table 6 shows.[37]

TABLE 6

PROPORTION OF MEN AND WOMEN WORKERS WHOSE JOBS ALLOW THEM
TO TRY OUT OWN IDEAS, FOR SELECTED INDUSTRIES

INDUSTRY	MEN		WOMEN		TOTAL	
	Per Cent	Number	Per Cent	Number	Per Cent	Number
Textiles........	48	246	21	158	37	404
Apparel........	62	90	34	172	44	262
Leather........	42	76	17	54	32	130
Food..........	50	243	0	36	44	279
Machinery......	47	256	12	33	43	289
Paper..........	56	73	31	29	48	102

The sex difference in chances for job initiative is again more pronounced
in the southern mills. Among northern textile workers, 39 per cent of the
males, compared to 28 per cent of the females, can try out their own ideas,
an important but small difference. However, in the South, 61 per cent of the

[36] Theodore Caplow has contributed one of the most comprehensive analyses of the role of
women in the labor force in his *Sociology of Work* (Minneapolis: University of Minnesota Press,
1954), pp. 230–47.

[37] This interpretation cannot be conclusively supported by my data, since the differences may
not be a simple reflection of objective variations in the jobs men and women hold. I cannot
tell how much more the men value initiative than the more tradition-oriented women workers
and thus exaggerate the extent to which their jobs permit this.

men and only 15 per cent of the women feel they are able to exercise initiative.[38]

Women employees also have less free movement than men, and southern workers are more restricted than northern workers. Women workers, particularly in the South, are more highly supervised, and in these mills the technology is more advanced and more restrictive. Table 7 shows these differences.

TABLE 7

PROPORTION OF TEXTILE WORKERS, BY REGION AND SEX, WHO CAN
LEAVE JOBS FOR THIRTY MINUTES WITHOUT RELIEF

REGION	MEN		WOMEN		TOTAL	
	Per Cent	Number	Per Cent	Number	Per Cent	Number
North................	56	148	48	83	53	231
South................	50	101	35	74	43	175
All textile workers.....	53	249	42	157	49	406
All factory workers....	70	2,157	54	756	66	2,903

Thus, on every indicator of powerlessness, the Roper study suggests that women textile workers have less freedom and control than men, and southern employees have less freedom and control than northerners. The female employee's disadvantageous position is much more striking in the South than in the North; in addition, some of the regional differential shown by Roper's survey is due to the fact that there were proportionately more of these especially deprived women workers in the southern mills. The pronounced powerlessness of southern women suggests the need for union organization to increase their freedom and improve the working conditions which result in 61 per cent being too tired at the end of the workday.

MEANINGLESSNESS

Textile technology intensifies powerlessness, and its highly subdivided organization of work contributes to the alienation of meaninglessness. Most work in textile mills lacks the variety of operations common in the printing industry. When jobs are so fractionized, it is difficult for textile workers to feel they play an important part in the company's total scheme of production. The problem of meaninglessness may be aggravated in textiles because craft methods of work once predominated in the industry.[39] Many

[38] This finding is striking but also difficult to interpret with any certainty. The objective difference between the work of men and women may be more pronounced in the South, but hardly enough to account for such discrepant figures. Traditional conceptions of sex roles are probably stronger in the South. Southern male workers may be disposed to say their jobs permit independence as an assertion of their manliness. On the other hand, southern women may be expressing traditional notions of the propriety of submissive female behavior.

[39] Smith, *op. cit.*

older workers still remember when mill occupations commanded great skill and considerable variety.

Weavers were at one time the most highly skilled and prestigeful craftsmen in the industry. Even after the automatic loom eliminated many of their traditional skills, their jobs retained considerable variety and interest. But as work organization has been more and more rationalized, many of the tasks which made up the weaver's job have been parceled out to loom-cleaners, battery hands, doffers, and other weaving-room operators. The same is true for the second largest occupation in the mills, that of the spinners. Before the realignment of jobs, a spinner blew off her frames with an air hose, cleaned or "picked" rolls, set in new bobbins of roving in her machines, put up the ends after doffing, and put up broken ends of yarn. At present she performs only the latter of these five operations. The rest are consigned to other specialized workers or are taken care of by automatic processes.[40]

On the other hand, it is quite possible for the textile operator to understand the processes of production of the mill as a whole. Though highly rationalized, machine operations and work flow are simple enough to make sense. Many plants are small, and their organization of production is readily comprehensible to the workers.

There are few data available on the intensity and importance of meaninglessness alienation for textile workers. If, as it seems likely, the extreme division of labor makes it difficult to achieve a sense of individual purpose in the actual operation of work, this may not be a critical matter. Tradition-oriented workers rarely expect to derive meaning from the work process itself. And as I attempt to demonstrate in the next section, the industrial community provides their work life with social meaning.

TRADITIONAL INDUSTRY AND COMMUNITY INTEGRATION:
CONSEQUENCES FOR POLITY AND PERSONALITY

In the textile industry, technology, work organization, and economic conditions all are powerful alienating factors. The social organization of the industry, on the other hand, integrates the worker into an industrial community. Because the millworker is not alienated socially, his powerlessness does not lead to the discontent common among other industrial workers who lack both control and integration. Social cohesion in textiles results chiefly from the worker's relation to the larger community rather than from the integration of functional work groups in the factory.[41] With the industry located almost entirely in the South today, most mills are situated in small

[40] Harriet Herring, personal communication to the writer.
[41] As is the case in the steel industry, where production is carried out by crews. See Charles R. Walker, *Steeltown* (New York: Harper & Bros., 1950), pp. 63–89.

towns or villages, where the family and the church are the dominant institutions and where traditional patterns and social relationships that reflect the isolation of both the region and the village community still prevail.

In the smaller mills, there may be considerable opportunity for social interaction on the job. In a knitting mill observed by the writer, women machine operators sat close to one another in rows, talked to each other while working, and even at times broke into spontaneous group-singing of religious songs. But in the larger spinning and weaving mills, there are few natural working groups and relatively few opportunities for socializing while carrying out the job. Machine-tenders do their jobs individually. Functional work teams are prevented by the overlapping of machine assignments. In one weaving room, each weaver was assigned 72 looms, each loomfixer, 94; each battery hand, 53; and each cloth-doffer, 965; so that no sense of collective responsibility developed among different workers for a common machine patrol.[42] Furthermore, there are relatively few workers in the machine rooms because each person has a heavy work load over a large area, as Plate 4 clearly shows. Although employees adapt to the noise of machinery, most pronounced in weaving rooms, opportunities for socialization are also lessened because of the pressure of work and because management openly frowns on worker conversation.[43] Yet because the work force is very homogeneous, shorthand communication is readily developed, and rumors spread rapidly through the mill.[44]

The mode of integration in the textile industry differs greatly from that of other industries in this study. Unlike printing's integration, it is not based on identification with a craft and the internalization of the standards and rules of the occupation and the craft associations. It is not based on the formal rules and procedures which emerge from the conflict of management and workers, as is the case in the automobile industry. Though the high degree of loyalty to the company which characterizes the textile industry is similar to that found in the chemical industry, this integration is based much more on the common backgrounds of workers and management within a homogeneous community than it is on functional interdependence in an industrial enterprise.

Although it is sometimes dangerous to generalize about the textile industry, because particular villages and companies differ greatly and conditions are changing, integration in the industry (especially in the South) tends to be based upon traditional rather than bureaucratic norms. It is a situation which contrasts strikingly with more modern industries. There is less of an emphasis on formal systems of rules, particularly written procedures; the regularizing influence of labor unions is lacking. Instead, the accent is on

[42] Smith, *op. cit.*, pp. 31–32.
[43] Barkin, *op. cit.*, p. 7.
[44] Harriet Herring, personal communication to the writer.

personal relations with management, loyalties of kinship and neighborhood, and a religious sanction on submission to things as they are. These traditional patterns are most pronounced in the smaller mills and villages.

When administration is traditional, it is based on customary ways of doing things, and policy is implicit and unwritten. In many medium-sized as well as many small southern mills, Glenn Gilman reports that "there are no elaborate supervisor's handbooks to which additional leaves are added each week, no continuing codification of policy." [45] Larger companies, of course, have developed bureaucratic routines. They cannot simply rely on "the golden rule" as a general manager of a Georgia mill claims to do! In Gilman's view, the quotation from this man epitomizes the informality and traditionalism of industrial relations which characterize the southern textile industry:

You can't possible develop a written body of policy that's extensive enough and yet detailed enough to deal with the situations you meet. Either you have to be constantly making exceptions to your policy, or else you stick to the policy and make a lot of decisions that actually aren't fair. We have a few simple rules and regulations about tardiness and absences and vacations and drunkenness on the job and things like that; but for the most part, we stick to the Golden Rule as our personnel policy—and with the exception of that one, we haven't got a rule or regulation we can't break if it stands in the way of doing the right thing. [46]

The arbiter of what is "fair" and "the right thing" is of course management—as is characteristic of the prebureaucratic factory. None of the twenty-three mills which provided Gilman with his data used a formal grievance procedure. Informal grievance procedures operated in about half the mills. Only 16 per cent of the workers in the southern textile industry are in mills covered by union contracts. [47]

When a union is successfully organized in a southern mill, textile management is less likely than management in bureaucratic industries to accept it as a partner in the rule-making process. Textile companies try to nullify collective-bargaining machinery. Supervisors resent the union's intrusion; top management emphasizes its open-door policy for dealing with the complaints of individuals, instead of recognizing the union committee. "Rules are promulgated without consultation, and union suggestions for revision and adjustment are arbitrarily rejected simply to re-emphasize the union's limited power." [48]

In bureaucratic work organizations, impersonal and objective criteria of performance predominate over personal qualities such as family connections

[45] Glenn Gilman, *Human Relations in the Industrial Southeast: A Study of the Textile Industry* (Chapel Hill: University of North Carolina Press, 1956), p. 266.

[46] *Ibid.*

[47] U.S. Department of Labor, *Wage Structure: Cotton Textiles*, p. 2.

[48] Barkin, *op. cit.*, p. 12.

and religious affiliation. But in the traditional textile industry, family and kinship relationships penetrate the work situation. Husband, wife, and children (as well as other members of the close extended families characteristic of southern villages) often work in the same mill. In considering job applicants, the recommendations of people working for the company are given great weight. "Family connections and where the applicant was born and reared are important. . . . A good part of the employment interview . . . may be devoted to establishing just 'who' the applicant is in terms of his kinfolk and in terms of people who he and the interviewer know in common." [49]

Although such close family ties give the worker emotional security important in sustaining himself under difficult conditions of existence, they also inhibit striving for freedom and control. A worker who is self-assertive or joins a union may fear that not only he but other members of his family will lose their jobs. Direct company domination is less powerful than in the past, since mills in most company towns have sold their housing to the workers.[50] But partly because of tradition and partly because of the submissive personalities of textile workers, mill managements still retain considerable paternalistic control.

Religion is another institution which integrates the community and inhibits the independence of the workers. In southern towns, the church teaches the worker the importance of obedience to authority and reinforces his submissiveness and resignation to the conditions of this world by promising him substitute gratifications in the afterlife. When labor-management conflicts do arise, the church is generally a strong supporter of the employer's position.[51] Finally, the highly emotional expression of the fundamentalist churches and the frequent revivals are an important safety valve for those tensions created by the stifling conditions of the cotton mill.[52]

When cotton mills were first built in the southern states, the new factories were viewed as community projects invested with the philanthropic goal of restoring the region which had been devastated economically by the Civil War and its aftermath.[53] Even today, industry which locates and prospers in the South contributes to the economic resurgence of an area less developed

---

[49] Gilman, *op. cit.,* p. 272. In the long run the importance of such particularistic factors will probably decrease. At least one of the largest employers in the industry does not permit relatives to work in the same plant.

[50] Harriet Herring, *Passing of the Mill Village* (Chapel Hill: University of North Carolina Press, 1949).

[51] Pope, *op. cit.*

[52] In his classic work, *The Mind of the South,* Wilbur Cash points out that the period of the most rapid expansion of southern industrialism was also the time of the greatest growth of emotional religious sects and the heyday of the traveling evangelist (New York: Alfred Knopf, 1941), pp. 291 ff.

[53] Broadus Mitchell, *Rise of the Cotton Mills in the South* (Baltimore: Johns Hopkins Press, 1921).

than the North, and this provides a basis for the identification of the textile industry with the community. In addition, mill villages are small, and the people are homogeneous in cultural background. For all these reasons, work in the southern textile industry is more highly integrated with the local community than in the multi-industry northern cities, where the diversity of manufactures prevents close identification with any one industry, and a man's occupation is therefore less visible.

The Roper study appears to confirm the fact that kinship, religion, and community loyalties reinforce feelings of identification with the mills. Despite the working conditions described earlier, textile workers score high on all indicators of company loyalty. Eighty-four per cent felt that their company was about as good a place to work as any other in the same line of work, compared to only 73 per cent of all factory workers (see Table 38, Appendix B). This procompany attitude was strongest in the South, where 89 per cent of the millworkers concurred, despite the fact that there was more objective powerlessness in southern mills. Ninety-five per cent of the textile workers felt that their jobs were essential to the success of the company, compared to 89 per cent of the whole sample—only one industry had more positive responses (see Table 39, Appendix B). Finally, textile workers gave relatively few cynical responses to the question of what gives a person the best chance to advance. Male workers, usually somewhat skilled, emphasize "the quality of his work"; female workers, in the lower-skilled jobs, stress a person's "energy and willingness to work" (see Table 46, Appendix B).

Like northern printers, southern textile workers possess an occupational community. In fact, the insulation of millworkers from people in other walks of life is so pronounced that some observers view them as a separate caste in the southern system of stratification. As a leading southern social scientist puts it:

The mill workers were in many respects actually more segregated than the Negro elements of Kent society. It is difficult to see how they were less despised and discriminated against by the dominant white elements. If one were a member of a mill village, he had no more chance of being invited to dinner by "respectable" white families than had a Negro, nor could he entertain much greater expectations of marrying into a "respectable" white family, going to the same college where their children go, belonging to their clubs. . . . The mill people lived very much in a world of their own. Although they spent their lives within walking distance of the town people, the culture of their villages was, in many ways, something apart.[54]

Another student of the industry, Glenn Gilman, feels that conditions have so improved for southern cotton workers that they should no longer be

[54] John Gillin, "Introduction," in Morland, *Millways of Kent,* p. ix.

considered a caste. He feels that occupational status is no longer synonymous with total community status and that millworkers now feel equal to anyone.[55] Gilman's views must be treated cautiously because he tends to romanticize mill culture; however, one would expect that the modernization of the South, reflected in increasing industrialization and urbanization, would reduce the isolation of its textile workers. Yet, as recently as 1949, in one mill community 65 per cent of the employed children of millworkers were also working in the cotton plants.[56] And ten years later, 52 per cent of the children who had meanwhile completed high school or dropped out of school in this same community were working in the mills.[57] On the basis of these studies, Morland feels that there is a tendency "toward establishing an inbred occupational group" and that this solidifies differences between mill people and others in the community. He feels that the social stigma which town people apply to textile workers promotes feelings of *esprit de corps* and security among the mill villagers.[58]

Although it, too, is a source of normative integration and cohesion, the southern textile worker's occupational community is very different from that of the printer's, described in the previous chapter. It is not the expression of the worker's freedom, because it is virtually a compulsory membership group reflecting the occupation's subjected castelike status. For a printer, membership in the occupational community represents voluntary choice. However, the textile worker's community, although largely spontaneous and informal, is not fully autonomous. Paternalism is on the decline, but the worker's community is still controlled by the powers in the industry, in contrast to the printer's occupational community, which is a reflection of the independent power of the craft and the unions. Voluntary associations are rare in the traditional culture of textile communities, and those which do exist cannot become independent centers of power. In contrast with the situation in printing, the occupational community in textiles does not further participation in the civic and political life of the industry and society, but instead discourages contact with, and independent activity in, the larger community. The millworker's occupational community, then, is not an expression and vehicle of personal dignity, but rather another adaptive element in his pattern of submission.

The most significant consequence of any community is its effect on individual personality. Morland, in his study of the Kent mill village, employed depth psychological tests and long interviews to construct the typical personality of the southern millworker. As he himself summarizes his findings:

[55] Gilman, *op. cit.*, pp. 284 ff.
[56] Morland, *Millways of Kent*, p. 51.
[57] John Kenneth Morland, "Educational and Occupational Aspirations of Mill and Town School Children in a Southern Community," *Social Forces*, xxxix (1960), 174.
[58] Morland, *Millways of Kent*, pp. 51 ff.

The typical textile worker (1) accepts life as he finds it, and is not aggressive in seeking to change his condition. He is resigned to his lot. (2) He seems to be more noncompetitive than competitive, more dependent than independent, more submissive than dominant. (3) He lacks confidence in himself and feels inadequate, especially when faced with new or difficult tasks. He is humble. (4) He is reserved, quiet, and cautious, particularly when with strangers. He seems to repress his feelings more than to give them expression. (5) He is suspicious of and even hostile toward outsiders. (6) The most prevalent feeling states, particularly for children, seem to be fear and anxiety.

Morland also includes a few more "positive" traits in his personality sketch: devotion to the kin group, warm friendship to those who are friendly and uncritical, a reliable and co-operative attitude toward work, and generosity in giving time and money to help those in need.[59]

The ego of the southern textile worker is therefore as characteristically weak as that of the craft printer is strong. Although industry and occupation are not the only factors (certainly the difference between the milieu of the northern city and the southern village is very critical), these polar types demonstrate how significantly a man's relationship to his work affects his entire personal and social being.[60]

THE LOW ASPIRATIONS OF A TRADITIONAL LABOR FORCE

And yet because of the nature of its labor force, the intense objective powerlessness involved in textile work leads to relatively few subjective manifestations of self-estrangement. Textile workers have been drawn largely from traditional elements of society—the foreign-born, rural southerners, women, and the uneducated. These workers generally entered the mills without previous industrial experience. Because of their social backgrounds and isolation from the main currents of American culture, their aspirations, needs, and perspectives differ from those of more modern workers—typically, the American-born, northern, urban, and more highly educated males. Workers with traditional orientations do not value control and self-expression as much as do more modern industrial workers; the absence of these factors therefore does not result in felt self-estrangement.

From its beginnings, the textile industry has been a low-wage industry with little attraction to the native American outside the South. In the New England branch of the industry, foreign-born workers dominated the labor

[59] *Ibid.*, pp. 227–51.
[60] Although textile workers rarely leave their community to find jobs in other industries, there is some out-migration of young people and the more volatile workers. Since the social structure of the textile industry provides so few outlets for independent spirits, such people tend to leave the community entirely. This further reduces the already small pool of potentially independent leaders and intensifies the homogeneity of the community's character types.

A FUNDAMENTAL TEXTILE PROCESS: *Spinning*

A spinner pieces together two ends of broken yarn. The textile operative must patrol several long alleys of spinning spindles looking for breaks in the material. (Courtesy of the American Textile Manufacturers' Institute, Inc.)

A FUNDAMENTAL TEXTILE PROCESS: *Weaving*

Semiautomatic looms in the weaving room shuttle back and forth producing cloth from spools of yarn. Note the visual evidence of heavy work loads: there are more than two hundred looms visible in this picture, but only three workers can be seen. (Courtesy of the American Textile Manufacturers' Institute, Inc.)

force. As Herbert Lahne puts it: "What the immigrant was to the New England mill, the native farmer was to the Southern mill. Both were without previous experience in industry, and both came to the mill with rural habits of work and standards of living." [61] Even the low wages and restricted freedom in the mills were an improvement over the worker's former destitute status as a submarginal farmer.[62]

The industry has also been a large employer of women; today 43 per cent of its employees are female. The high concentration of women in low-skilled, unfree industrial jobs seems to be a major safety valve against the consequences of alienating work conditions. As we have seen, women textile workers are concentrated in jobs which are the least skilled, the most repetitive, and the least free. This makes it more likely for men to have jobs with the opposite attributes. And as we shall see shortly, women in the industry are not dissatisfied with such work. Work does not have the central importance and meaning in their lives that it does for men, since their most important roles are those of wives and mothers.

The textile worker's lack of education is especially critical. Studies of job attitudes suggest that formal education increases a worker's need for control and self-expression in work. In the Roper study, textile workers were the least educated of the sixteen industrial groups; 69 per cent had grade-school educations or less, compared to 50 per cent of the entire sample (see Table 44, Appendix B). Lack of education means less exposure to the communication channels of the larger society; it means narrow horizons and thus unfamiliarity with other occupations and possibilities for gratification.

In the last chapter, we saw that the non-alienated work relationship characteristic of a craft industry had a number of subjective consequences for printers: work was involving and interesting, provided an opportunity for personal growth, gave a positive occupational identity, and was viewed as an end in itself. When we look at the situation of textile workers with respect to each of these aspects of self-estrangement, we do not find the expected relationships between objective alienation and its subjective expression. The traditional-oriented workers in the industry have few aspirations for work with control, challenge, and growth potential, and are therefore not greatly frustrated by the absence of these qualities.

Involvement and interest.—Whereas craft work requires constant attention to the task at hand, since the craftsman is controlling and manipulating his materials, a machine-tending technology produces a large number of jobs which become highly routine. The work of minding semiautomatic machines

[61] Herbert A. Lahne, *The Cotton Mill Worker* (New York: Farrar and Rinehart, 1944), pp. 76–78.

[62] For a discussion of the impact of these social origins on the southern workers' political response to industrialization, see Robert Blauner, "Industrialization and Labor Response: The Case of the American South," *Berkeley Publications in Society and Institutions*, IV (1958), pp. 29–43.

is not deeply involving; workers, therefore, can let their minds wander and be detached from any intense immersion in the activity. Fifty-four per cent of the textile workers in the Roper survey said they could do their work and keep their minds on other things most of the time, in contrast to 43 per cent of all factory workers. This was the highest proportion of non-involvement among all sixteen industries, equaled only by a similar percentage among apparel workers (see Table 41, Appendix B).

To be sure, there is considerably more involvement in skilled jobs. Among male textile workers, only 27 per cent of the skilled can let their minds wander off course, in contrast to 48 per cent of the other workers.[63] Women are concentrated in the least-skilled and most repetitive jobs; their work is therefore the least involving. Sixty-four per cent of the women employees and 46 per cent of the men can let their minds wander. Table 8 shows that this sex differential is even more pronounced in other industries which have significant numbers of female employees, although the leather industry is an exception.

TABLE 8

PROPORTION OF MEN AND WOMEN WORKERS WHO CAN THINK
OF OTHER THINGS WHILE WORKING, FOR SELECTED INDUSTRIES

INDUSTRY	MEN		WOMEN		TOTAL	
	Per Cent	Number	Per Cent	Number	Per Cent	Number
TEXTILE.......	46	246	64	158	53	404
Apparel........	37	90	61	181	53	271
Food...........	39	244	63	54	43	298
Machinery.....	38	257	44	39	39	296
Leather........	36	76	30	54	33	130
Paper.........	19	73	52	33	29	106

Among printers, involvement in work was associated with a striking degree of job interest. Considering the detachment possible in most textile jobs, we would expect these workers to express little interest in their work and to experience instead considerable monotony. Yet only 18 per cent of the textile workers feel that their jobs are dull or monotonous most or all of the time—this is less than the over-all sample norm of 20 per cent (see Table 42, Appendix B).

Why do textile workers find objectively unchallenging work interesting rather than monotonous? Because of their traditional backgrounds, they do not expect variety in work tasks or inherent interest in millwork and therefore do not define repetitive, non-involving jobs as monotonous. The survey data further revealed that unskilled and low-skilled male textile workers are

[63] There were 48 male respondents who were skilled and 169 respondents in the other three categories of lesser skill. For the definition of the four skill categories in the Roper sample, see n. 24.

much less dissatisfied than these workers in other industries; that women in the industry are less bored than men when they work on similarly repetitive jobs; and that southerners suffer less from monotony than northern mill-workers.

In virtually all industries, the degree of work interest for men varies directly and markedly with the skill level of the job. In a high-skilled craft industry such as printing, only 4 per cent find their jobs dull or monotonous; in a low-skilled assembly-line industry such as automobile manufacturing, 34 per cent complain of monotony. And in textiles, too, the degree of monotony is a "function" of skill, for male workers. Of the unskilled, 27 per cent find their jobs dull; of the low-skilled, 16 per cent are bored; of the medium-skilled men, 19 per cent complain of monotony; and of the skilled group, only 3 per cent find their jobs dull. Yet the unskilled and low-skilled male textile workers are less likely to be bored than workers with similar training in other industries. Compared to 27 per cent in textiles, 38 per cent of the un-skilled in the entire sample find their jobs monotonous. In the automobile industry 61 per cent in this category are dissatisfied! Compared to 16 per cent in the textile industry, 25 per cent of the low skilled in the entire sample find their jobs monotonous. Among the medium-skilled and skilled male textile workers, the proportion dissatisfied is strikingly similar to that in other industries (see Table 47, Appendix B).

Though skill level affects the degree of felt monotony, unskilled and low skilled male textile workers are less dissatisfied and bored than their counter-parts in other industries because of their relatively low aspiration level. And women workers, concentrated in non-involving jobs which permit little control or initiative, also find these "objectively dull" jobs interesting. In the entire industry, only 20 per cent of the women workers find their jobs monotonous, compared to 16 per cent of the men—despite the contrast in the actual nature of the work.

A final reason for the low level of felt monotony in the textile industry is its high proportion of southern workers. Because of their relative lack of education and aspiration, southerners are less likely to find routine work monotonous than northerners. Only 11 per cent of the southern textile em-ployees found their jobs dull, in contrast to 23 per cent of the northerners. As Table 9 shows, the regional difference is striking for both men and women.[64]

Personal growth.—Another aspect of self-estrangement is concerned with opportunities for the expression of a worker's resources and skills and the development of new potentialities. Because of the technology and social relations of textile production, the majority of workers have no possibility for personal growth and development in their work. Few jobs involve any

---

[64] Part of the regional difference may be due to the fact that the over-all skill level was higher in the South for both men and women and therefore fewer jobs were "objectively" dull.

challenge or demand judgment. In addition, the paternalistic attitudes of management and supervisors discourage the responsibility of the worker, who is viewed as a child that must be directed and looked after. The constant supervision and work pressure develop a dependent, rather than an independent, attitude. The lack of collective institutions, particularly unions,

TABLE 9

PROPORTION OF TEXTILE WORKERS WHO FIND JOBS DULL AND MONOTONOUS, MOST OR ALL OF THE TIME, BY REGION AND SEX

REGION	MEN		WOMEN		TOTAL	
	Per Cent	Number	Per Cent	Number	Per Cent	Number
North..........	20	149	28	83	23	232
South..........	10	103	12	75	11	178
Total........	16	252	20	158	18	410

to provide a textile worker with protection and dignity, reinforces this dependency.[65]

Considering the nature of textile work, one would expect that few employees would feel that their jobs were sufficient outlets for their capacities. Yet only 23 per cent of the textile workers feel that their jobs are "too simple to bring out [their] best abilities." This is somewhat less than the over-all sample norm of 25 per cent (see Table 43, Appendix B).[66] These data do not indicate that textile jobs are fulfilling. Instead they clearly suggest that textile

[65] Only 38 per cent of textile workers feel that they can try out their own ideas on the job, in contrast to 49 per cent of all factory workers in the Roper study (see Table 35, Appendix B). Although skilled workers have more initiative than the unskilled in all industries, including textiles, even the skilled male employees in this industry are at a disadvantage because of its distinctive technology and social institutions. Fifty-seven per cent of the male textile workers with more than two years' job training can try out their own ideas; in the entire sample 66 per cent of the male skilled workers have such opportunity for self-expression. As we have seen earlier in this chapter, women, particularly in the South, are least likely to say that their jobs allow them to try out their ideas (see pp. 72–73).

[66] To be sure, the skilled workers are the most satisfied on this score, the unskilled the most dissatisfied. Yet the textile workers' low level of aspiration is suggested by the fact that at each skill level there are fewer male employees who consider their jobs too simple than there are at comparable levels in the automobile industry (Table 10).

TABLE 10

PROPORTION OF MALE TEXTILE AND AUTOMOBILE WORKERS WHO FEEL JOBS ARE TOO SIMPLE TO BRING OUT BEST ABILITIES, BY SKILL LEVEL

SKILL LEVEL	TEXTILE WORKERS		AUTOMOBILE WORKERS	
	Per Cent	Number	Per Cent	Number
Unskilled.............	36	69	49	73
Low skilled...........	16	37	35	23
Medium skilled.......	19	59	27	33
Skilled..............	9	45	17	29

workers have very low estimates of their own abilities and possibilities. A low level of aspiration is most striking in the South and among women. In the South only 16 per cent felt that their jobs were too simple, and women in objectively less challenging work were no more likely to express dissatisfaction than men[67] (see Table 11).

TABLE 11

PROPORTION OF TEXTILE WORKERS, BY REGION AND SEX, WHO FEEL
JOBS ARE TOO SIMPLE FOR THEIR BEST ABILITIES

REGION	MEN		WOMEN		TOTAL	
	Per Cent	Number	Per Cent	Number	Per Cent	Number
North..........	27	148	31	83	29	231
South..........	15	91	16	75	16	166
Total........	23	239	24	158	23	397

The textile industry also restricts the development of its employees' potential because of its limited opportunities for advancement. There are few skilled jobs. The occupational ladder is limited, and there is a narrow wage spread. In 1954 about half the workers in the southern part of the industry were earning between $1.00 and $1.20 per hour.[68] Of the major industries, only the wage distribution in automobile manufacturing is more compressed.

Advancement possibilities are also reduced because of economic stagnation. As an old industry, textiles has long since passed through the periods of expansion and growth which bring increased promotion opportunities. In the present period of economic decline, textile workers are indeed fortunate simply to hold on to their jobs.

In the Roper study, only 40 per cent of the textile workers say their jobs lead to promotions if they do them well. This is the fourth lowest industrial figure: only the leather; stone, clay, and glass; and automobile industries have lower proportions (see Table 45, Appendix B). Advancement into management ranks is even more unlikely because of the mill hands' low education, lack of social skills, and castelike status. Only 11 per cent thought they had good chances of getting jobs above the level of foreman, considerably less than the 20 per cent so optimistic among the entire sample (see Table 49, Appendix B).[69]

[67] That these data reflect levels of aspiration, rather than reluctance to express discontent, is supported by the fact that southern women employees were quite forthright in expressing dissatisfaction with job pressures and fatigue.

[68] The wage spread is more compressed for women than men. The interquartile range is approximately eighteen cents for the female and twenty-six cents for the male workers. U.S. Department of Labor, *Wage Structure: Cotton Textiles*, p. 3, pp. 10–11.

[69] Only the leather industry had a lower proportion of workers who thought they might attain such a position.

Some students of the southern textile industry suggest that advancement may be held back

When there are many women in an industry, the advancement chances of the male workers are increased. Women are concentrated in the lowest-skilled jobs which are usually dead ends. In industries such as textiles, where strong traditional attitudes about the relative status of the sexes prevail, women are rarely considered for higher positions. Male textile workers can therefore be somewhat more optimistic about advancement, since they can hope for one of the few skilled jobs or a job supervising the ranks of women. Indeed, more than half of the male textile workers, 53 per cent, said that their jobs lead to promotions; only 16 per cent of the women workers felt this way. In apparel, another industry with a predominantly female labor force, 54 per cent of the men and 33 per cent of the women expected promotions.[70]

ARE TEXTILE WORKERS SELF-ESTRANGED?

Occupational identity.—Though the low aspirations of tradition-oriented textile workers permit relative satisfaction with work lacking freedom, control, and self-expression and though the community integration in the mill towns result in loyalty to employers, work in the textile industry does not provide an occupational identity which is approved of by the self and by others. The low status of mill hands in the community, the low wages,

by the attitudes of the workers themselves. In traditional communities, to better oneself may be viewed as a group betrayal, an attempt to stand apart from the collective in a society which does not sanction individuation. These attitudes would seem more likely when considerable social distance exists between workers and supervisors, as is now the case in the textile industry. Morland, for example, mentions the typical resentment of villagers toward those who have become foremen through their own efforts. The circumspect worker who is pushed into the job is not resented, and often this is the only way such jobs can be filled. He cites the case of a young worker studying textiles by correspondence in order to get ahead, who feared that the other "workers would run me out of the mill if they found out." Morland, *Millways of Kent*, p. 35.

My analysis of the Roper study does not support the idea that southern textile workers are apathetic toward promotion. Forty-eight per cent of the southern men said they would like to be foremen some day, compared to 35 per cent of the northern men. Sixty-five per cent of the southern men expected promotions if they did well, compared to 45 per cent of the northerners. And 18 per cent of the southerners thought they might rise above the foreman level, compared to 15 per cent of the northerners. Perhaps another reason for these differences is the fact that the more favorable economic conditions in the southern part of the industry made such ambitions more realistic.

The individualism of southern textile employees is also suggested by the fact that they were much more likely than either northerners or southern women to feel that ability, rather than seniority, should be the major criterion for promotion to foreman.

[70] Other industries with sizable minorities of women workers show even greater differences. In the food industry, 52 per cent of the men and only 3 per cent of the women expect promotions; in machinery, 53 per cent of the men and 9 per cent of the women; in paper manufacturing, 66 per cent of the men and 26 per cent of the women. Among leather workers, men and women were equally pessimistic about their chances to get ahead.

With regard to rising above the foreman level, 16 per cent of the male textile workers and only 3 per cent of the females were optimistic. Similar differences by sex appear in all industries.

economic insecurity, and lack of freedom and control, inevitably tend toward a deflation of self-esteem.

The submissiveness required of male textile workers must be damaging to the maintenance of a sure sense of masculinity;[71] the low wages and status undoubtedly threaten the sense of worth and success in life. Despite the greater physical discomforts of her job, textile employment for the female worker is not as damaging to her sense of identity, since successful work is not part of the traditional female role. Thus, in the Roper study, 62 per cent of the male workers said that if they could go back to the age of 15, they would choose different trades or occupations. Only 43 per cent of the women felt this way. (Table 12 also suggests that the status of the textile worker rankles somewhat more in the North than in the South.)

TABLE 12

PROPORTION OF TEXTILE WORKERS, BY REGION AND SEX,
WHO WOULD CHOOSE A DIFFERENT OCCUPATION

REGION	MEN		WOMEN		TOTAL	
	Per Cent	Number	Per Cent	Number	Per Cent	Number
North.........	64	148	45	83	57	231
South.........	59	104	41	74	51	178
Total........	62	252	43	157	54	409

Work as a means to an end.—A final consequence of objectively alienating conditions is that work becomes instrumental, a means to an end, rather than an activity fulfilling and meaningful in itself. For textile workers, work has been neither an end in itself nor a means to an end. Work can only become instrumental when it has been compartmentalized as a separate aspect of life. As we have seen, in the textile worker's folk community, work has been highly integrated with family and kinship, with religion, and with local ties. In such a context, similar to preindustrial society in general, even work which is objectively distasteful is not alienating.

Again the question of aspiration is paramount. Objectively alienated work is less likely to be viewed primarily as a means to an end when workers have not been exposed to alternatives which are potentially more self-realizing. Work in the textile industry, particularly because of its location in small southern communities, fosters a narrow provincialism and lack of exposure to new stimuli and experience. Workers are physically isolated and cut off from the larger society; few have traveled outside their own county.[72]

[71] Solomon Barkin suggests that the family in southern textile communities is typically dominated by a mother or grandmother, another factor which contributes to a submissive male personality. Personal communication to the writer.

[72] In 1958, Morland revisited the ninety-six mill families he studied in 1948. Only eleven of these had moved from Kent, and of these eleven, nine lived within forty miles of the town. "Stability and Change among Mill-Village Families" (unpublished manuscript).

In the long run, the situation in the textile industry may be considerably more dynamic than what has been depicted here. The isolated mill village may become less typical of the industry as the larger, more modern plants tend to locate in small towns and middle-sized cities. In such locations, the old paternalistic control of the employer holds less sway, as jobs in other mills and even in other industries become increasingly available. Company power, already weakened by the sale of mill housing to the employees, will decline further as economic improvements and educational upgrading raise the level of expectations of the work force. As the traditional worker develops a more modern outlook, alienation and dissatisfaction are likely to increase. It may be a long time before the cohesive industrial community based on the loyalty of the worker to the company and the integration of work with non-work concerns gives way to the more normal industrial model of class conflict, bureaucratic union-management relations, and alienation. Trends, however, are in this direction.

But, at present, the southern textile industry is perhaps the best example in modern America of an industry where objective tendencies toward subjective alienation are overcome, not by fulfilling or creative work, but through the traditional integration of work and non-work concerns, particularly its connections with family, religion, and community. Depending on one's perspective, the situation can be viewed as an almost idyllic folk society or as a rather totalitarian community dominated by paternalistic management.[73] The evidence on the reaction of management to union threats suggests that the folk element is not totally spontaneous and that an important component of coercion exists. Industry tends to dominate religion, kinship, and neighborhood,[74] instead of religion, kinship, and local ties dominating work activity, as is typical in primitive and agrarian societies. Even so, the interlocking of work and life in an integrated industrial community probably makes the job of a textile worker meaningful, if not necessarily highly gratifying and rewarding.

In the following chapter, we look at another industrial environment with strong alienating tendencies, but where the compartmentalization of work from other areas of life has developed to its greatest extent. Automobile workers, products of an impersonal assembly-line technology and a northern urban milieu, are an industrial type very different from textile hands and therefore react in quite other ways to alienated work conditions.

[73] The two clearest proponents of these contrasting positions are Gilman, *op. cit.*, and Barkin, *op. cit.*
[74] Pope, *op. cit.*

5

THE AUTO WORKER AND THE ASSEMBLY LINE: ALIENATION INTENSIFIED

The automobile assembly line has dominated the perspective of writers on work and technology in the past decades and has become "the classic symbol of the subjection of man to the machine in our industrial age." [1] The alienated automobile worker, as I remarked in the beginning chapter, is somewhat mistakenly viewed as the typical industrial employee of today.[2] The industry itself stands out as the prototypal industry of the period of advanced industrialism, especially its early stages, just as textile manufacturing is the industry representative of the period of early industrialization

In contrast to printing and textiles, the automobile industry is a characteristically modern industry. Its economic and social structure is bureaucratic rather than traditional. A few large firms, employing up-to-date methods of factory and personnel organization, dominate this highly concentrated industry. Production plants are very large and contain elaborate hierarchies of authority. The assembly line continues and intensifies the trend toward greater division of labor, rationalization, and efficiency, which began with the machine industries, the most advanced form of manufacturing in the nineteenth century. Relations between workers and management have also become formalized. In the impersonal atmosphere of the large factory, a system of formal rules and regulations has developed out of labor union and company conflict.

The automobile industry is today one of the largest employers in American industry. Eight hundred thousand workers are employed in manufacturing motor vehicles alone. Almost two and a half million are employed

[1] Charles R. Walker and Robert Guest, *Man on the Assembly Line* (Cambridge, Mass.: Harvard University Press, 1952), p. 9.

[2] Students of the automobile industry are not themselves responsible for this image. The present chapter is indebted to two outstanding sociological studies of automobile workers for much of its descriptive and analytical material: *Man on the Assembly Line* by Charles Walker and Robert Guest and *Automobile Workers and the American Dream* by Ely Chinoy (New York: Doubleday & Co., 1955).

in the automobile-industry complex, which includes new-car showrooms, used-car lots, garage and repair shops, and service stations. Such major industries as steel, rubber, petroleum, and glass developed chiefly with the growth of the automobile industry and still depend upon it as their most important consumer.

The automobile manufacturing industry has two major branches that differ considerably in their characteristic technologies: the parts division, which includes plants producing engines, transmissions, bodies, batteries, and other components; and the assembly division, which produces the complete vehicle from these component parts. Although many of my observations apply to the automobile industry as a whole, this chapter concentrates on work in the assembly plants, where the distinctive conveyer-belt technology of the industry is located.

The essential feature of a craft technology is its lack of standardization of the product. In a machine-tending industry like textiles, standardization is considerably advanced. In assembly-line industries, standardization reaches an even higher level. During each model year, an automobile company produces only a limited number of different vehicles. Although these variations in design, size, appearance, and purpose are important for the consumers, a black two-door coupé differs very little from a two-tone station wagon in over-all structure, basic components, or method of production. And, ideally, every car is identical to every other one of the same model line in standards of quality and workmanship, although this is not always so in practice.[3]

In those assembly-line industries which produce durable, "hard" goods (in contrast to the "soft" products of the food industries), the assembly-line technology depends not only on the standardization of the end product but even more on the standardization of the individual parts and components which make up the completed product. Automobiles can be produced on a mass basis because parts and assemblies for the same make of automobile are interchangeable.

The assembly of these interchangeable components takes place along a conveyer belt, which regularly and rapidly brings the cars past the worker's station. The hundreds or thousands of individual operations necessary to complete the car are organized into an uninterrupted time-space series, and the jobs of the individual workmen are almost as subdivided as the parts which they assemble. The highly rationalized conveyer-belt form of production is the most distinctive aspect of the automobile industry, a technological innovation which has been admired and copied throughout the world. Its remarkable efficiency enabled Henry Ford to pay workers the unheard-of wages of five dollars a day; it can send a complete automobile off a single

[3] As any automobile owner who has bought a "lemon" knows from sad experience.

assembly line every 45 seconds; it has produced several hundred million cars, trucks, and buses in the relatively short history of the industry; and, of course, to a great degree it has transformed the folkways of American society.

In the extremes of praise and censure which have been leveled against this dramatic mode of production, the magnitude of its distribution has been exaggerated. What is most characteristic of present-day industry is not its domination by the assembly-line factory, but its diversity—the wide range of very different industrial environments. The majority of manual workers today are not employed in factories but work in various non-factory settings, e.g., construction, transportation, and service industries, which are usually not as highly mechanized as manufacturing industries. Even among factory industries, there are only a few where an assembly-line technology predominates: the electrical-equipment industry; the very new electronics industry; the rubber industry; and certain branches of the food industry, particularly canning, meat-packing, and dairy products.

Finally, even in one of the most clear-cut assembly-line industries, automobiles, the majority of manual workers do not work directly on the conveyer belt. In many of the parts plants there are no assembly lines, and production processes may be similar to those in craft and machine industries. In the assembly plants, a conveyer-belt technology and method of work organization predominate, but many blue-collar operatives work in departments or on jobs producing parts or subassemblies to supply the needs of the line, rather than work directly on the belt itself. It is estimated that only 18 per cent of the manual workers in the automobile industry actually work on the line.[4] And in the labor force as a whole it seems likely that less than 5 per cent of American manual workers today are assembly-line workers.[5]

But these facts do not belie the importance of the assembly-line mode of production in the modern period. As Daniel Bell has emphasized, the assembly-line concept has greatly influenced all forms of work organization.[6] In automobile manufacturing itself, the conveyer belt is the final stage of production, and all other operations in the industry, including those of the parts plants, must be co-ordinated to its needs. Because the line sets the standards and determines the rhythm of production in the industry, most off-line jobs, particularly in assembly plants, take on many of the characteristics of assembly-line work, though not in such an extreme form.

Conveyer-belt technology in the automobile industry requires large-sized

---

[4] U.S. Department of Labor, *Occupational Outlook Handbook, 1959* (Bulletin No. 1255 [Washington: U.S. Government Printing Office, 1959]), p. 505.

[5] Unfortunately no census or business statistics record the number of workers on assembly lines, either in individual industries or in the economy as a whole. Instead of having precise figures, I am, therefore, limited to an estimate based on the characteristics of various industries.

[6] Daniel Bell, *The End of Ideology* (Glencoe, Ill.: Free Press, 1960), pp. 247–48.

plants with many thousands of workers. About 55 per cent of the automobile workers are employed in establishments with more than 2,500 employees.[7] The transportation equipment industries, which include aircraft, shipbuilding, and railroad-car manufacturing as well as motor vehicles, average 334 employees per establishment, more than any other manufacturing industry (Table 22, Appendix A). Eighty-two per cent of their employees are in plants with 1,000 or more workers, whereas only 34 per cent of all factory workers are employed in such large establishments. The transportation equipment industries have a smaller percentage of employees working in small and middle-sized plants than any other manufacturing industry (Table 23, Appendix A).

The companies that operate these plants include some of the largest organizations in American industry. General Motors has more than 300,000 employees and is the largest private employer in the country. The "Big Three" —General Motors, Ford, and Chrysler—account for more than 90 per cent of the domestic production of motor vehicles. Although there were hundreds of manufacturers in the early days, today only six American firms make a complete automobile. The industry is therefore highly concentrated, in contrast to printing and textiles, where small and medium-sized firms still predominate. The concentration ratio statistics dramatize this difference: the concentration index is 96.3 in automobile manufacturing, 11.9 in textiles, and 2.3 in printing (see Table 21, Appendix A). In automobiles the assembly branch of the industry is most dominated by a few producers; there are considerably more small enterprises in the parts division, where individual plants also tend to be smaller.

ECONOMIC CONDITIONS AND EMPLOYMENT

Because they are relatively new industries, the economic situation of the assembly-line industries is generally more favorable than that of older machine industries such as textiles. Because they are modern large-scale industrial organizations, automobile firms utilize market research and advertising to maintain their positions. And if the relatively young automobile industry is no longer a growth industry, the period of its most rapid expansion has been fairly recent.

During almost the entire first half of the twentieth century, motor vehicles was one of the most rapidly expanding industries in the United States. Even as late as the 1940's, total employment in automobile manufacturing increased 4 per cent, from 575,000 workers in 1940 to 825,000 in 1950. However, during the 1950's employment leveled off. In 1960 44,000

---

[7] U.S. Department of Labor, *Occupational Outlook Handbook, 1959*, p. 499.

fewer workers were employed in the manufacture of motor vehicles, a decline of 5 per cent since 1950.

The industry has been quite vulnerable to short-term business fluctuations. Because the purchase of an automobile can be more easily deferred than the purchase of food and other necessities, the industry has been hit extremely hard by recessions and depressions. Another cause of employment fluctuation has been the annual retooling shutdowns for new models; the length of these layoffs, however, has decreased greatly in recent years.

Cyclical and seasonal fluctuations notwithstanding, the most important source of instability in the industry is more basic. The industry's very success in providing the majority of Americans with relatively new automobiles involves a crisis in marketing. As the number of car owners increases, the continuing willingness of so many Americans to buy a new automobile each year becomes more and more problematic. This fact, combined with growing mechanization and its threat of permanent technological unemployment, makes the long-term growth picture in the industry uncertain and means that automobile workers are subject to considerable economic insecurity.

The pronounced insecurity is borne out by census statistics and by the Roper attitude survey. In 1949, 67 per cent of the nation's male wage and salary workers employed in all manufacturing industries worked fifty weeks or more; the remaining one-third had less steady employment, being out of work more than two weeks during the year. The frequency of layoffs in the automobile industry is suggested by the fact that only 57 per cent of its employees worked fifty weeks. In contrast, 78 per cent of those in printing, 79 per cent of those in the chemical industry, and 68 per cent of the textile workers worked virtually a full year (see Table 27, Appendix A).

During an average month of 1958, more than 5 automobile workers out of every 100 were likely to be laid off; the ratio for all factory workers was less than 2 per 100. The automobile figure was the highest layoff rate for any industry. The lowest rates were in the unusually stable continuous-process industries. Only 1 chemical worker per 100 was likely to be laid off; the rate for oil refining was 0.3 per 100.[8]

Unemployment figures for individual industries tell the same story. In 1958, 21 per cent of the automobile workers were unemployed, compared to 9 per cent of all factory workers. The economic upturn of 1959 and 1960 reduced this figure, but automobile workers were still more likely to be unemployed than men in other industries. In 1961, 14 per cent of the labor

---

[8] "Current Labor Statistics," *Monthly Labor Review*, lxxxiv (1961), 678. Thus if we compare the automobile rate of 5.3 per 100 with the oil refinery rate, we see that during a typical month in 1958 an automobile worker was eighteen times more likely to be laid off than an oil refinery employee.

force in this industry was out of work; unemployment was twice as prevalent in the automobile industry as in the textile industry and four times more frequent than in printing and chemicals (see Table 29, Appendix A). The average unemployment rate for this four-year period was higher in automobiles than in any other industry.

At the time of the Roper survey in 1947, automobile workers were more apprehensive about job security than workers in any other industry. Twenty-nine per cent expected to be laid off during the next six months, compared to only 14 per cent of the entire sample (Table 32, Appendix B). And only 73 per cent felt that they could have their jobs as long as they wanted, compared to 81 per cent of all factory workers (Table 31, Appendix B).

Although insecurity due to economic market conditions remains, automobile workers are not as powerless to control their conditions of employment as they were in the past. In contrast to the textile workers, the vast majority are organized in a strong industrial labor union. The United Automobile Workers (UAW) has eliminated much of the arbitrariness of past industrial relations. Through a series of conflicts with management (bitter in the past, but more and more routine in recent years), the union has successfully instituted a system of industrial rules, the most important cornerstone of which is the principle of seniority. Much of the union's energy since World War II has been directed to the problem of stabilizing employment in the industry: this, of course, is the purpose of the so-called guaranteed annual wage, or Supplementary Unemployment Benefits Plan (SUB).

Because of the structure of the textile industry, economic distress has been expressed by the many bankruptcies and shut downs of small and middle-sized firms. The automobile industry has a different economic structure, and economic problems are manifested in other ways. General Motors, Ford, and Chrysler will not go bankrupt, and therefore the bulk of the workers do not face the prospect of a permanent loss of employment. Occasionally, of course, a major automobile manufacturer shuts down his entire operations or at least an entire plant,[9] but unemployment in the industry is more typically expressed by periodic layoffs and frequent short work weeks. In contrast to the situation in the older small-firm industries, such as textiles and leather, insecurity falls most heavily on the younger worker in the automobile industry. The older worker is protected by his seniority from most reductions of force and therefore gains a considerable degree of job security.

Before examining the dimensions of alienation among automobile workers, we must look more closely at the technology and organization of the

---

[9] One of the most dramatic recent examples is the Packard shutdown. For an account of this situation and its impact on the discarded workers, see Harold Sheppard, Louis Ferman, and Seymour Faber, *Too Old To Work, Too Young To Retire* (Ann Arbor and Detroit: University of Michigan and Wayne State University, 1960).

assembly line and the occupational structure and typical jobs which it produces.

TECHNOLOGY AND WORK ORGANIZATION:
THE ONE-MINUTE JOB

The level of mechanization is quite high in the automobile industry as a whole. Capital investment per production worker is $19,000, compared to $11,000 in the printing industry, $9,000 in textiles, and $15,000 in all manufacturing (Table 18, Appendix A). However, heavy machinery is concentrated in the parts branch of the industry. Plants which fabricate and machine engines and transmissions, cast wheels, and stamp fenders and other body parts are highly mechanized. In the assembly plants, it is materials-handling rather than production which is carried out by machine systems. The advanced character of automobile assembly production lies in its rationalization of materials-handling and work organization, rather than in the development of elaborate machinery or automatic processes.

From this viewpoint, the machine-tending technology of the textile industry is actually more advanced than that of automobile assembly. In textiles, the basic manufacturing operations are performed by complex machinery. Since the machines are only semiautomatic, workers must still perform such minor tasks as removing yarn parcels, tying up broken strings, and starting up the process. On the automobile assembly line, the major operations are performed by the workers themselves rather than by machinery. Though the work is carried out by hand with the aid of small power tools, such as electric drills and ratchet screwdrivers, it is not craft work, since the highly rationalized organization of work assignments and work flow standardizes the basic manual operations.

In a final assembly plant, the frame of the automobile starts down the conveyer belt and passes through a series of departments, in each of which workers who are relatively stationary attach a particular part to the chassis or body.

Final assembly is the process of putting together in sequence the individual parts of the subassemblies, with the completed vehicle rolling off the end of the line. Overhead wires feed electric power to nut tighteners, welding equipment, and other tools used by workers on the assembly line. A conveyor carries the motor vehicle forward while men at work stations attach the necessary parts and subassemblies in proper sequence.

Generally, the assembly of a car starts with the frame which forms the foundation of the motor vehicle. All other parts and subassemblies are attached to it. Large and heavy subassemblies, such as the engine and the body, are lowered by hoists into position on the chassis as it comes down the line. The finishing accessories, such as bumpers, hubcaps, and floor mats, are added near the end of the line. Finally, the headlights are adjusted, the wheels are aligned, and gasoline is pumped into the fuel tank, and thus another new motor vehicle is driven off the line under its own power.[10]

In assembly-line production, work operations are broken down into their simplest components. The extremely precise and synchronized work flow and production schedule guarantee a high degree of co-ordination, so that each worker performs his operation in the right sequence.[11]

Because of the extreme subdivision of the work process, most jobs in the automobile industry do not call for the traditional skills characteristic of printing and other craft industries. According to the 1950 Census, 29 per cent of the manual workers in the industry were skilled craftsmen and foremen. Skilled journeymen are more common in automotive parts plants, however, than in assembly plants. And most of the skilled men in the latter plants work away from the main conveyer belt.

Almost three-quarters of the workers in the automobile industry are classified as semiskilled or unskilled by the Census. The jobs of these workers require few of the qualities that characterize work in craft industries: judgment, experience, and subtle co-ordination of hand and eye. Adequate performance depends instead on an easily developed "knack" that is perfected in a brief practice period.[12] The learning time of the typical job in the assembly plants may be only a few hours or a few days. In the Roper survey, the automobile industry had the highest proportion of workers in the unskilled category of all sixteen industries. Forty-eight per cent felt that their jobs could be learned in less than one month. Thirteen per cent said that their jobs took between one and three months to learn; 21 per cent, between three months and two years. Only 18 per cent had jobs that took more than two years to learn. Only one other industry had a lower proportion of skilled workers (see Table 51, Appendix B).[13]

[10] U.S. Department of Labor, *Occupational Outlook Handbook, 1959*, p. 502.

[11] Walker and Guest, *op. cit.*, p. 10. There have been a number of attempts to arrive at a general and more formal definition of the assembly line. The German Labor Commission, cited by Alain Touraine, says it is "an uninterrupted series of elementary tasks, each one having a limited duration, and which is accompanied by a progression of the object in the course of its fabrication." Touraine himself views the assembly line as "a type of organization of work such that the diverse operations, reduced to the same duration or to a multiple of that duration, are executed without interruption between them and in a constant order in time and space." *L'évolution du travail ouvrier aux usines Renault* (Paris: Centre National de la Recherche Scientifique, 1955), p. 40.

[12] Walker and Guest, *op. cit.*, pp. 41–42.

[13] And these figures probably exaggerate the skill level of work in the automobile industry, since workers are likely to upgrade the time it takes to learn their jobs. The level of skill was even lower in Walker and Guest's X plant sample because they concentrated on assembly-line workers. Of this group, 65.5 per cent said it took them less than a month to learn their jobs and only 34 per cent more than a month (*op. cit.*, p. 35). The Walker and Guest figures are probably more representative data for the assembly-line situation, the Roper data for the automobile industry as a whole.

Assembly-line technology divides the process of production into simple, unskilled elementary tasks, and assembly-line work organization gives each operative the responsibility for one, or at most a very few, of these subdivided tasks. The immense fractionization of labor in the industry can be seen in the brief time span of each individual job, and in the small number of the operations which make it up.

The average time span of operations on the assembly line is one minute. Fifty to sixty cars pass by each worker on the conveyer belt every hour, and he repeats basically the same task on a different car every minute, eight hours a day (see Plates 5 and 6).

In craft industries there is no definite time span of operations because production is not standardized. And the work of a skilled journeyman consists of an almost infinite number of operations: variety is an inevitable aspect of the jobs in this kind of technological setting. In the machine-tending textile industry, mass-production techniques have greatly reduced the variety of work, and repetition is characteristic of the large majority of unskilled jobs. Jobs in the automobile industry are at least as highly fractionized. In the plant which Walker and Guest studied, the largest proportion of workers, 32 per cent, had jobs which consisted of only one operation; 13 per cent had two operations; 23 per cent from three to five operations; 16 per cent from five to ten operations; and 16 per cent had more than ten operations.[14] Thus two-thirds of the jobs consisted of fewer than five operations.

The assembly-line workers themselves can best describe the highly subdivided jobs that result from such rationalized work organization. Typical is a man who installs toeplates; his job consists of two operations in a two-minute cycle:

I put in the two different toe-plates. They cover the holes where the brake and clutch pedals are. I am inside the car and have to be down on the seat to do my work. On one kind of car I put in the shift lever while another man puts in the toe-plates.

After finishing the work cycle in the car which has carried him a few feet along the line, he returns to his station, climbs into another car, and begins another installation.[15]

One of the least repetitive jobs on the line is that of an assembler of the "baffle windbreaker" in the "Trim Department":

As the body shell moves along the line, I start putting on a baffle windbreaker (two fenders fit on it) by putting in four screws. Then I put nine clips at the bottom which hold the chrome molding strip to the body. On another type of car there is a piece of rubber which fits on the hood latch on the side and keeps

[14] *Ibid.*, p. 40.
[15] *Ibid.*, pp. 44–45.

the hood from rattling. I drill the holes in the rubber and metal and fit two screws in. Also I put four clips on the rubber in the rear fender.

On another type of body, I put the clips on the bottom molding, and in the trunk space I put two bolts which hold the spare tire clamp. I repeat these things all the time on the same types of car.

This worker rides along the conveyer and completes his cycle of operations in less than two minutes, while the conveyer is moving over a distance of about thirty feet. He then goes back to his starting point and starts over again.[16]

There is little variety, then, in the work of the automobile assembler, because the majority of jobs involve only a few operations. Even so, workers are quite aware and appreciative of the difference between a job with one or two operations, such as putting in screws and tightening them with an air-driven screwdriver, and a job with three or four operations.[17]

MAN AND THE CONVEYER:
THE FIGHT FOR CONTROL

In a craft industry, as we have seen, the worker has considerable freedom and controls his immediate sociotechnical environment; this freedom and control is almost a technological necessity for the work to get done. In certain machine industries like apparel and shoe manufacturing, the technology often permits the worker who operates a machine to control his work process. In the machine-tending textile industry, however, technology, work organization, and economic pressures all contribute to the powerlessness of the individual. Similarly, in the automobile industry, the worker lacks control over his immediate work process. The conveyer-belt technology dominates this work environment and pre-empts the worker's movement and choices.

The essential feature of the automobile assembly line is the fact that the pace of work is determined by the machine system rather than by the worker. As a foreman in an assembly plant explains it:

The line here, the moving line, controls the man and his speed. Then no matter how slow a man is, he has to keep moving. We're all human, we like to go as slow as we can unless we are pushed, and this line controls him perfectly.[18]

[16] *Ibid.*
[17] Another source of variety is the production of different models on the same line. The assembler may have to perform his basic job in a slightly different fashion, depending on whether the vehicle is a station wagon, a coupé, a compact, or the standard four-door sedan. But because the automobile worker does not control the pace at which he works, these mixed-model runs generally add to the pressure and discomfort of the line, which minimizes the potential advantage of more varied work.
[18] C. Walker, R. Guest, and A. Turner, *The Foreman on the Assembly Line* (Cambridge, Mass.: Harvard University Press, 1956), p. 11.

Since the speed of the line is mechanically set, the cars move down the conveyer belt at a predetermined rhythm. Often it is necessary to work at top speed to keep up with the line. Most workers do not have much chance to vary their pace at their own discretion. The most intensive study of automobile workers concluded that this was the aspect of the job most disliked.[19]

Workers whose jobs are off the conveyer belt have considerably more control over their work pace. This is why such jobs are so highly valued:

> Work at a machine may be just as repetitive, require as few motions and as little thought as line assembly, but men prefer it because it does not keep them tied as tightly to their tasks. "I can stop occasionally when I want to," said a machine operator. "I couldn't do that when I was on the line." Production standards for a particular machine may be disliked and felt to be excessive, but the machine operator need only approximate his production quota each day. *The line-tender must do all the work that the endless belt brings before him.*[20]

A machine operator whose quota is 150 pieces a day may go all out in the morning to produce 100 pieces and take it easy in the afternoon, only putting out 50; at any rate, it is his own decision. The technology and work organization of the assembly line, however, eliminate the possibility of the worker's legitimate control over his work pace. Some employees adapt to the predetermined rhythms of the belt without great strain. Walker and Guest report that a minority of workers in the X plant actually "liked the challenge and excitement of keeping up with the line." One man derived satisfaction from "keeping up with a rapid-fire job" and got bored on days when the cars came off slowly.[21] More commonly, workers conform to the mechanically set work pace but experience a degree of resentment against the constant infringement of their autonomy. The major annoyance is not the belt's rapid pace but its unchanging speed, which takes no account of the fact that in the course of eight hours most workers need to vary their efforts in line with rhythmic alterations in mood and fatigue.

Still other workers, presumably those with the greatest need for autonomy, are forced to innovate illegitimate, subterranean arrangements in order to maintain some control over their work pace. One such illegitimate innovation is "doubling-up." In doubling-up, a worker proceeds furiously for an hour, performing not only his own job but also the job of the man stationed next to him. They then alternate every hour. While one works, the other takes off. But, as Frank Marquart observes, "Such crazy racing against the clock is always an invitation to management to retime jobs and tighten up production standards." [22] Another way of getting ahead and gaining time is to work

[19] Walker and Guest, *op. cit.*, p. 62.
[20] Chinoy, *op. cit.*, pp. 71–72. (My emphasis.)
[21] Walker and Guest, *op. cit.*, p. 52.
[22] Frank Marquart, "'The Auto Worker," in *Voices of Dissent* (New York: Grove Press, n.d.), p. 144.

on the vehicles "up the line" before they have reached one's own work station, but because of the serial nature of assembly-line work organization this is not possible in all jobs. These examples show that conveyer belt production does not make control over pace impossible for all workers. The technology does make it extremely difficult, and the standardized work assignments require that these variations from protocol be kept hidden as much as possible from management.

Because assembly-line workers cannot control the speed of the line, they are relatively powerless to influence the degree of pressure in their work situations. Pressure in the automobile industry as a whole is greater than in most other industries.[23] However, important differences exist among the major companies. For a number of years, General Motors has been known for its extreme work pace, which has been 30 per cent faster than that of Chrysler. The work pace at Ford plants has been somewhere in the middle.[24] When an assembly line is operated at a high speed, the pressure may be so constant that free time and breathing room are almost totally lacking. The X plant studied by Walker and Guest evidently operated such a high-pressure line, as these typical worker comments suggest:

> The line speed is too great. More men wouldn't help much. They'd just expect more work out of an individual. There's an awful lot of tension.
> The work isn't hard, it's the never-ending pace. The guys yell "hurrah" whenever the line breaks down.
> It's not the monotony, it's the rush, rush, rush.
> On the line you're geared to the line. You don't dare stop. If you get behind you have a hard time catching up.[25]

All automotive lines do not operate at such a fast pace, however. Most observers agree that line speeds in the industry are less pressured than they were twenty or thirty years ago. Both technological improvements and the policing functions of the union have contributed to the relatively more relaxed atmosphere.[26] And since the co-ordination of the timing of individual jobs can never be 100 per cent efficient, some workers may have 10 or 15 seconds "idle time" in each one-minute work cycle. This permits the possibility of working up the line, getting a few minutes ahead, and conspicuously consuming one's leisure by walking away from the line or engaging in "horseplay."

But because pressures are extremely great in some plants, automobile workers have been intensely preoccupied with "speedup," the fear that man-

---

[23] Maurice Kilbridge ("The Effort Bargain in Industrial Society," *Journal of Business*, xxxiii [1960], p. 12), classifies automobiles as a "fairly fast pace" industry.

[24] *Ibid.*, p. 13.

[25] Walker and Guest, *op. cit.*, pp. 51–52.

[26] Herbert R. Northrup, "The UAW's Influence on Management Decisions in the Automobile Industry—An Outsider's Point of View," in *Proceedings of the Seventh Annual Meeting of the Industrial Relations Research Association, December, 1954 (Detroit, 1955)*, pp. 39–40.

agement will increase line speed in order to get out more production.[27] The speed of the conveyer belt is a constant issue of negotiation and conflict between union and management. The union's legitimate concern with line speed is symbolized by the fact that in certain plants the mechanical box which incloses the regulator of the conveyer belt's speed can be opened only by the joint insertion of two keys, one of which belong to the union president.[28]

A constant, even very rapid, work pace does not necessarily result in the discomfort that defines high speed as pressure. In some conveyer-paced systems, workers are able to "swing" with the job, to adjust their own rhythms to those of the machine process, thus experiencing what Baldamus has called "traction": "a (pleasant) feeling of being pulled along by the inertia in a particular activity." [29] On the automobile line, such traction is often prevented by the variations in work load caused by the different models. For example, a man's operations on station wagons may take 10 seconds longer than his regular task on four-door sedans. But since the line cannot slow down for station wagons, the worker must speed up a little. This can be done without serious discomfort when the more difficult jobs are widely dispersed in the progression of vehicles. The over-all speed of the line takes into account the fact that a certain proportion, perhaps one out of every ten cars, will be station wagons. But either through inefficient scheduling or unusually heavy demand, station wagons or other more time consuming jobs may "bunch up" on the line. If a worker's job cycle does not have enough idle time to take up the slack, he will get further and further behind. And because the belt moves inexorably at the same speed, it is not possible to catch up. Variety in work task and work loads may therefore be a more important cause of pressure than the actual speed of the line.[30]

Three conclusions emerge from a consideration of data from the Roper survey on the question of work pressure. First, most workers in the industry do not complain of excessive job pressure. Second, that minority of employees who do feel that they have to work too fast is larger than in any other industry. Third, feelings of excessive work pressure are much more common among the unskilled automobile workers, presumably those who man the assembly lines. Unfortunately this study does not permit a direct

[27] The automobile worker's fear of speedup parallels the textile worker's fear of stretchout. Because the latter employee is mobile and follows the work, he may be extended in "space"; the relatively immobile assembly-line operative may be extended in "time."

[28] I am grateful to Maurice Kilbridge for this information.

As Marquart has observed, there is no satisfactory definition of what is and what is not speedup. The definition of a fair day's work is determined not only by "scientific" time study, but by the traditional practices and labor policies of individual companies, the progress of mechanization in the plants, the degree of militancy of the local union, and the vulnerability of the company to union pressure (*op. cit.,* p. 145).

[29] Wilhelm Baldamus, *Efficiency and Effort* (London: Tavistock Publications, 1961), p. 59.

[30] I am indebted to Robert Guest and William Friedland for calling my attention to the importance of this factor.

comparison of the attitudes of line workers with those of off-line employees.

Of workers in all sixteen industries in the Roper survey, automobile workers were the most likely to say that their jobs make them work too fast most of the time. Thirty-three per cent were subjected to such extreme pressure, in contrast to 24 per cent of all factory workers. Only 10 per cent of those in the printing industry felt they had to work too fast (see Table 33, Appendix B).

The unskilled automobile workers were particularly subject to the most intense pressure. Forty-eight per cent felt they had to work too fast, in comparison with 26 per cent of the low-skilled men, 24 per cent of the medium-skilled, and only 10 per cent of the skilled.[31] The fact that there was no other industry in which such a high proportion of the unskilled complained of job pressure suggests that it is the assembly-line technology and work organization and not just the lack of skill which is crucial. In the textile industry, for example, only about half as many, 26 per cent, of the unskilled male workers felt they had to work too fast.

A third of the automobile workers surveyed by Roper reported that their jobs left them "too tired" at the end of the work day. Although only two industries, textiles and apparel (industries in which many workers are women), had slightly higher proportions of fatigued workers, the figure for the automobile industry is not much higher than the sample norm of 30 per cent (Table 34, Appendix B). However, the unskilled male automobile workers, concentrated on the conveyer belt, were more likely to be tired than their counterparts in other industries. Forty-four per cent of them got too tired, compared to 35 per cent of the unskilled workers in the entire sample and 17 per cent of the skilled automobile workers.

The mechanical pacing of work rhythms by the conveyer belt rather than by the worker himself is the central aspect of work on an automobile assembly line. Many, although not all, workers view the line's insistent rhythm as oppressive and extend this negative attitude toward other aspects of the job. In examining other elements of powerlessness, we shall see how assembly-line technology colors the entire work environment.[32]

Lack of control over quantity.—Because the conveyer belt so largely determines his pace, the assembly-line worker cannot control the quantity of

---

[31] See n. 24, chap. 4, pp. 67–68 for the definitions of the four skill groups in the Roper study.

[32] The French industrial sociologist and humanist, Georges Friedmann, has warned against a stereotyped notion of the assembly line, emphasizing the large differences among them in the humaneness of the work, and the pressures they exert on their operatives. "Work on the assembly line merits excesses neither of honor nor of indignity, neither the naïve or crude apology of certain technicians nor the pathetic malediction of some romantics" *Ou va le travail humain?* [Paris: Gallimard, 1950], p. 245. (My translation.) Friedmann distinguishes between two types of assembly lines—*chaines tendues,* where the work is fast, tense, strained, and nervous, and *chaines sociales,* where the pace is much more relaxed and the team element of the line predominates. Unfortunately, *chaines sociales* are few today, as Friedmann himself observes, and *chaines tendues* are the rule. Certainly the assembly line in the automobile industry is one of the more extreme forms of the *chaines tendues.*

his output. The worker who finishes his own operations cannot speed up the number of units which move through his particular station; nor can he increase the total number of units to be produced per hour. He can, of course, temporarily decrease his own work speed by not completing all the units brought to him by the conveyer and in so doing will eventually force a slowdown of the entire line.[33] But such a practice, if kept up, would quickly lead to discovery, reprimand, and eventual discharge.

Automobile workers on subassembly operations off the main conveyer belt often can control their output somewhat by building up "banks." If a man prepares instrument panels or seat-cushion assemblies, he can work faster than the speed of the line and accumulate a store of these finished parts around his work bench. Such a bank allows him to slow down and relax at other times. Besides permitting some control over work pace, Walker and Guest note that the growth of a sizable bank is a "visible, tangible, and controllable evidence of accomplishment" for the worker. "Bank builders" had a higher than average degree of job satisfaction.[34] But the conveyer belt denies the large majority of automobile workers in an assembly plant even this limited opportunity to control quantity of output.[35] Workers in parts plants are more likely to have this job freedom.

Partial control over quality.—The assembly line works against a worker's desire to measure up to his own standards of excellence. In the X plant, approximately 44 per cent of the workers "felt that it was difficult to sustain the kind of quality performance which was expected of them or which they themselves wanted to sustain. To most of [them] this was a discouraging and negative feature of the job." Predictably, this lack of control over quality was most common among those whose jobs were strictly paced by the line. The other half of the work force, particularly those off the line, considered that they could usually achieve "good quality work" in their jobs.[36]

The difficulty in producing both "quality and quantity," of which many line workers complained, is due, of course, to the constant rhythm of the conveyer belt and the lack of control over its pace. As one man expressed the problem, "The bad thing about assembly lines is that the line keeps moving. If you have a little trouble with a job, you can't take the time to do it right." [37]

Some of the variations in workmanship standards that show up in new

---

[33] Walker and Guest, *op. cit.,* p. 85.

[34] *Ibid.,* p. 146.

[35] The famous study of the Hawthorne plant was perhaps the first to note the presence and analyze the function of the banks. Fritz Roethslisberger and W. Dickson, *Management and the Worker* (Cambridge, Mass.: Harvard University Press, 1939). Probably "banking" is most common in technical systems where workers operate machines. It is unnecessary in craft production, rare in assembly-line settings, and of course impossible in automated continuous-process plants.

[36] Walker and Guest, *op. cit.,* p. 59.

[37] *Ibid.,* p. 51.

car showrooms may be due to the attitudes of the workers as well as conveyer belt pressures. Because jobs are so standardized and the atmosphere of
large assembly plants is rather anonymous and impersonal, workers do not
get individual credit and recognition for high-quality work, in contrast to
the situation in craft and continuous-process industries. The social structure
of the plant does not generate the incentive to maintain personal standards
of excellence. And since there is no opportunity to perfect difficult jobs when
routine operations take place on a moving belt, a worker may paradoxically
experience more of a sense of control over the quality of his product through
occasional sloppy work than through the constant achievement of uniform
standards.

Predetermination of techniques.—Mass production in the automobile industry is the ultimate example of work organization in which the tools and
techniques to be used on each job have been completely. predetermined by
engineers, time-study technicians, and supervisors. Only a few workers, e.g.,
maintenance machinists, have some freedom to choose the way they do a
particular job. The automobile work environment is so highly rationalized
that workers have practically no opportunity to solve problems and contribute their own ideas.

The great majority of employees and particularly those on the line cannot
vary the sequence of operations that make up their standardized jobs. Many
jobs consist of only one or a few operations. Because of the serial nature of
assembly production, jobs with several operations are designed so that they
can be done only one way. If you drill two holes for a toeplate, fasten the
plate on the floor by inserting a screw in each hole, and tighten the screws
with a screwdriver, you cannot decide to put in the screws before you drill
the holes or to tighten them up before you put them in. Routine tasks in
the continuous-process industries, such as instrument-reading, can be done in
almost any order.

Automobile workers do not always easily give up all control in this area.
Some are quite ingenious in devising ways to beat the system. But since the
organization of work does not permit the workers to show initiative, control
over job methods, like control over pace, is also subterranean and illegitimate.
Because all jobs are standardized and time-studied in terms of prevailing techniques, tools, and work loads, men who find ways of doing their jobs faster
or with less effort hide this information from management. Besides the
doubling-up already referred to, some automobile workers make minor
improvements in their tools. By shortening or lengthening the extension of
a wrench socket, the assembler may be able to make the movements that
he repeats all day long more easily and gracefully than with the standard
equipment. Such illegitimate tools will be hidden in tool boxes to delay
management detection and the consequent retiming of the job to the worker's
disadvantage.

Forty-seven per cent of the automobile workers in the Roper study reported that their jobs gave them a chance to try out ideas of their own. This figure is considerably lower than in the printing industry, where 79 per cent of the workers gave this response (Table 35, Appendix B). Still, it is very close to the sample norm and seems surprisingly high, considering the routine, mass-production character of the industry. When these statistics are computed separately for the various skill groups, they reveal that the automobile figure is relatively high because low- and medium-skilled workers are more satisfied with their opportunities for initiative than are employees of equal skill levels in other industries. Possibly these automobile workers are off the line and, comparing themselves with the unskilled men on the conveyer belt, feel relatively privileged. Table 13 shows that about two-thirds of high-, medium-, and low-skilled male auto workers feel they can try out their ideas; in contrast, only 21 per cent of the unskilled auto workers feel this way.

TABLE 13

PROPORTION OF MALE AUTOMOBILE WORKERS WHO CAN
TRY OUT IDEAS ON JOB, BY SKILL LEVEL

SKILL LEVEL	AUTOMOBILE WORKERS		ALL MALE FACTORY WORKERS	
	Per Cent	Number	Per Cent	Number
Unskilled...........	21	73	39	605
Low skilled..........	70	23	43	258
Medium skilled.......	64	33	51	582
Skilled..............	66	29	66	571

Looking at the opportunities for job initiative among the unskilled workers in a number of industries illustrates the special deprivation of the assembly-line situation. Of the twelve industries with more than ten male unskilled workers in the sample, the automobile industry had the smallest proportion of workers who could try out their own ideas. In most industries, approximately two in five of the unskilled had such chances for initiative, in automobiles, only one in five did (Table 14).

Lack of free movement.—The typical automobile worker on the line has few possibilities for physical movement except for those motions necessary to make his minute contribution to the assembly of the car. Unless he is able to work ahead, he must stay constantly near his place because of the speed with which the conveyer brings car after car to him. Were he to leave his place and not add a brake drum or an instrument panel, his workmates up the line would not be able to do their jobs. A line worker must get relief even to go to the bathroom, and for this reason a number of workers are "utility men," capable of doing any job on the line, who fill in for those on relief and also for absentees. The importance of even this modicum of

physical freedom is shown in the frequency with which the number of
relief men assigned to a particular line becomes an issue of dispute between
the union and the company. In fact, during the 1960 contract negotiations,

TABLE 14

PROPORTION OF UNSKILLED MALE WORKERS WHO CAN
TRY OUT IDEAS ON JOB, BY INDUSTRY

INDUSTRY	PER CENT	NUMBER
AUTOMOBILES	21	73
Leather	23	26
Machinery	24	66
Iron and steel	30	113
Food	33	91
Textiles	35	68
Transportation equipment	35	20
Chemicals	39	18
Furniture	40	68
Stone, clay, and glass	41	29
Sawmills and planing	45	22
Apparel	54	11
All industries	39	605

disagreement over relief time was the cause of wildcat strikes in a number
of plants.[38]

The automobile worker, thus, has very little control over the technological
environment in which he works. The assembly line's inexorable control over
the pace and rhythm of work is most critical; it is largely responsible for the
high degree of pressure, the inability to control the quantity of work, and
the lack of free movement. The extreme rationalization of work organization
results in the lack of freedom to determine the techniques of work. Many
assembly-line workers react to their basic lack of control over technology
by trying to find their own ways of asserting some autonomy in the work
situation. Building banks, working up the line, doubling-up, and altering
tools may serve as safety valves which, for some, minimize the frustrations
resulting from an extremely unequal (and unchallenged) power relation
between the worker and the technical system.

A consequence of this lack of control may be the persistence of industrial
sabotage among some automobile workers today. Machine-breaking was a
common response in the early stages of industrialization when new factory
conditions appeared oppressive; it has largely disappeared among factory
workers in advanced industrialism. Is it possible that throwing handfuls of
bolts and nuts in motors and welding parts inside fenders are not simply

[38] According to the Roper study, 60 per cent of the automobile workers were free to leave
their jobs for thirty minutes without relief (Table 36, Appendix B). These were workers on
jobs off the line or in parts plants, which allow considerably more physical movement. This is
another important reason why such jobs are preferred.

anticompany gestures, but instead are ways of getting even with a dominating technology? The sabotage attitude is also expressed in the joy with which automobile workers greet a breakdown of the assembly line, provided it does not send them home and cut into their pay checks. A worker interviewed by Chinoy said, "You get the feeling, everybody gets the feeling, whenever the line jerks, everybody is wishing, 'breakdown, baby.'" [39] And an X plant worker informs us that "the guys yell 'hurrah' whenever the line breaks down. . . . You can hear it all over the plant." [40]

Since the automobile worker is so thoroughly controlled by the assembly line, he is relatively free from close, overbearing personal supervision. The automatic conveyer belt takes over many of the control functions of supervisors in other industries. Foremen do not have to pressure workers; the assembly line can do that. They don't have to push for a certain output and check the workers' production. Instead, they achieve full production capacity by making sure that every work station on the line is manned by someone who can do the job (here absenteeism is their major headache) and by developing the kinds of personal relationships with their men which can lessen the frequency of flareups and other manifestations of discontent endemic in a tense work environment.[41]

THE PROBLEM OF MEANING

Assembly-line workers, in general, and automobile workers, in particular, are more subject to the alienation of meaninglessness than workers in other industries. They work on a much smaller part of the total product than workers in craft, continuous-process, and even most machine industries. Their scope of operations has been reduced to the minimum by the extreme functional rationality of the assembly line. A man who attaches steering columns or instrument panels all day has nothing to do with any part of the vehicle besides his own restricted specialty.

Automobile workers who are employed off the line or in parts plants are more able to derive some sense of purpose from their work because they may work on an entire part or subassembly themselves. Their tasks may be very repetitive, but they can see some tangible evidence of their labors, a growing pile or a binful of completed parts. The cyclic nature of work on

---

[39] Chinoy, *op. cit.*, p. 71.

[40] Walker and Guest, *op. cit.*, p. 51.

[41] Walker, Guest, and Turner, *op. cit.* Walker and Guest also suggest in *Man on the Assembly Line* that the workers displace onto the conveyer belt some of the hostility that employees might direct toward foremen in other industries: "It may be said that the workers who disliked assembly line work rarely projected their feelings into dislike of their foremen. This appears to us an important finding. Even when a foreman appeared to be reinforcing disliked characteristics of the line—its pace, repetitiveness, or fatigue, for example—the worker tended to exonerate him by implying that such factors were beyond his personal control" (p. 99).

the line makes it difficult to gain a sense of purpose by orienting one's efforts toward the completion of a task, since the vehicle to which one has added a part immediately moves onward, out of the range of one's vision and concern. Perhaps it is only the inspector who test-drives each car after it rolls off the end of the line who can feel some kind of a personal identification with a completed product. From this viewpoint conveyer-belt work is even less meaningful than the routine tasks of textile operatives who, in tying up yarn breaks, are at least making minor repairs and who have a personal responsibility for a number of spinning frames, looms, or other mill machines.

The alienation of meaninglessness is further intensified by the worker's lack of a clear identification with a particular job. The division of labor is so extreme that most jobs are basically the same. In addition, because there are many lines operating at once, there are a number of men performing exactly the same tasks. One cannot therefore derive a sense of function as *the* left-front–hubcap assembler. Fractionized job assignments, cyclic rather than task-directed work rhythms, and the anonymous atmosphere of the large plants—all dilute the sense of meaning, purpose, and function on the assembly line.

The automobile worker's lack of a sense of purpose and function in work does not come primarily from a lack of understanding of how his highly subdivided job fits into the total rationalized scheme of production. Automobile workers have a large amount of such understanding. Their technical competence is probably higher than workers in other mass-production industries because of their great knowledge of the manufacture and maintenance of automobiles, a knowledge learned not in the factory but off the job, working and puttering on their own cars. It is highly ironic that in the industry where the average American worker is most equipped to perform a large number of jobs, technology has reduced his job operations to the ultimate in minuteness.[42]

Yet with respect to the meaningfulness of their work, it is irrelevant that automobile workers could do so many other jobs. The critical fact is that they don't have to know anything more than their limited jobs in order to perform efficiently. Meaninglessness is combated only when the worker's job makes him responsible for a larger scope of the productive process and when, for technical reasons of production, he is required to take into account the work of other employees and of other departments. In assembly-line plants, only the jobs of utility men, craftsmen, repairmen and inspectors make such demands; the majority of workers are unable to counteract the alienation of meaningless work.

---

[42] Marquart reports that the typical automobile assembler has a home workshop where at his leisure he can satisfy the need for meaningful craft work that the plant job frustrates (*op. cit.*, p. 149).

INDUSTRIAL SOCIAL STRUCTURE:
MASS SOCIETY AND ANOMIE

Work in the automobile industry rarely entails membership in a cohesive industrial community. The technology and social organization of assembly-line production have encouraged social alienation as well as powerlessness and meaninglessness. An integrated normative system is implicit in the formal relations between unions and companies, but the informal social structure does not integrate the worker sufficiently to develop the strong sense of loyalty to occupation or company which is characteristic of the printing and textile industries.

Few industries are as bureaucratic as the automobile industry. Companies are large and stable, and utilize modern methods of personnel relations. The union is strong, relatively secure, and accepted as a legitimate participant in the rule-making process. The relative anomie of the non-union period of the 1920's and the early 1930's has been greatly reduced, as formal rules and procedures have emerged, and continue to emerge, out of the now institutionalized conflicts of management and union.[43]

However, this formal normative structure is not well supported by the informal social structure of the industry, and for this reason there is less normative integration than in the other industries. The informal and often restrictive work rules which make up part of the occupational culture in printing, railroad, steel, and other industries are virtually absent in the automobile industry. Because of frequent changes in work assignments and the mobility of employees between jobs, departments, and companies, "custom and practice have little opportunity to take root in the automobile industry." [44]

In addition, the technology of the assembly line is a divisive rather than an integrating force because it results in (1) large, centralized factories, (2) a compressed wage and skill distribution, (3) infrequent advancement opportunities, and (4) relatively few close-knit, functional work groups.

The large factory.—In contrast to textiles, which began as a small-town

[43] The fact that labor-management conflict, in the automotive and other industries, now takes place within a framework of agreed upon "rules of the game" instead of being based purely on power, is another reflection of the bureaucratization of industrial social organization. In a sense, the union-management contract is the most concise statement of the formal norms governing the bureaucratic employment relationship, and it is especially important in such industries as automobiles, where integration is also not based on an informal community consensus. The contract spells out the minimum obligations of the worker to the company and the company to the worker. It contains rules for conferring such "negative sanctions" as layoffs and discharges and such "positive sanctions" as promotions, vacations, and overtime work. Its provision for orderly grievance procedures to deal with complaints, disputes, and feelings of inequity are especially critical, since these procedures are the means through which new norms arise out of situations of normlessness and normative conflict.

[44] Jack Stieber, "Work Rules and Practices in Mass Production Industries," *Proceedings of the Fourteenth Annual Meeting of the Industrial Relations Research Association, 1961* (New York, 1961), p. 404.

and small-plant industry and has maintained its cohesive features in the context of southern traditional communities, automobile manufacturing has always been based in large factories located in northern metropolitan settings. The assembly of motor vehicles requires large plants, and factories in the automobile industry are larger than in any other manufacturing industry, as we have already seen. As Karl Marx emphasized a century ago, large factories increase the social distance between workers and management, reduce the loyalty of the work force to the enterprise, and heighten the potential for class consciousness.[45] In the 1930's and 1940's automobile workers were among the most militant of the new factory workers; visionary radicals viewed them as the most promising core of a class-conscious American proletariat.

While the UAW now is a moderate rather than a militant influence on industrial relations, the automobile worker's sense of loyalty to his company and his degree of identification with management is probably considerably less than that of most other factory workers. Assembly-line production, according to Alexander Heron, results in the greatest cleavage between workers and management, a hypothesis supported by the Roper study and other findings.[46] Only 62 per cent of the automobile workers in the Roper survey feel that their company is as good a place as any in the industry, compared to 92 per cent of the chemical employees, 84 per cent of the textile workers, and 78 per cent of the printers (see Table 38, Appendix B).[47] And in a survey of eight manufacturing industries conducted by the Opinion Research Corporation in 1954, only 30 per cent of the automobile workers said that their "company takes a real interest in its employees." [48] This was the lowest proportion of the eight industries (Table 15).

The insecurity of employment in the industry is another factor which contributes to the over-all lack of normative integration. When a worker is temporarily laid off or required to work short weeks several times a year, he is likely to feel that management views him only as a number, an instrument of production, and not as a human being.

Atomization.—Another causal factor is the relative lack of internal levels of status within the blue-collar world of the automobile industry. Social

---

[45] Karl Marx, "Germany: Revolution and Counter-Revolution," in V. Adoratsky (ed.), *Selected Works of Karl Marx* (New York: International Publishers, Inc., n.d.), II, 470, cited by Seymour Martin Lipset, Martin Trow, and James S. Coleman, *Union Democracy* (Glencoe, Ill.: Free Press, 1956), pp. 151–52.

[46] Alexander Heron, *Why Men Work* (Stanford: Stanford University Press, 1948), p. 161. Peter Drucker has made similar observations with respect to the automobile industry.

[47] The norm for the whole sample is 73 per cent. Only one industry, non-ferrous-metals manufacturing had a lower degree of "loyalty," 57 per cent, than automobile workers.

[48] Worker loyalty is not uniformly low in all automobile companies. The level of consensus and integration is probably quite high at certain of the smaller companies, such as American Motors, which do not have the same history of intense labor conflict as the giants, General Motors and Ford.

stratification and differentiation themselves contribute to the normative integration of a social system because differences in status and rewards symbolize inferior and superior contributions to the goals of the system. Those in superior positions generally uphold most clearly the norms and values of

TABLE 15

PROPORTION OF WORKERS WHO FEEL THEIR COMPANY TAKES
A REAL INTEREST IN ITS EMPLOYEES, BY INDUSTRY*

INDUSTRY	PER CENT	NUMBER
AUTO AND AUTO EQUIPMENT.......	30	102
Textiles........................	39	144
Machinery......................	40	156
Aircraft, transportation..........	42	60
Other manufacturing.............	43	298
Iron and steel..................	44	109
Electrical machinery.............	53	137
Food...........................	54	70
Chemical and paints.............	54	121
Total......................	43	1071

* Source: Opinion Research Corporation, *Automation—Friend or Foe of the Workingman?* tabular supplement to *Public Opinion Index for Industry,* XII (1954), No. 6, p. A-1.

the enterprise and wittingly or unwittingly encourage those lower in status to identify with these norms in order to achieve greater rewards in turn. The extensive subdivision of labor in assembly-line technology results in a relatively undifferentiated blue-collar labor force, epitomized by the most compressed wage spread in the American economy. In 1957 the interquartile range in regular hourly wage rate for the nation's automobile workers was only 14 cents. More than half (53 per cent) of all auto workers were earning between \$2.25 and \$2.40.[49] Seventy-five per cent were compressed within a 30 cent range between \$2.15 and \$2.45. In contrast to 14 cents in the auto industry, the interquartile range in the highly differentiated oil refining industry was 70 cents an hour.[50]

This lack of differentiation, symbolized by the narrow wage spread, contributes to a situation which Walker and Guest have aptly called "depersonalization," or the increase of "the individual worker's sense of anonymity within the general mass of his fellow workers."

[49] H. M. Douty, "Wages in the Motor Vehicle Industry, 1957," *Monthly Labor Review,* LXXX (1957), 3. See also L. Earl Lewis, "Wage Dispersion in Manufacturing Industries," *Monthly Labor Review,* LXXIX (1956), 780–86.

[50] Calculated from data in U.S. Department of Labor, Bureau of Labor Statistics, *Factory Workers' Earnings, May 1958* (Bulletin No. 1252 [Washington: U.S. Government Printing Office, 1959]), p. 29.

For the idea of studying the social structure of blue-collar industries from the viewpoint of stratification and mass-society theory, I am indebted to William Kornhauser and his seminar in political sociology, 1956. For a systematic analysis of mass-society theory, see William Kornhauser, *The Politics of Mass Society* (Glencoe, Ill.: Free Press, 1959).

Again, at the end of every two-week period when the worker receives his pay envelope, the wages inside it will be roughly of the same amount as the wages of hundreds of others. Every job on the line is slightly different—and these differences he appreciates keenly, but there is only a slight difference in what one pays as against another, together with little if any difference in status or prestige. Therefore, any production worker can, and sometimes does, say: "There are hundreds of jobs like mine, not much better, not much worse. The differences are so slight, or seem so slight to management, that I am *interchangeable*" [my emphasis]. . . . We suggest that the sense of becoming depersonalized, of becoming anonymous as against remaining one's self, is for those who feel it a psychologically more disturbing result of the work environment than either the boredom or the tension that arise from repetitive and mechanically paced work.[51]

The lack of advancement.—The "massified" wage, skill, and status structure produced by conveyer-belt technology also increases alienation because it reduces the opportunities for advancement. In assembly-line plants there are relatively few skilled jobs toward which low-skilled operatives can aspire. In addition, because skilled jobs often require formal apprenticeships or on-the-job training not easily available to most workers, "there is a deep gulf between skilled and non-skilled jobs." [52] In one auto plant, only 6 per cent of the skilled maintenance workers had started their careers on the assembly line.[53] Another study found that 80 per cent of the unskilled workers were not even actively interested in skilled work.[54]

Blue-collar work in the automobile industry has no natural ladders of promotion, by which each job systematically leads to a higher one, and so on. A man is hired for one job, and he expects to stay on that job. Only 4 of the 47 unskilled workers in Chinoy's sample had the next best paying job in their department or division as a goal.[55] In the Roper study, only 39 per cent of the automobile workers said that their jobs led to promotions, if they did them well. Only two other of the sixteen industries had lower proportions of workers without expectation of advancement (Table 45, Appendix B).[56]

Only a small proportion of automobile workers want and expect to become

---

[51] Walker and Guest, *op. cit.*, pp. 160–61.

[52] Chinoy, *op. cit.*, p. 62.

[53] Robert H. Guest, "Work Careers and Aspirations of Automobile Workers," in W. Galenson and S. M. Lipset (eds.), *Labor and Trade Unionism* (New York: John Wiley & Sons, 1960), p. 322.

[54] Chinoy, *op. cit.*, p. 62.

[55] *Ibid.*, pp. 63–64.

[56] Advancement opportunities are worst for the unskilled workers, whose more alienated work situation makes the chance to get a better job most important. Of the 73 male automobile workers with less than one month's job training, only 30 per cent feel their jobs lead to promotions, compared to 50 per cent of the 92 workers with more than one month's training.

THE AUTOMOTIVE ASSEMBLY LINE: *Mass Production and Efficiency*

New Plymouth automobiles can roll off the final assembly end of the conveyer belt at the rate of one per minute per line because of the extreme rationalization of work organization and work flow that characterizes this form of production. (Courtesy of the Chrysler Corporation.)

THE AUTO LINE: *Subdivided Jobs and Restricted Freedom*

Assembler with cap, back left, places lug nuts on rear wheels as assembler without cap, front left, uses power nut-tightener to fasten wheels securely to vehicle. These men perform the identical tasks shown above all day long and may fasten from eight hundred to one thousand wheels in eight hours. The movement of the cars along the conveyer belt determines the pace of their work and keeps them close to their stations, virtually "chained" to the assembly line. (Courtesy of the Chrysler Corporation.)

supervisors but this situation is not peculiar to the industry.[57] The advancement barrier between the ranks of the blue-collar workers and the supervisory level results not only from the scarcity of higher positions but also from differences in social status and the manual worker's general lack of social and leadership skills. And a considerable proportion of qualified manual workers do not want to leave the solidary relations with their mates and assume the responsibilities and aggravations of foremanship.[58]

A special factor contributing to the automobile worker's high degree of social alienation is the nature of work both off and on the line. Unskilled, repetitive, and stereotyped, it does not permit a man to demonstrate those qualities of skill, initiative, leadership, and resourcefulness which are usually the requirements for a higher position. Often, the worker does not know what to do in order to qualify for promotion.[59] The standards of selection are not clear, and there is a tendency for workers to feel that pull and connection get a man ahead. Automobile workers are particularly likely to be cynical and feel that the advancement pattern is unjust rather than equitable. Workers were asked to choose what "gives a person the best chance to advance in the plant" from among such possibilities as the quality of work, work attitude, length of company service, etc. The proportion of cynical responses,[60] 50 per cent, given by automobile workers was the second highest among the sixteen industries. Only the steel industry had a slightly higher percentage of cynical responses (Table 16, Appendix D). In the more highly integrated printing and textile industries, cynical answers were offered by only 30 per cent of the respondents.

Auto workers were considerably less likely than others to feel that the quality of a man's work and his energy and willingness to work were the key factors that contributed to advancement. The generally cynical attitude suggests that there is little consensus between workers and management concerning the standards of distributive justice, a critical aspect of normative integration. It is significant that the three industries which are the most anomic on this point—steel, transportation equipment, and automobiles—are those which have the highest proportions of workers employed in very large factories.

An atrophied group structure.—Finally, assembly-line technology reduces

---

[57] Only 34 per cent of the 30 per cent who said they would like to be foremen some day, thought that things would work out so that they would actually be foremen. This means that only about 10 per cent of the total automobile sample actually expect to become foremen. Similar results were found in Chinoy's study where 10 per cent of the workers both wanted and expected to become foremen. E. Chinoy, *op. cit.*

[58] See Lloyd Reynolds, *The Structure of Labor Markets* (New York: Harper & Bros., 1951), pp. 146–48 for an excellent discussion of these factors.

[59] Chinoy, *op. cit.*, p. 52.

[60] "How well he gets on personally with his immediate bosses"; "how good a politician he is"; and "whether he is a friend or relative of a high official or foreman."

the cohesion of the work force because it sets up obstacles to the formation of the informal, functional work groups common in many industries. Most automobile jobs are done individually, rather than by teams of employees. On an assembly line a worker may be able to talk with the men on both sides and those across from his work station, but each man is in contact with a different set of workers. Therefore, as the sociologists Walker and Guest discovered, few are "conscious of being members of any identifiable social group." [61]

Workers on the line may have more opportunity to communicate than do isolated workers who tend individual machines. Many X plant workers reported that the chance to talk and joke with others was one reason, although not necessarily the principal one, for liking their jobs.[62] For a few it was probably the major compensation (aside from wages, of course) in an otherwise totally unsatisfactory work situation. But this social interaction tends to be restricted to superficialities, because the conditions of work on the assembly line make any sustained or deeper sociability impossible. On many jobs noise makes it extremely difficult to be heard. In addition, a large number of jobs require close attention because of the speed of the line and the necessity to keep up. Restricted physical mobility also affects social interaction, limiting contacts to those directly at hand. Thus, automobile employees are less able to derive the social satisfactions in work which are very important in many other industries.

Although a sense of group membership is rare, it sometimes does develop. First-line foremen can become the focus for group identity in their department when they identify with their workers as well as management and view their role as that of group leader. Such foremen "stick up" for their workers rather than simply transmit management directives and delegate among the men some degree of responsibility for the assignment of work loads and the prevention of production bottlenecks.[63]

Finally, automobile workers do not have an occupational community as developed as printers and textile workers. Because their work is unskilled and unsatisfying, they have relatively little pride in it and do not identify with their occupation. They do not have the network of union and social and recreational clubs which printers and some other craft workers have.

With social alienation so intensified by all these elements of the industry's social structure, the union might appear to be the logical focus for an industrial community which could provide the worker with a sense of membership and belonging. Certainly the UAW has been important as a guardian of the workers' interests and as a rule-making institution. In this capacity, it has reduced through the years the worker's individual and collective

[61] Walker and Guest, *op. cit.*, p. 79.
[62] *Ibid.*, p. 68.
[63] Walker, Guest, and Turner, *op. cit.*, pp. 126–41.

powerlessness against the forces of technology and management. Loyalty to the union is basic, and it intensifies particularly in times of crisis. Still, relatively few automobile workers participate in the union's political life.[64] The UAW is not only more than ten times as large nationally as the biggest printing union; individual locals are proportionally larger because they are based on huge individual plants. To some extent then, the automobile worker finds himself facing two massive and somewhat impersonal bureaucracies, the company *and* the union. The union's capacity to overcome social alienation is therefore limited, important as its other functions have been and continue to be.

CONSEQUENCES OF SELF-ESTRANGING WORK AND MODES OF ADAPTATION

We have seen that automobile workers exert little control over their immediate work processes, rarely find purpose and distinctive function in their jobs, and lack a sense of belonging to an integrated industrial community. Conveyer-belt technology makes alienation, particularly powerlessness, most severe for those employees who work directly on the line. However, the influence of the assembly line's constant and mechanically paced rhythm extends beyond its immediate domain, and the highly standardized organization of work into minutely subdivided jobs is characteristic of the industry as a whole. Relative to other industries, the objective dimensions of alienation are more pronounced in automobile production, and a high degree of subjective alienation, or self-estrangement, might be expected to follow, unless other factors intervene as they do in the case of the textile worker. Let us consider the question of self-alienation in the automobile industry.

On the assembly line proper, the speed of the belt does not permit the detachment that is common with respect to repetitive work on machines. A certain present-time involvement is inevitable, to the extent that the assembler must strain simply to keep up with the line. Work off the line and in parts plants permits more detachment. On the whole, automobile workers in the Roper study were somewhat less likely than other factory workers to be able to keep their minds on other things while working. Thirty-seven per cent could do this, compared to 54 per cent of the textile employees, and 43 per cent of the entire sample (see Table 41, Appendix B).

A craftsman's involvement is based on the technical necessity and his internalized need to organize raw materials into an integrated product through the solution of the major and minor problems which impede the craft task. The automobile worker's immersion in the immediate situation is based more on external pressures. Since he resists and resents the very pressures that prevent detachment and idle daydreaming, involvement in his tasks

[64] Marquart, *op. cit.*, p. 150.

does not express or enhance his dignity and sense of well-being. When jobs are standardized and without challenge, workers prefer tasks that do not demand constant attention. Therefore, another dissatisfying feature of many automobile jobs is that they permit neither challenge nor detachment.[65]

Monotony.—Automobile workers were more likely to find their jobs always dull and monotonous than workers in any other industry in the Roper study. Eighteen per cent gave this response, compared to 6 per cent of the entire sample. Another 16 per cent said their jobs were dull and monotonous most of the time; thus, one automobile worker out of three complained of boredom, compared to one out of five of all factory workers (Table 42, Appendix B). It was primarily the unskilled, those concentrated on the assembly line, who found their jobs monotonous; the majority of the others felt that their work was interesting.

The proportion who complained of monotony was 61 per cent among the unskilled male auto workers, 27 per cent among the low-skilled, 16 per cent among the medium-skilled, and only 6 per cent among the skilled workers. The regular and consistent relationship between rising skill level and increased job interest is common to factory industries in general, as Table 16 shows. But in the automobile industry the gap between the unskilled and low-skilled employees is strikingly greater, a fact that suggests the especially alienating conditions of the assembly line, where the majority of the unskilled men are working.

TABLE 16

PROPORTION OF MALE AUTOMOBILE WORKERS AND ALL FACTORY WORKERS WHO FIND
JOBS DULL AND MONOTONOUS MOST OR ALL OF THE TIME, BY SKILL LEVEL*

SKILL LEVEL	AUTOMOBILE WORKERS		ALL MALE FACTORY WORKERS	
	Per Cent	Number	Per Cent	Number
Unskilled....................	61	69	38	604
Low skilled................	27	22	25	260
Medium skilled..............	16	37	19	622
Skilled.....................	6	31	5	738

* See Table 47, Appendix B for data for all sixteen industries.

Table 16 makes it clear that it is only the unskilled automobile workers who experience monotony more frequently than their counterparts in other industries. In fact the 61 per cent thus dissatisfied is the highest proportion among unskilled employees in all the industries Roper surveyed. For ex-

[65] Yet these external pressures of the conveyer belt are not wholly negative. We have already mentioned the Walker and Guest finding that a minority of the workers they studied liked the challenge and excitement of keeping up with the line, including the X plant worker who derived satisfaction from "keeping up with a rapid-fire job" and got bored on days when the cars came off the line slowly.

ample, only 36 per cent of the unskilled in the iron and steel industry find their jobs boring, 27 per cent of those in textiles, and 12 per cent of those in chemicals (Table 47, Appendix B).

Statistics do not express the monotony of the assembly line as well as the men who work on it. Walker and Guest found that the repetitive character of the work was one of the job's most objectionable features for a majority of the men, as the two comments below suggest:

The job gets so sickening—day in and day out plugging in ignition wires. I get through with one motor, turn around and there's another motor staring me in the face. It's sickening.

The assembly line is no place to work, I can tell you. There is nothing more discouraging than having a barrel beside you with 10,000 bolts in it and using them all up. Then you get a barrel with another 10,000 bolts, and you know every one of those 10,000 bolts has to be picked up and put in exactly the same place as the last 10,000 bolts.[66]

Of course, everyone does not find repetitive work frustrating and dis-satisfying. Only 33 per cent of the automobile workers Roper surveyed find their jobs monotonous; two-thirds say that their work is interesting most or all of the time. Yet standardized routines are characteristic of automobile production as a whole and not only the conveyer belt. The average worker is able to make an adjustment to a job which, from the standpoint of an intellectual appears to be the epitome of tedium.[67] Even among the un-skilled, so much more dissatisfied with their job routines than men in other industries, a sizable minority, 39 per cent, find such work interesting. Similarly, in the assembly plant Walker and Guest studied, a minority preferred the repetitive character of their work or at least were indifferent to it.[68]

Personal stagnation.—With jobs so standardized, there is little possibility for the average automobile worker to grow and develop personally in his work. The learning time required for most jobs is extremely short. In the X plant two-thirds of the jobs could be learned in less than a month. Even for those jobs that require a few months' training, once the work is mastered there is nothing more to learn.

Here the worker in automotive parts plants may be at an advantage, for the technology is considerably more advanced and dynamic in this branch of the industry. Highly automated processes have been introduced in the manufacture of engine blocks, and workers in these plants have had to learn

[66] Walker and Guest, *op. cit.*, pp. 54–55.

[67] See Arthur N. Turner and Amelia L. Miclette, "Sources of Satisfaction in Repetitive Work," *Occupational Psychology*, XXXVI (1962), 215–31 for a perceptive discussion of the conditions under which this takes place.

[68] Walker and Guest, *op. cit.*, pp. 53–55.

new methods of work.[69] The conveyer-belt technology in assembly plants, however, has been remarkably static for many decades. The annual model change usually results in only minor innovations. Workers are rarely able to gain new technical knowledge or experience from their work environment. Because of the fractionization of jobs and the general anonymity of the large factory, a man will not learn from new processes unless they affect his individual job directly. The pressure of line work and his inability to move freely through the plant also limit the knowledge he may gain from changes that take place in other parts of the factory.

The average automobile employee accepts the lack of challenge in his work environment just as he adapts to the repetitive character of the work. In the Roper study only 35 per cent complained that their jobs were too simple to bring out their best abilities, a figure approximately equal to the proportion who found these jobs monotonous. But again the minority of dissatisfied employees is larger than in other industries. In the entire Roper study only 25 per cent found their jobs too simple, and only two industries—sawmills; and stone, clay, and glass—had more workers proportionately who felt thwarted in this way (see Table 43, Appendix B). And again the unskilled auto worker is much more likely to feel frustrated than either the other men in his own industry or unskilled employees in other types of factories.[70]

Among young auto workers, the process of adapting aspirations to objective possibilities has not yet taken place, and they are therefore both more dissatisfied with the negative aspects of their present work and more optimistic about their chances of getting ahead. Workers under forty years old were considerably more likely than workers over forty to report that their jobs made them work too fast and left them too tired at the end of the day, even though in the Roper sample as a whole it was the older workers who were more likely to complain of fatigue. In the two lower-skilled groups the majority of the young workers found their jobs monotonous, while only a minority of the older men expressed dissatisfaction with uninteresting work. Fifty-nine per cent of the unskilled auto workers under forty feel that their jobs are too simple to bring out their best abilities, whereas only 37 per cent of the men in this skill category who are over forty feel frustrated. The younger men are more likely to be hopeful about changing this situation. Among all male automobile workers, 48 per cent of the young, in contrast to 29 per cent of the old, feel that their jobs lead to promotions.

But as Chinoy has pointed out, automobile workers redefine the meaning

[69] William Faunce, "Automation in the Automobile Industry: Some Consequences for In-Plant Social Structure," *American Sociological Review*, XXIII (1958), 401–7 and "Automation and the Automobile Worker," *Social Problems*, VI (1958), 68–78.

[70] Forty-six per cent of the unskilled automobile workers find their jobs too simple, compared to 35 per cent of the low skilled, 24 per cent of the medium skilled, and 16 per cent of the skilled. At each skill level, and particularly at the lowest, automobile workers are more likely to feel thwarted than men in most other industries (Table 50, Appendix B).

of advancement, as they get older, to fit the context of the assembly line. Instead of wanting a more skilled or even higher-paying job, the major goal becomes an easier, less rapidly paced job off the assembly line, at the same pay level.[71] As they gain seniority many workers are able to do this, and therefore the older workers tend to be less dissatisfied than the young. However, in those automotive plants which do not include a number of fabricating departments as well as a final assembly division, the older worker may be stuck on a line job long after his physical stamina and agility of movement have declined.

The instrumental attitude.—For printers the most satisfying and important aspects of their jobs are the intrinsic features; as we saw in chapter 3, external considerations such as wages and security are de-emphasized. It is the opposite story for automobile workers, and this, of course, is the essential meaning of self-estrangement. The only aspects of their jobs that the X plant workers liked were the high pay and the level of employment security, which was relatively high for an economically depressed area. None of the intrinsic features of the work was attractive; in fact, Walker and Guest found that the five most disliked characteristics of the job situation were all inherent aspects of the work as activity.[72]

The high pay and the security which is possible for the older employee with many years of seniority reduces the auto worker's discontent and results in moderate satisfaction with the job as a whole, in contrast to the frequently strong dissatisfaction with the actual work routines. Even more than with other factory workers, the principal meaning of work for automobile employees, and particularly for those on the assembly line, tends to be the pay check and those opportunities for a better off-work life that a fairly steady job at high wages provides. The job is a means to an end and not an end in itself, since the activity of work in the automobile industry is fundamentally unrewarding. The automobile worker, particularly the man on the conveyer belt, approaches the classic model of the self-estranged worker. In a moving passage, Chinoy demonstrates this self-estrangement by means of the workers' own comments:

These features of work in mass-production industry which alienate the worker from his labor and from himself lead to deprivations which are not easily verbalized. Yet they do show themselves in various ways; in the sad comment, "The only reason a man works is to make a living"; in the occasional overflow of resentment, "Sometimes you feel like jamming things up in the machine and

[71] Similarly Guest reports that most of the workers he studied were not very ambitious. They wanted to get away from their jobs but had resigned themselves to the fact that upward movement was not possible (*op. cit.*, pp. 322–23).

[72] These were: (1) cannot set own pace, (2) is physically tiring, (3) do not have interesting work, (4) cannot do different things, (5) cannot use my brains. Walker and Guest, *op. cit.*, p. 62.

saying goodbye to it"; in the cynical observation, "The things I like best about my job are quitting time, pay day, days off, and vacations"; in the complaint, "There is no interest in a job in the shop"; and in the resigned answer to questions about their work, "A job's a job." [73]

When work is generally unrewarding in itself and the status of the occupation is relatively low, a job will contribute little to a man's sense of worth and self-esteem. Standardized mass-production work in the automobile industry does not provide an occupational identity which is approved of by the community at large and by the worker himself. When asked whether they would choose the same line of work if they could start their lives over again at the age of fifteen, only 23 per cent said yes. Sixty-nine per cent would prefer different occupations than automobile work, 8 per cent were undecided. Of all sixteen industries in the Roper study, in only one, leather manufacturing, were there fewer workers who would have made the same life decision once again (Table 37, Appendix B). Even among the skilled automobile workers, 59 per cent would prefer to be in different occupations. In contrast, only 36 per cent of the skilled printers thus reject their occupational identity.

Adapt or quit?—As they grow older and gain seniority on their jobs, automobile workers gradually feel themselves trapped in the situation. Although frustrated by an alienating work relationship, they have gained too much economic security to make a move. Alternatives are few and uncertain. Wages are high; a house has been bought which demands monthly payments; children are growing and thinking about college—the automobile worker is stuck. Two common psychological adaptations to his self-alienation are fantasy and the projection of his own frustrated ambitions on his children. Chinoy informs us how frequently automobile workers daydream about quitting the shop and setting up some independent business of their own, such as a turkey farm or a string of motels. In most cases these remain fantasies; few of the older men quit. Their daydreams serve as a safety valve for day-to-day frustrations. The other response is to plan college educations for the children; they, at any rate, will not work on an assembly line. This attitude is far different from that of the textile workers, who seem to accept it as a matter of course that their sons will follow them in the mills.

Those workers who have not yet been trapped by age or other circumstances have another alternative, quitting the job. Not surprisingly, automobile workers quit more frequently than manual employees in other industries, despite their high wages, which exceed the average for all manufacturing. From 1946 to 1958, the average quit rate was 2.4 in the assembly branch of the motor vehicles industry. This means that for every 100 employees, between 2 and 3 quit every month. This was one of the highest

---

[73] Chinoy, *op. cit.*, p. 85.

rates for the entire economy; it compared with a rate of 1.0 for industrial chemicals.[74]

An additional factor makes the situation of the automobile worker especially poignant. In other industries the majority of the low-skilled and highly repetitive jobs that involve little freedom and control are not physically heavy. For this reason, most unfree and unfulfilling jobs in such industries as textiles, leather, apparel, and electronics are held by women rather than men. As in the textile industry, this means that many of the more challenging jobs and most advancement possibilities belong to the male workers. A high proportion of women raises the "satisfaction level" of an industry, both because it upgrades the objective situation for men and because women are more content than men with work that is of little challenge. However, the work which is among the most objectively alienating in all industry, automobile manufacturing, is also heavy manual work and therefore must be performed by men, who are, in a sense, trapped by the high pay and the lack of alternatives.[75]

Dissatisfaction as dignity.—There is, therefore, a much greater frequency of active dissatisfaction with alienated work among automobile workers than among textile employees. In fact, the result of assembly-line technology and work organization may be the highest level of dissatisfaction in all industry. On virtually every indicator of job satisfaction in the Roper study, the automobile industry ranks close to, if not at, the very bottom—as a quick inspection of the tables in Appendix B indicates.

[74] I have computed this average from quit rates appearing in the monthly labor statistics of the *Monthly Labor Review*. As much as possible I tabulated the rates for the automobile assembly industry and did not include the parts section of the industry. A number of times during the period analyzed, the Bureau of Labor Statistics changed its industrial classifications, and it was necessary to use the most comparable category. In 1959 when labor turnover data were resumed after some months, individual figures for the automobile industry were not given separately but as a part of the transportation equipment group of industries. For this reason, I do not have more recent figures.

Since 1956 the automobile industry quit rate has dropped considerably. Quit rates drop sharply in times of recession as well as in the winter months. In the past years, a sharp and seemingly permanent decline in quit rates for industry as a whole has taken place.

Although many factors influence quit rates, the high rate in the automobile assembly industry is at least partially the result of dissatisfaction with routine, dull jobs and the mechanically determined pace of the conveyer belt. This inference is supported by the finding of Walker and Guest that quit rates in the X plant were almost twice as high among men on the assembly line as among men off the line. They also found that the men with the most repetitive jobs and those on the conveyer belts were much more likely to take time off from work than were men in other types of work (*op. cit.*, pp. 116–17, 120).

[75] As Gladys Palmer puts it, "The sense of frustration reflected in the studies of men in automobile assembly plants may be an extreme case, because relatively high rates of pay and seniority privileges tend to keep them attached to plants that have limited transfer and promotion opportunities." "Attitudes toward Work in an Industrial Community," *American Journal of Sociology*, LXIII (1957), 18.

Sawmills is another industry in which the work is both unfree, unskilled, and heavy, so that production workers are also men. This industry is not however as numerically and socially important as automobile production.

The automobile worker's job dissatisfaction is a reflection of his independence and dignity; he does not submit as easily as other manual workers to alienating work. This independence and dignity is expressed in other ways beside a generalized dissatisfaction. The auto worker quits his job more frequently than other workers. He is characteristically a griper, a man who talks back to his foreman, in contrast to the more submissive textile employee. He presses grievances through a union steward system and engages in wildcat strikes and revolts against the union bureaucracy itself more frequently than other workers. On the job, he resorts to illegitimate methods of asserting some control over his immediate work process. And he may even express contempt for a dominating technology and the company product in occasional minor acts of industrial sabotage.

The automobile worker is an alienated worker because his work has become almost completely compartmentalized from other areas of his life, so that there is little meaning left in it beyond the instrumental purpose. Unlike the textile worker, he does not live in a traditional society where work is highly integrated with the major social institutions: family, religion, and community. Although many automobile workers were born in traditional southern communities, the industry is primarily located in northern urban industrial cities—in modern mass society rather than traditional folk society.

With his alienated relation to his work and his emphasis upon leisure and consumption, the automobile worker is, in a sense, the blue-collar prototype of "the mass man in mass society." His work is unfree and unfulfilling and exemplifies the bureaucratic combination of the highly rational organization and the restricted specialist. In relation to the two giant bureaucracies which dominate his life, he is relatively powerless, atomized, depersonalized, and anonymous. Yet, as the producer of motor vehicles, he is a vital factor in an automobile civilization, as well as a ready consumer of its mass culture and mass leisure.

Somehow it is quite fitting that the man who builds automobiles should be the worker prototype of the mass man. More than any other product, the automobile has created the mass society, and it remains its symbol. Motor-vehicle production was the first major successful example of mass production and mass consumption. The automobile has contributed immeasurably to the speed and physical mobility of a mass society. It has also affected the tone of classlessness and contributed to status mobility in American society; for the affluent masses can buy and drive these powerful objects which, in the past, were the playthings of the elite classes. And Detroit automobiles are among the major targets of those critics of mass society who decry its vulgarization of taste and aesthetic style. The automobile worker builds cars; he understands them. He identifies with his own vehicle and works on it constantly. The automobile is a large part of his world.

Yet the automobile worker, as we have noted, has also been the "proletarian hero," the hope of Marxist intellectuals who saw in the working class the possibility of a revolutionary reorganization of society. And there is some justice in this image, for the conditions of his work sometimes make him the prototype of the militant worker as well. He works in the largest factories, where conflicts of interest between worker and management are intensified. Through his union, he has engaged in much class action, some even violent; and he is probably more class conscious than most American workers.[76] It is perhaps because the automobile worker represents in an especially clear way the conjunction of the mass and class influences in modern society and therefore highlights better than any other type the position of the factory worker in mass society that he has become the symbol of the modern industrial employee.

[76] Ely Chinoy comments on this point (in a personal communication to the writer) that many automobile workers express their alienation by the "petty bourgeois" aspiration of small-business ownership rather than by the collective orientation of the class-conscious individual. This mentality, which Marxists term "false-consciousness," is of course common among American industrial workers as a whole.

6

THE CHEMICAL OPERATOR:
CONTROL OVER AUTOMATED
TECHNOLOGY

The coexistence today of craft industries like printing, machine-tending industries like textiles, and assembly-line industries like automobile manufacturing, each of which represents a different period in the development of technology and division of labor, is an indication of the diversity of America's industrial scene. A recognition of this diversity cautions us against generalizing too facilely about the American factory worker. A further expression of the picture's complexity is the growing importance of a fourth, and still different, work environment: that of the automated factory.

Automated production was well developed in oil refining and industrial chemical plants long before the recent concern with this new industrial trend; in fact, these industries were "automated" years before the term "automation" was invented. Oil and chemicals are the two most important examples of continuous-process technology. Extremely advanced technologically, economically, and socially, these industries may portend the conditions of factory work and employment in a future dominated by automated technology. Therein lies the special importance of an intensive analysis of alienation in these industries. At the same time we must guard also against overgeneralizing from this limited case, for even a predominantly automated economy will have considerable diversity, and present knowledge already indicates that automation takes many different forms, depending on the industry's technology and economic situation before automation.

A continuous-process plant is quite different from a typical factory. There are no recognizable machines and very few workers visible. Except for a few maintenance workers in colored helmets welding or painting pipes, you see very few people doing anything and nobody making anything. Instead, one sees a large number of individual buildings with vast areas of open space between them, huge networks of pipes, and large towers and other equipment which one later learns are various types of distillation units or chemical reactors. The chemicals which are made and the oils which are refined flow through these pipes from one stage of their processing to another, usually without being handled at all by the workers. They are processed in large reactors where raw materials are combined or separated. Generally, oils and chemicals must pass through a number of reaction operations before the product is completed. The flow of materials; the combination of different chemicals; and the temperature, pressure, and speed of the processes are regulated by automatic control devices. The automatic controls make possible a continuous flow in which raw materials are introduced at the beginning of the process and a large volume of the product continually emerges at the end stage. Ultimately, it is the liquid or gaseous nature of most products and raw materials that makes possible a continuous-flow technology (see Plate 7 for automatic control devices and Plate 8 for the networks of pipes and reactor units).

Continuous-process technology is the most highly mechanized of the various forms of manufacturing. Capital investment is enormous. So much of the process is carried out by the machine system that relatively few manual workers are required. Thus in the most highly automated industry, oil refining, the capital investment per production worker is $110,000, compared to the average of only $15,000 in all manufacturing industry. In the chemical industry as a whole, the ratio is $28,000 per production worker; and in the branch of this highly diversified industry which manufactures heavy chemicals, it is considerably greater (Table 18, Appendix A).

The oil refining industry is a key industry in the economy. The value of its products shipped in 1954 was almost twelve billion dollars, a figure exceeded only by the food industries and perhaps by the steel and automotive industries.[1] And yet it has only two hundred thousand employees, ranking nineteenth in size of employment among the twenty major manufacturing industries.[2] Not surprisingly, the individual worker in a continuous-process industry is more productive than workers in other industries, in terms of the value he adds to the product by his participation in the manufacturing process. Thus, another indicator of the high level of mechanization is the fact that the value added by manufacturing, per production worker, is highest in the chemical and petroleum industries. Each chemical production worker adds $12,772 a year to the total value of the products of the industry, in contrast to the $4,577 which a textile worker adds (Table 19, Appendix A). The more highly mechanized an industry's technology, the greater is the investment in the physical plant and machinery, and therefore expenditures for maintaining and repairing this equipment increase. In oil refining, 44

[1] National Industrial Conference Board, *Economic Almanac, 1960* (New York: National Industrial Conference Board, 1960), p. 184. No data were available for steel or motor vehicles.
[2] *Ibid.*, p. 183.

per cent of the entire payroll is earmarked for maintenance expenses, the highest figure among twenty manufacturing industries. In chemicals the proportion is 22 per cent, the third highest industrial figure, and almost twice the proportion for manufacturing industries as a whole (Table 20, Appendix A).

The continuous-process industries are both relatively new industries. Industrial chemicals is still at an early stage of its growth cycle. The industry has experienced meteoric expansion in the war and postwar years and is now the fastest growing major manufacturing industry. Whether measured in terms of capital investment, trends in total output, or employment, oil and chemicals are dynamic growth-industries. Important factors sustaining this growth and economic prosperity are the high level of scientific research and the expenditures for new plants and equipment, which far surpass those in other industries.

The dynamic change inherent in the chemical industry is due to its competitive market situation; its youthfulness; and particularly its close relationship with, and dependence on, science. Chemistry, like all sciences, is inherently dynamic; the discovery of new chemicals and processes is sooner or later reflected in new forms of industrial production. Although the chemical industry does not have the kind of price competition we find in the older small-firm industries, there is considerable competition among the major companies in developing new products and processes. It spends more money on basic research than any other manufacturing industry.[3]

The science and research emphasis is naturally reflected in the industry's occupational structure. Twelve per cent of its total labor force in 1950 were professionals (including 23,500 chemists and 21,000 engineers), compared to only 4 per cent of the labor force in the automobile industry.[4] The large number of professionals and scientists in the industry is a cause, as well as an effect, of its dynamic character, since the role of an industrial scientist is to stimulate change and experimentation.

Because of the extremely complex technology and the high level of capital

---

[3] Thirty thousand, or almost 20 per cent, of the 165,000 people engaged in basic research for all industry are in the chemical and allied products industries, according to an estimate of the National Research Council. E. B. Alderfer and H. E. Michl, *The Economics of American Industry* (3rd ed.; New York: McGraw-Hill Book Co., 1957), p. 251. In 1959, the chemical industry spent more money on new plants and equipment than any industry except the even more highly automated oil refining industry—1.3 billion dollars, approximately twice as much as the $.6 billion expended by the automobile industry. National Industrial Conference Board, p. 303. The research director of the International Chemical Workers Union (ICWU) mentions that the chemical industry in 1954 "spent $2,240 per production worker for new plant and equipment . . . two and a half times more than the average for all manufacturing industry, which was $877." Statement of Otto Pragan, in "Automation and Technological Change," *Hearings, Subcommittee on Economic Stabilization,* 84th Cong., 1st Sess. (Washington: U.S. Government Printing Office, 1955), p. 152.

[4] U.S. Department of Commerce, Bureau of the Census, *Occupation· by Industry* (Washington: U.S. Government Printing Office, 1955), p. 36.

investment necessary to produce industrial chemicals and the products of the oil industry, the continuous-process industries are dominated by large companies. Oil refining is one of the most concentrated of all industries; it has a concentration ratio of 99. The chemical industry, with a ratio of 59, is somewhat less concentrated; however, small operators predominate in sectors of the industry other than heavy industrial chemicals (see Table 21, Appendix A). In 1949, the three largest companies—DuPont, Union Carbide, and Allied Chemical and Dye—held 50 to 60 per cent of the total assets in the industry;[5] the eight largest companies control approximately 80 per cent of the total assets.[6]

Despite the size of the major companies, individual plants do not employ as many workers, on the average, as in the automobile industry. Whereas 55 per cent of the automobile workers are employed in plants with more than 2,500 men, only 19 per cent of the chemical employees and 28 per cent of the oil workers are in such large establishments.[7] This is because automation has reduced the size of the work force in the continuous-process industries and also because of a conscious policy of decentralization. The large companies have preferred to operate many middle-sized plants rather than a few big establishments. Large establishments are more characteristic of the oil industry, 53 per cent of whose employees work in plants with more than 1,000 people, than the chemical industry, only 40 per cent of whose employees work in factories with more than 1,000 (Table 23, Appendix A). The average chemical plant has about 69 employees; the average oil refinery, 142 employees; the average automobile factory, about 334 employees (Table 22, Appendix A).

Decentralization is a decisive feature of the continuous-process industries, expressed not only by the distribution of the plants of a single company but also by the organization of individual plants. Continuous-process technology results in a layout of work that is very different from textile and automobile production, where the bulk of machine and assembly-line operations and the majority of the workers are concentrated under one roof. Chemical and oil refining operations are divided among many buildings or subplants with large stretches of open space between the buildings. In a sense, a chemical factory or a refinery does not consist of one plant, but of a large number of plants, in each of which a particular product or a particular reaction is processed. The 400 blue-collar employees of the Bay Chemical Company are dispersed throughout the ammonia plant, the caustic plant, the chlorination plant, the latex plant, the methionine plant, the xanthate plant, the mercaptan plant, and the electrolytic-cell plant, in addition to several maintenance

[5] Edmund H. Lambert, Jr., "Labor and the Chemical Industry" (Master's Thesis, University of California, Berkeley, 1949, in files of the Institute of Industrial Relations, Berkeley), pp. 17–19.

[6] *Hearings, Subcommittee on Economic Stabilization*, 84th. Cong., 1st sess.

[7] National Industrial Conference Board, *op. cit.*, p. 183.

buildings. The danger of fire and other hazards, as well as the range of products and processes, makes such decentralization necessary. Even in the largest continuous-process establishments, the "social density" of the work force is very low. The 3,500 workers employed at one of northern California's largest oil refineries are spread out over 3,500 acres of grounds.

In this chapter, I shall examine the ways in which the distinctive technological, economic, and sociological features of the continuous-process industries affect the alienation of the blue-collar workers. In contrast to the numerous studies of the automobile assembly line, there has been little research on work in continuous-process plants, an indication of their newness, but more importantly of the concentration of research on negative work environments.[8] The emphasis will be on the chemical industry, particularly its most automated heavy industrial chemicals branch, rather than oil refining, since the former was the major focus of my field investigations.[9] Before considering the specific dimensions of alienation, let us look at the employment situation, occupational structure, and the new type of blue-collar work brought about by continuous-process technology.

JOB SECURITY AND CAREERS:
THEIR TECHNOLOGICAL AND ECONOMIC BASES

Workers in the continuous-process industries are far more secure in their employment than employees in most other industries. In an automated technology, the volume of output is not a function of the number of production workers, as it is in pre-automated systems, but depends largely on the capacity of the technical equipment. Individual plants do not hire and fire as consumer demand rises and dips, as is common in the automotive industry. The number of workers necessary to operate and maintain the equipment has already been reduced by automation to the minimum number required for safety and efficiency. For these reasons, labor tends to be a semifixed or fixed cost in production rather than a variable cost, and the "core labor force" in an automated technology therefore has an unusually high degree of job security, as James Bright has emphasized.[10]

Another contributing factor has been a persistently steady demand for

---

[8] Floyd Mann and Richard Hoffman's investigation of electric power plants is the most relevant case study. Though classified as a utility rather than a manufacturing industry, the electric light and power industry also uses a continuous-process technology. See F. C. Mann and L. R. Hoffman, *Automation and the Worker* (New York: Henry Holt & Co., 1960).

[9] Another reason for concentrating on chemicals is that there were more chemical employees (78) in the Roper study than oil workers (52), and the general industrial comparisons are therefore somewhat more reliable. However, it must be pointed out that work attitudes in the chemical industry may be more positive than those in oil, and concentration on chemicals may minimize some of the alienating tendencies of continuous-process production.

[10] James Bright, *Automation and Management* (Cambridge, Mass.: Harvard University Press, 1958), pp. 202–3.

oil and chemical products which has made the long-run economic situation in the continuous-process industries extremely favorable. The oil industry's most rapid growth was in the 1920's; however, production levels remained high even during the depression, and oil workers had considerably greater job security during the 1930's than other factory workers. Oil employment stabilized during the 1940's and actually declined for a period in the 1950's as economic recessions and continued automation took their toll. On the other hand, the chemical industry's growth rate has not slowed down. Between 1940 and 1960 the number of its wage and salary employees increased by approximately 100 per cent. In the ten years between 1950 and 1960, while the number of production workers in oil refining decreased from 136,000 to 116,000, the blue-collar work force in chemicals expanded from 494,000 to 539,000.[11]

The chemical industry is also considerably less subject to short-run business fluctuations than the automobile industry, for example.[12] This is partly due to the wide range of its products,[13] which means that a drastic drop in demand for any one product does not depress the entire industry. The industry is also less dependent on the vagaries of consumer spending, since much of its production is sold to other companies (often other chemical firms) for use in production, maintenance, and sanitation.

Of all major manufacturing industries in 1949, the oil refining and chemicals industries had the highest proportions of employees who worked fifty or more weeks. Eighty-eight per cent of all oil workers and 79 per cent of the chemical workers worked virtually the entire year, compared to only 57 per cent of the automobile workers and 67 per cent of all factory workers (Table 27, Appendix A). Between 1958 and 1961, when the average monthly layoff rate in the automobile industry was 3.6, it was only 0.8 in the chemical industry and 0.6 in the oil refining industry. In all factory industries, 2.1 workers were laid off per month, on the average, in this period (Table 28, Appendix A).

The attitudes of continuous-process workers in the Roper survey suggest almost no fear of job loss. Only 2 per cent of the oil and chemical employees thought they were likely to be laid off in the next six months. These were the lowest figures for any industry and contrast with 29 per cent of the automobile workers and 14 per cent of all factory workers (Table 32). Similarly, 94 per cent of the chemical employees and 92 per cent of the refinery workers felt that they could have their jobs as long as they wanted,

---

[11] U.S. Department of Commerce, *Statistical Abstracts of the United States, 1961* (Washington: U.S. Government Printing Office, 1961), pp. 208–10.

[12] It is also somewhat more fortunate than the oil refining industry in this regard.

[13] The main branches of the industry illustrate the diversity of its production: industrial organic chemicals; industrial inorganic chemicals; drugs and medicines; soaps; paints, pigments, and fillers; gum and wood chemicals; fertilizers; vegetable and animal oils and fats; and countless miscellaneous chemicals.

so again oil and chemicals were the two most optimistic industries (Table 31, Appendix B).

Because of the high degree of responsibility that continuous-process technology demands, management is particularly interested in a permanent, stable work force; and indeed, employment in the oil and chemical industries is often for life. The economist Richard Lester has stated that these industries have moved from a commodity to a welfare concept of employment: "The employer and the prospective employee think of employment in terms of a whole work career—a long-term relationship in which the employer takes on an increasing burden of fringe benefits covering the man and his family, and the employee acquires tenure, job rights, and rights to promotion opportunities." [14]

Job security in the continuous-process industries is enhanced by the proliferation of welfare benefits. The petroleum industry (and, to a lesser extent, the chemical industry) has a "cradle-to-the-grave" series of employees' benefits which includes paid sick leave, company contributory savings plans, pensions, and death benefits. In 1959 a survey of the National Industrial Conference Board found that almost 40 per cent of all the company savings plans in the country were in the oil industry.[15] In 1957 this industry averaged 78 cents per payroll hour for fringe benefits, compared to only 45 cents for all manufacturing.

The welfare concept of employment in these young industries partially reflects the socially progressive viewpoints of their managerial elites, who are usually college trained. It is a conscious policy, but one which stems naturally from the economic basis of production in continuous-process plants. These policies are made financially possible by the high profits of the industries and the relatively small numbers of blue-collar workers. Because these industries are so highly capital-intensive, labor is a relatively minor aspect of cost; high wages and fringe benefits therefore do not "hurt" as much as they would in such relatively labor-intensive industries as automobiles and textiles.[16]

Workers in the continuous-process industries are therefore able to face the future with fewer economic anxieties than workers in other industries. In the Roper study the highest proportion of employees who said it was likely that they'd be able to retire from work at the age of 65 and live the rest of

[14] Richard Lester, "The New Dimension of Industrial Employment," in Robert Gray (ed.), *Frontiers of Industrial Relations* (Los Angeles: California Institute of Technology, 1959), pp. 3.1–3.11.

[15] Harland Fox, "Employee Savings Plans in the Oil Industry," *Management Record*, XXII (1960), 2.

[16] In 1957, in chemicals and petroleum, wages were only 19 and 26 per cent of "value added by manufacture," as compared to 39 per cent in the transportation equipment industry and 51 per cent in the textile industry. The figure for all manufacturing industries was 36 per cent. National Industrial Conference Board, *op. cit.*, p. 211.

their lives "in reasonable comfort on . . . savings, pensions, and social security payments" was in the chemical industry, where 63 per cent were this optimistic. Fifty-one per cent of the oil workers were optimistic, compared to 43 per cent of all factory workers and only 33 per cent of the automobile workers (see Table 52, Appendix B).[17]

BALANCED SKILL AND DIVERSIFIED JOB STRUCTURE

Craft production results in an occupational distribution in which the majority of the manual workers are highly skilled. Machine-tending and assembly-line technologies result in distinctive occupational structures characterized by low levels of skill and little internal differentiation. Continuous-process technology also produces a distinctive occupational structure because sizable numbers of workers are required at all levels of skill and training—high, medium, and low. The result is what might be called a balanced skill mix.

The more highly developed the continuous-process technology, the more balanced is the skill distribution among skilled, semiskilled, and unskilled workers. Thus in the oil refining industry, 38 per cent of the manual workers are skilled; 46 per cent, semiskilled; and 16 per cent, unskilled laborers. In the somewhat less mechanized chemical industry, 30 per cent are skilled; 30 per cent, semiskilled; and 18 per cent are unskilled. The blue-collar skill distribution for all major manufacturing industries is given in Table 26, Appendix A.[18]

The developing mechanization in continuous-process technology results in an internal distribution of the blue-collar labor force that is different from the assembly-line mass-production industries. The most dramatic change is the reduction in the number of semiskilled operatives (as we saw in chapters 4 and 5, the semiskilled worker is often quite unskilled), since automatic processes do the work which these men would do in other technological situations. There is also a striking increase in the number of skilled craftsmen, who are needed to maintain and repair the expensive, delicate automatic machinery. In the Bay chemical plant, pipe fitter-welders, machinists, millwrights, construction men, electricians, instrument repairmen, and other

---

[17] The Roper survey preceded the UAW's pension gains, so it is quite likely that automobile workers, and perhaps many workers in other industries as well, would today be less pessimistic about their long-range security.

[18] The distribution of workers by length of training is more precise and detailed in the Roper survey than the census categories, though based, of course, on a much smaller sample. It shows a similarly divergent pattern of occupational structure by industry. Printers are clustered at the high-skill pole; automobile workers and textile workers at the low-skill pole; chemical workers and oil refinery employees are fairly evenly distributed among the various training categories—with the distribution in the oil industry somewhat more balanced (see Table 51, Appendix B).

maintenance workers make up 40 per cent of the blue-collar force; only 6 per cent of the workers in the ABC automobile plant Chinoy studied were maintenance men.[19]

The occupational structure in the continuous-process industries is further differentiated by a highly elaborate system of job classification. Most work in automobile plants is concentrated in a few job grades. In the X automobile plant there was an average of fourteen workers in each job classification.[20] In the Bay chemical plant there were only three workers per job category.[21]

This highly refined job-grading is paralleled by a more highly dispersed wage distribution. While 50 per cent of the automobile workers are clustered in a wage-spread differential of 14 cents an hour, the interquartile range for chemical workers is 80 cents an hour.[22] In oil refining, the range is 70 cents an hour. As we saw in chapter 4, the wage distribution is also concentrated in the textile industry, where the range is 20 cents an hour.

Thus the blue-collar world in continuous-process industries is highly stratified along the lines of skill, status, job grade, pay scale, department, and type of work. These features of the industrial social structure have significant consequences for the integration of the worker into the factory community.

AUTOMATED WORK:
RESPONSIBILITY AND VARIETY

It is the work of operating the automatic equipment which exemplifies the distinctive technology of continuous-process production, just as the assembly-line operative's job epitomizes the work situation of the automobile industry. Jobs in maintenance and distribution do not differ greatly from similar work in other industries. For this reason, my analysis of the work and the alienation of the chemical worker focuses on the chemical operator.

Very little of the work of chemical operators is physical or manual, despite the blue-collar status of these factory employees. Practically all physical production and materials-handling is done by automatic processes, regu-

[19] The sizable maintenance sector of the blue-collar work force in continuous-process plants has a high skill concentration: Davis' study of the Bay Chemical Company found that 85 per cent of the maintenance workers had jobs which required more than one year to learn adequately. Jobs in operations and distribution are clustered more at the low and medium skill levels; only 18 per cent of the operators required more than a year to learn their jobs in the same survey.

Unfortunately, the Roper survey does not distinguish maintenance and operating employees, so it was not possible to make separate tabulations on this and other pertinent questions.

[20] Charles R. Walker and Robert Guest, *Man on the Assembly Line* (Cambridge, Mass.: Harvard University Press, 1952), p. 167. My calculation.

[21] Statement of Bay Company industrial relations representative.

[22] Computed from data in U.S. Department of Labor, Bureau of Labor Statistics, *Factory Workers' Earnings May 1958* (Bulletin No. 1252 [Washington: U.S. Government Printing Office, 1959]), p. 28. The automobile figure is from L. Earl Lewis, "Wage Dispersion in Manufacturing Industries, 1950–1955," *Monthly Labor Review*, LXXI (1956), 2.

lated by automatic controls. The work of the chemical operator is to monitor these automatic processes: his tasks include observing dials and gauges; taking readings of temperatures, pressures, and rates of flow; and writing down these readings in log data sheets. Such work is clearly of a non-manual nature.

Workers characterize their jobs as being more "mental" or "visual" than physical. When asked if they do any manual work, they will often say that they turn valves occasionally, an expenditure of physical energy which is not much greater than the office manager's adjustment of the controls on the office thermostat. On the whole, the operators interviewed like this lack of physical effort, although it was not a major element in their over-all work satisfaction. A few regretted the absence of physical activity. They felt jobs were becoming too easy and that a man could get soft with too much "push-button stuff." Workers with farm backgrounds seemed more likely to express such opinions.

The development of machine and assembly-line technologies greatly reduced the number of traditional craft skills necessary for manufacturing production; with the emergence of automated continuous-process technology, traditional craft skill has been completely eliminated from the productive process.[23] Even the talent for unskilled manual work, or "knack," so important on the assembly line, has been eliminated by the automated processes. In the place of physical effort and skill in the traditional, manual sense, the major job requirement for production workers in continuous-process technology is responsibility. As the French sociologist Alain Touraine phrases it, "Their responsibility defines their professional skill." [24]

Within each of the buildings that make up a continuous-process plant, a small crew, generally numbering from three to seven workers per shift, is responsible for the particular products or processes of their subplant. Each team is directed by a head shift operator who has considerable training and experience, and each is made up of workers of diverse levels of training and with varying degrees of responsibility.

Chemical operators are responsible for the quality of the product, for the continuing, trouble-free operation of the processes, and for the extremely expensive automatic equipment. Almost all of the Bay Company operators interviewed felt that their jobs involved a high degree of responsibility. Only two out of twelve had worked previously at jobs in other industries which they felt required more responsibility than their work in the chemical plant. However, the extent of an operator's responsibility depends on his position in the hierarchy of his departmental work team. The closer to the bottom his job, the more likely the worker was to minimize his own responsibility

---

[23] Traditional skills do persist, of course, in maintenance.

[24] Alain Touraine, *L'évolution du travail ouvrier aux usines Renault* (Paris: Centre National de la Recherche Scientifique, 1955), p. 123.

and to stress the over-all responsibility of his head shift operator upon whom he could call when something was seriously wrong.

The responsibility of a head shift operator is extremely great; he co-ordinates the work of all the members of his team, arranges for maintenance priorities and for the transport of materials and products to and from his plant, and serves as the link between his work team and management.

As we shall see later, the long-run change in the nature of blue-collar work from manual skill to responsibility provides new avenues for meaning and self-expression in work.

Variety and diversity.—The extreme rationalization and division of labor in the textile mill and on the automobile assembly line result in jobs which are the ultimate in repetition and routine. The variety of the jobs of chemical workers in a continuous-process plant is considerably greater. For maintenance workers, who make up 40 per cent of the plant force, the very nature of their work disallows a repetitive cycle of operations, except for those tasks involved in regular preventive checks of equipment. Scheduling of maintenance work is determined by what piece of equipment breaks down, and there is obviously no way to standardize this. There is also an inherent variety, though to a lesser extent, in the jobs of the distribution workers who load and unload trucks and tank cars or pump the product from one part of the plant to another.

Process operators have a certain amount of standardized work, but the contrast with the repetitive, subdivided operations of the automobile worker is striking. Virtually all jobs require more than the ten operations that only a favored minority of auto workers enjoy. While the typical job cycle of the assembly-line worker is one minute, the chemical operator's most standardized operation is his periodic round of readings, which he takes every two hours. On such a round, an operator may check the readings on more than fifty different instruments located at widely dispersed points in his patrol area. There is a considerable variety, then, even in the most routine of the chemical operator's job tasks.

Jobs are not as limited in scope in the continuous-process industries because chemical processes cannot be subdivided to the extent that the mechanical operations in assembly can be. Chemicals are not discrete units upon which a number of operations can be performed very quickly, but liquids and gases that flow continuously through a series of automatic operations, each of which takes a considerable amount of time. Job design must be organized around the entire process the chemical undergoes in its production. Automation also greatly reduces the number of operators necessary for production, so that the work is divided among fewer employees.[25]

---

[25] In his study of automation in a large number of industrial contexts, James Bright observes that it invariably results in a larger span of operations for the individual worker. However, Bright found that automation does not necessarily raise skill requirements. In some cases it actually reduces skill levels (*op. cit.*, pp. 177–195, 201).

The large number of subplants, products, and processes in an industrial chemical factory makes for a highly diversified work environment. This diversity adds greatly to the variety in work, especially when job rotation allows many workers to divide their time between different parts of the plant. At the Bay Company, many craftsmen and distribution employees were on a job-rotation program. The maintenance responsibilities of the instrument repairmen, for example, are divided into five zones, each of which includes one or more buildings of the plant. A man works in one zone one week, another zone the second week, and so on, in a five-week rotation cycle.

Even the work of those operators who do not rotate from one subplant to another gains variety from the large number of chemicals produced in a single process. An automobile worker might produce scrap that can be shoveled into a scrap barrel; there is no equivalent to the waste products, by-products, or coproducts made in a chemical process, each of which must be controlled and looked after.

FREEDOM IN THE AUTOMATED FACTORY: FREE TIME AND FREE MOVEMENT

The special technological and economic characteristics of the continuous-process industries give workers a great deal of control over their immediate work processes. Due to the interplay of a large number of factors, the alienating tendencies of modern industrial organization, so pronounced in the case of the automobile assembly line, are reduced to a virtual minimum and the personal on-the-job freedoms of the operatives are enhanced.

A new work rhythm in the factory.—Unlike textile and automobile workers, chemical workers are free from constant pressure on their jobs and, in fact, have a great deal of free time. The Bay Chemical Company workers interviewed were virtually unanimous on this point. A typical comment of a middle-aged operator was:

There's no great pressure. They give you a job to do, and you do it. If things are running smooth, there's no problem. Nobody is pushed around here unless you're lax. There's no real incentive to get out two pounds more than yesterday, nothing like that.

The lack of constant job pressure in continuous-process plants is not a product of management's humanitarian concern for the employees but is principally due to the nature of an automated technology. The monitoring of automated processes and equipment need be done only periodically, not constantly. Because it is mental work and requires great care and responsibility, if not necessarily elaborate knowledge, workers cannot be rushed or pressured. The defective work of an automobile assembler is usually easily remedied by the repairmen after the car is off the line. But in continuous-process production mistakes are extremely costly. Turning the wrong valve can ruin thousands of pounds of product. And because of the inevitability of problems and breakdowns which must entail all the energy of the work force, the standardized operations are scheduled to take up only part of a worker's time, leaving large quantities of free time to deal with such emergency situations if they arise.

Therefore, instead of the steady work characteristic of other types of manufacturing, the work of the chemical operator has an irregular, even erratic, rhythm. It is a rhythm which consists of long periods of relative inactivity and occasional, though unpredictable and usually brief, periods of extremely arduous activity. Most of the time, things are going well. The operator has only his regular monitoring to do, which takes up about half his time. When a stranger enters the control room of a chemical plant or an oil refinery, he sees many operators sitting around and talking. He wonders why so many more men are kept on the job than seem to be needed, particularly since unions in the oil and chemical industries generally have not been strong enough to maintain the "featherbedding" that exists elsewhere. The answer is that all these men are needed, and needed badly, in crisis situations. When something goes wrong with the process, it is necessary for everyone to work extremely hard in order to locate the trouble and set things right as quickly as possible, so that the loss of the product is minimized.[26] The extra cost that management incurs by such work-scheduling is much less than the savings it can gain by getting production quickly back to normal, since the huge capital investment makes "down time" exceedingly expensive. An operator's story captures management's attitude:

I remember once the boss came into the control room and he said, "When I see you guys sitting around I know everything is going all right. When I see everybody up and running around then I know something's wrong."

Although the chemical worker's freedom from pressure is principally caused by technological factors, it is supported by the economic conditions of the industry. High profits and economic prosperity and growth greatly contribute to the relaxed atmosphere. The cost structure of the industry also works to the advantage of the manual workers. In a highly capital-intensive industry, it is more profitable to exploit technology than the work force itself. In the labor-intensive textile industry, as we have seen, the worker rather than the machine system is pushed and pressured.

[26] Alain Touraine has observed the same situation in the automated workshops of the Renault automotive works: "In ordinary times, they seem unoccupied, bored, before the measuring and control apparatus. But an important event happens and their qualities are called forth; rapid decisions must be made; an error can have enormous consequences." Touraine, *op. cit.*, p. 123 (my translation).

Mann and Hoffman similarly note that the operator in electric power plants is needed for his ability to "react effectively to breakdowns in the system" (*op. cit.*, p. 210).

It is therefore not surprising that only 12 per cent of the chemical workers in the Roper study complain that their jobs make them "work too fast," compared to 33 per cent of the automobile workers[27] and 32 per cent of the textile employees. Only three of the other fifteen industries had smaller proportions of workers who had to "work too fast"; significantly, the lowest proportion of all, 6 per cent, occurred in the oil refining industry (Table 33, Appendix B).

The chemical workers' freedom from pressure is also confirmed by the results of Davis' questionnaire survey at the Bay Chemical Company. The overwhelming proportion of his 223 respondents reported that they had enough time to do their jobs. Seventy-four per cent had enough time always or usually (13 per cent always, 61 per cent usually); 19 per cent had enough time sometimes; and only 8 per cent replied "rarely" or "never." The operators of automatic equipment were freest from pressure: 82 per cent usually or always had enough time to do their jobs. Workers in distribution felt more pushed than others.

Because continuous-process work is physically light and free from constant pressure, workers are less likely to be overfatigued than in other industries. In the Roper study only 14 per cent of the oil workers and 19 per cent of the chemical workers complained that their jobs left them too tired at the end of the day, compared to 30 per cent of the entire sample. Printing was the only industry with a smaller proportion of tired workers (see Table 34).

Some writers who have noted a similar decline of physical tiredness with automation have also observed an increase in mental tension and mental fatigue in these work environments.[28] Perhaps in these cases mental strain and tension may have been due to the change-over from manual to automated methods, rather than a response to automated work per se. Mental fatigue does not seem to be much of a problem in the oil and chemical industries probably because workers have had sufficient time to adapt to the new job requirements.

Work pace and output.—The relaxed work atmosphere during smooth operations allows chemical workers to control their pace of work. A young employee who had been recently "bumped" from a more skilled job and was one of the few dissatisfied operators makes this clear:

You can set your own pace. If you want to work fast, you can do so and then take a break. Or you can drag it out to make time go faster. We do this lots of

---

[27] The contrast between the unskilled in the two industries is even more striking. Forty-eight per cent of the seventy-three automobile workers with less than one month's job training felt they had to work too fast, compared to only 11 per cent of the eighteen unskilled chemical workers. This comparison must be treated cautiously because of the small size of the chemical worker sample; however it does suggest that the differences are due to industrial variations in technology rather than skill differences.

[28] Charles Walker, *Toward the Automatic Factory* (New Haven: Yale University Press, 1957); Mann and Hoffman, *op. cit.;* William Faunce, "Automation and the Automobile Worker," *Social Problems,* VI (1958), 68–78.

time. Sometimes when it's close to the time for 2 o'clock readings, we might have soup on the stove. You can eat the soup first and do the work later or take the readings at 1:45 and then eat your soup.

Davis asked the Bay Company workers how regularly they could choose their own working speeds. Fifty-two per cent reported that they could choose their own speeds "usually"; 27 per cent had this freedom frequently; only 15 per cent replied "seldom"; and 6 per cent, "never." As Table 17 shows, the maintenance workers were most able to set their own pace.

TABLE 17

HOW FREQUENTLY BAY CHEMICAL WORKERS CAN CHOOSE THEIR
OWN WORKING SPEED, BY TYPE OF WORK

CAN CHOOSE OWN SPEED	WORK DEPARTMENT			TOTAL
	Maintenance	Distribution	Operations	
Usually...................	60%	46%	46%	52%
Frequently................	28	30	26	27
Seldom....................	11	17	20	15
Never.....................	2	9	9	6
Total per cent.............	101%	102%	101%	100%
Number of respondents......	(94)	(35)	(81)	(210)

Another question in Davis' survey points up the contrast with the textile and automobile workers' situation. Fifty-five per cent of the Bay chemical workers reported that they never "have to keep up with a machine or conveyor" in doing their jobs, 21 per cent seldom must do this, while only 25 per cent usually or frequently are tied to such a mechanical pace-setter. Thus approximately 80 per cent of the Bay chemical workers are free to set their own work pace; a good fortune enjoyed by only about 30 per cent of the sample of X plant automobile workers.[29]

Chemical workers control the pace of their work; they do not, however, control the pace of production. For operatives in other factory industries, work is production. The conveyer belt which forces the automobile worker to work at a predetermined rate compels him to produce at that rate. But with automated technology, the work of operators, even though they are still called production workers, becomes separated from direct production per se. The chemical operator can determine the pace at which he monitors the automatic equipment, but the automatic processes taking place within the chemical reactors determine the speed of production. The operator can, of course, and sometimes does, control this rate by adjusting the controls; but the approved pace of output is established by engineers in the front office, and not by him.

For this reason the chemical worker is similar to the automobile worker in

[29] Walker and Guest, *op. cit.*, p. 51. My calculations.

his inability to control the quantity of his output. But for him it does not appear to be a restriction of freedom but a necessary fact inherent in the nature of automatic technology. The automobile worker's lack of control over output is an integral part of his lack of control over work pace and the pressure of the assembly line and is therefore an additionally distasteful feature of his work environment.

Quality of product.—But unlike automobile workers, chemical workers are able to control the quality of their production. In fact, control of the quality of the product is their major job responsibility. Although the instinct of workmanship has been removed to a different level by the elimination of manual skill, it is still important. Putting out a good quality product is one of the most important sources of satisfaction and accomplishment for the operators interviewed.

Control over the quality of production can be frustrated not only by assembly-line pressure, forcing would-be craftsmen to work sloppily, but also by completely automatic quality control which insures a perfect product. The ability of an operator to feel a sense of accomplishment because "our product is now coming out 100 per cent yield . . . I'm tickled to see that," depends on the *problematic* nature of the process. It might be expected that improvements in automatic processes would eventually eliminate these areas of uncertainty and thereby eventually reduce the operator's sense of accomplishment. Industry experts deny this. Each advanced stage of automation, they say, brings its own technical problems and potential for breakdown.

Methods of work.—Chemical-process work is not as standardized as work on the automobile assembly line or in the textile mill. The worker has more freedom to determine techniques of doing his job. This results from the variety inherent in the work; the lack of time pressure, which allows experimentation and change; and the new situations for which new solutions must be found. Even on such a relatively routine job as instrument-reading, much variation in the sequence of work is possible.

The high level of this freedom is suggested by the fact that 50 per cent of the respondents in the Davis survey replied that they usually plan how they do their jobs; 34 per cent frequently do this; and only 6 per cent seldom or never are able to plan out their work. In the same study, 89 per cent of the workers reported that they "decide what needs to be done" on their jobs either usually or frequently.[30]

In the Roper survey, 64 per cent of the chemical workers and 59 per cent of the oil workers said they could try out their own ideas on the job, compared to only 49 per cent of the total sample, 47 per cent of the automobile workers, and 38 per cent of the textile employees. Only in two craft industries, printing and transportation equipment, did higher proportions of

---

[30] Detailed results show that the maintenance craftsmen enjoy a slightly higher degree of freedom in these respects, and the distribution workers consider themselves at a disadvantage.

workers command this job freedom (see Table 35, Appendix B). The technology and work organization of the continuous-process industries thus give the worker a certain amount of freedom to exercise choices and to make decisions in the course of his job.

However, even this degree of freedom is not as great as many workers desire. When I asked Bay Company workers whether they could try out their own ideas, many expressed a wish for more opportunities to display initiative in their work. The introduction of a suggestion system was frequently proposed to improve this situation.

Free movement.—The technological organization of chemical plants allows a great deal of physical mobility. Variations exist among occupations and departments of the plant, but no employees are as physically confined to a work station as are automobile assembly-line workers, nor is their physical mobility dictated by the pressures of the immediate job, as is that of the textile workers. An unusual degree of mobility results from the organization of the plant in a large number of individual buildings spread over a wide area, the high proportion of maintenance and distribution workers, and the generally relaxed pace of work. Maintenance craftsmen work out of a central shop, but their repair work and preventive checks take them to every department of the plant. Operators are assigned to a central control room in their particular process plant, but their job duties require them to make patrols of the surrounding outside areas in order to read meters and gauges and inspect the equipment. In automated production the operator has a responsibility for a large part of a productive process and therefore must be able to move from one end of a building to the other.

The physical environment of a continuous-process plant is also more free and less confining than that of a mass-production factory. Modern factories of all kinds are now often built with attractively landscaped grounds around the factory, but the worker does not really live within this more human environment, which is principally for the benefit of visitors and the community. The worker in a chemical plant or an oil refinery, however, actually carries out much of his work within the open spaces between the plant buildings.

CONTROL OVER AUTOMATED TECHNOLOGY

Of course chemical workers do not have total freedom of action in the work process. Like all factory workers, they must obey the rules of the work place and submit to the authority of management. The necessity of working night and weekend shifts is probably the most resented limitation of freedom. Since production is literally continuous, full shifts of operators must be in the plant twenty-four hours a day and seven days a week. The various crews rotate shifts, and each man works a normal day only one-quarter of the time. Changing shifts every two weeks prevented many workers from settling into satisfactory sleeping routines. Night and weekend work stands out as the number one source of dissatisfaction of the chemical operators.

Still, as compared to the textile mill and the automobile assembly line, continuous-process technology leads to considerable freedom from pressure, control over the pace of work, responsibility of maintaining a high-quality product, choice of how to do the job, and freedom of physical movement. It results in a lack of control over the quantity of output, but this is not seen as a serious restriction of freedom. However, might not the operator in the continuous-process industries who watches panel boards and adjusts dials still feel himself a small, ineffectual creature before the colossus of technological arrangements? For the huge networks of pipes, towers, and reactors certainly seem to dominate the scene and the workers. Each operator was therefore asked whether he controls the automatic processes and machines or whether the automatic processes and technology control him.

Seven operators felt quite strongly that they controlled the automatic equipment. Four operators felt that it was perhaps a little bit of both. They were in control when things were going smoothly but felt they had lost control when the operations were going haywire and they weren't able to fix the trouble. But, in contrast to automobile workers, none of the operators felt that in general they were dominated or controlled by their technology. The answers to this question seem convincing:

1. *A young head operator of the ammonia plant, ambitious and intensely interested in technology and science:* You have machinery working for you. Man is the master of the machine, and it works for him. If I want something to happen, I'll open a valve, and more product will be distributed to such and such a place. It's the operator who's definitely in charge, and he runs the machine. The machine does not run him.

2. *A young Mexican-American with ten years' seniority who is responsible for eight different chemical processes:* (*Laughing*) The machine's your robot. It does what you make it do.

3. *A former seaman and strong union man, who reads history at home and on the job and likes automatic equipment:* We're running it. If you leave it alone, it won't run. But sometimes when nobody's around, it seems as if it just keeps going. But we don't leave it though. . . . The thing is running, you've got to keep it running. You just accept the fact that you have to be there and watch it. . . . (*Then a suddenly occurring idea*): But we can stop it if we want to . . . (and a man on the assembly line cannot, which seemed to cinch the question for him).

4. *A former crane operator on the Mesabi iron range who moved west for*

better opportunities in a new industry: You control it. You can make the wrong move, and something serious will happen. It's the same way with a crane. Machinery can get away from you if you can't control it.

The statements of those who were ambivalent stressed that it depended on the situation:

5. *A middle-aged dryer operator who feels somewhat blocked in advancement and aspires toward his own business or selling:* Maybe both ways. This is because of the unpredictability of the damned stuff. When things go wrong, maybe then the process is controlling you.

6. *A former tapper in the aluminum industry, still somewhat nostalgic for his farm background:* It can work both ways. If it works right, you run it; if it isn't working right, then it runs you.

The responses to this question, as well as other evidence, indicate that chemical workers do not feel dominated by their imposing technological surroundings but, instead, get feelings of satisfaction from the control of complex automatic machinery. And, paradoxically, the feeling of control is probably greater because it is not always present and there are times when the processes seem to control them. If things were never out of control there would be no element of satisfaction in the struggle to maintain control: the game would be too easily won.

It is instructive to contrast chemical and automobile workers' attitudes toward breaks in production. As we have seen in the last chapter, auto workers welcome a line breakdown—it gives them a rest from the pressure of the conveyer and the disliked, repetitive jobs and allows them to breathe as free human beings for a few minutes until the bottleneck is stopped and they again surrender control. Unless it means being sent home and losing pay, the automobile worker wants the line to stay down as long as possible. The chemical worker, on the other hand, wants to solve the problem and restore production to normal as soon as possible. It is when there is a break in production that he must work most frantically and under pressure; normal operations allow him the opportunity to work at a leisurely pace—to breathe freely. Completely the opposite of the assembly-line worker, he feels in control when production is going smoothly. When it has broken down he feels he has lost control.

These contrasting attitudes toward technology also suggest that chemical operators are more functionally integrated with the goals of management and have more of a sense of purpose in their work. The following chapter takes up the question of social and personal alienation in the continuous-process industries.

7

PURPOSE AND INTEGRATION
IN THE CHEMICAL INDUSTRY

Continuous-process technology reduces the powerlessness of the blue-collar worker by giving him control over his immediate work process. The technology, work organization, and social structure of these industries also counteract tendencies toward meaninglessness. The result is that workers in continuous-process industries have more of a sense of purpose, understanding, and function in their work than workers in machine-tending and assembly-line technologies.

PROCESS TECHNOLOGY AND MEANING IN WORK

The most critical feature of automation is that it transfers the focus of emphasis from an individual job to the process of production. Although the process in which a worker is involved may not encompass the entire plant, his perspective shifts from his own individual task to a broader series of operations which includes the work of other employees. In this shift of emphasis from job to process, the worker's role changes from providing skills to accepting responsibility. His scope of operations also increases. Continuous-process technology thus reverses the historic trend toward the greater division of labor and specialization.

The responsibility demanded of the chemical worker is a collective, as well as an individual, responsibility. Since the process is integrated and continuous rather than divided in the manner that labor is divided, the responsibility of any one employee for his share of a plant's process is inevitably linked to the responsibility of other workers. An increasing interdependence develops, and automated plants tend to be based on team operations. The worker's shift from skill to responsibility therefore fosters thinking in terms of the collective whole rather than the individual part. The very definition of responsibility as a job requirement involves a meaningful connection between the worker's own function and the goals of the entire

enterprise. This link between responsibility and purposeful, functional integration has been made in a perceptive description of the sailor, whose duties
on watch are quite similar to the monitoring tasks of the automated operator:

Standing watches "sailorizes" the new man by virtue of the responsibility he
is given and the communication network he is tied into. When he is on lookout,
he is much influenced to be aware that the sleeping crew members are depending,
in part, on his diligence. If he accepts this role, he can't help but identify with
the crew. While on watch, he wears a set of headphones that connects him with
the bridge, and with all other men on watch, above and below decks. He hears
the men make reports, the OOD give engines speed or direction changes. He
hears the background noise of a ship alive. This is a team, and he cannot feel
alone.[1]

Rationality in continuous-process production is also enhanced by the
employee's ability to move freely around the plant. The automobile worker,
more or less confined to his place on the line, has little opportunity to view
operations in other sections of the factory. The chemical worker's mobility
increases his understanding of the total technical operations, and he becomes
aware not only of how his job fits into his department's processes—this is
functionally necessary—but also of how his department's processes contribute
to the total operations of the company.

The high degree of understanding resulting from continuous-process production is suggested by Davis' survey of Bay Company employees. Forty-six
per cent of the sample said they knew all of the stages required to complete
work on the product after their own job; 38 per cent said they knew most of
the stages. Only 14 per cent said they only knew some of the steps in future
processes, 1 per cent knew a few—no worker replied that he didn't know
any. The increased rationality inherent in process work may be further indicated by the fact that, among the operators, 60 per cent said they knew all
of the stages required to complete the product, a figure considerably higher
than that for maintenance repairmen and distribution employees.[2]

Whereas continuous-process production increases the worker's breadth of
knowledge and awareness of the factory as a totality, it does not necessarily
enhance the worker's depth of understanding of the technical and scientific
processes. In order to perform their jobs competently, workers need not
know, and the majority seem uninterested in, the complicated chemical
principles involved in the manufacture of their products. The respondents
were in agreement that it was not necessary to know much chemistry to be
a chemical operator. The fundamentals pertinent to the job are taught by

---

[1] Louis A. Zurcher, Jr., "Some Reflections on the Naval Vessel as a Total Institution" (Unpublished paper, San Francisco, 1962), p. 27. See also Paul L. Berkman, "Life Aboard an
Armed-Guard Ship," *American Journal of Sociology*, LI (1946), 386.

[2] Unfortunately, it has not been possible to find comparative data on this question from
industries with other forms of technology.

A NEW SOURCE OF DIGNITY IN BLUE-COLLAR WORK: *Responsibility*

Unlike the printing craftsman, the operator in a continuous-process plant uses no manual skills in carrying out his job. He neither sees nor handles the product but instead guides its progress through chemical reaction units by monitoring the gauges on the instrument panel boards of the control room. (Courtesy of the Cities Service Company, Anthony Linck, photographer.)

PERSONAL FREEDOM IN AN AUTOMATED WORK ENVIRONMENT

Networks of pipes and reactor units dominate the landscape of continuous-process plants, and through such networks the product flows in the course of its manufacture, unseen and untouched by blue-collar workers. The oil refinery employee setting a valve, above, does much of his work outdoors. He is free to leave the control room, his central work station, at his own volition, and he sets his own work pace. Compare the general atmosphere in this picture with the industrial environment of the auto assemblers in Plate 6: the conveyor belt and the automated process plant represent two extremes in personal freedom on the job. (Courtesy of the Cities Service Company, Anthony Linck, photographer.)

the company in on-the-job school sessions, held periodically. The minority of ambitious workers with strong scientific orientations are encouraged to take night-school classes, and they have a greater chance to advance into supervisory jobs where this knowledge is useful. But the very complexity of the scientifically based reactions means that there is more that is unknown to the average worker in the continuous-process industries than to the all-competent printing craftsman or the automobile assembler working in an ultra-simplified work situation.

There is another aspect of continuous-process technology which could conceivably increase the meaninglessness aspect of alienation. The worker's sensory relation to his product is totally eliminated. A craftsman, of course, works directly on his product; his senses of sight, touch, and even smell, are quite active. This is as true today for a printer or carpenter as it was for a cobbler in medieval times. Machine production eliminated much of the direct sensory relation between the worker and the work, but machine operators still must handle the product from time to time, use their eyes to inspect the machine's job, and occasionally perform hand operations on the product. Even on the fast-moving assembly line, the operative preserves some kind of tactile relationship to the automobile. He sees the product in process and he works on it.

In oil refineries and industrial chemical plants, the product is not worked on directly, nor even seen by the operatives, except for those products which are still made in "batches" rather than by continuous-production methods. The oil or chemicals goes through its entire cycle of operations in pipes and inclosed chemical reactors. It is only in a relatively rare emergency, when pipes burst or stills blow up, that the operatives see the product, whose progress they watch normally by means of dials and gauges.

In his study of automation in an engine-block plant in the automobile industry, William Faunce found that skilled machinists who had become automated operators were discomfited by this loss of a "direct feel" for their product.[3] Perhaps this was an important source of dissatisfaction because the change from manual skill to automated-machine monitoring had been rather abrupt. In the Bay chemical plant, working with an invisible product did not seem to be a source of alienation. Most of the operators appear never to have thought of this issue. A few replied that working indirectly through instruments made the job more challenging, in the sense that flying an airplane blind is a greater test of one's resources.

In summary, four aspects of the distinctive industrial environment of a chemical plant enhance the worker's sense of providing a unique, important function whose purpose he understands: process production; team operations; the job requirement of responsibility; and the possibility of physical

[3] William Faunce, "Automation and the Automobile Worker," *Social Problems*, VI (1958), 68–78.

movement. Of these, the technological factor of division of labor by process rather than by job seems to be the most important and also the most consequential feature of automation in general. The decline in the worker's sensory relationship to his product appears to be of little significance.

SOCIAL INTEGRATION IN CHEMICAL PLANTS

The technology, economic situation, and social structure of the chemical industry also contribute significantly to the integration of the work force in a cohesive industrial community. Of first importance is the small size of the plants in the industry and the decentralized organization within the plant. In small plants and small departments, the anonymity and the impersonality of bureaucratic large-scale organization are found less than in large, centralized factories. Communication between workers and management representatives is more frequent and is especially likely to be two-way communication in which advice is sought, as well as orders given.

A second critical factor, already discussed in the above section, is team production. Auto assembly workers are rarely members of clearly defined and interdependent work teams, and this consequence of assembly-line technology reduces the cohesion in the industry. But chemical-process operators are clearly identified with a particular shift and a particular department; the departmental work teams are not only clearly defined, they also have an explicit hierarchy of authority and status. Maintenance workers, too, are members of specific departments made up of others in the same craft. Work teams in the chemical industry develop identities: teams on different shifts strive to outdo each other in the quality of their product; retired workers often continue to inquire after their old work crews. As a pumper in one of the Bay Company's process plants, who had worked in the steel industry, puts it:

A chemical plant is more compact. There are less employees, and they are more closely knit. Just more people that you know. In a big plant like the steel mill you're one of many. Here there is closer knit contact. In a big company you are just a number to them. In my plant there's twenty shift men and two men on days. I got a chance to know all these people.

The high degree of cohesion brought about by team production within small, decentralized plants is suggested by a number of research findings. At the Bay chemical plant, Davis found that blue-collar employees ranked "friends at work" as that element of the total job situation which they most liked more consistently than ten other job factors, including interesting work, security, and pay. A number of workers mentioned their surprise at the readiness with which more experienced employees taught them their jobs and helped them with their problems—exclusiveness and withholding of skills and knowledge had been common in other industries. And in the Roper survey, 57 per cent of the chemical workers felt most of their fellow workers were doing very good work and 40 per cent felt that they were doing pretty well. Fewer workers proportionately than in any other industry said their workmates could do a lot better.[4]

A third element contributing to integration is the quality of supervision in continuous-process plants. The overbearing supervision characteristic of past industrial practices is unlikely in a modern continuous-process plant. Chemical production requires responsible workers who will not need to be watched too closely. Due to the decentralized operations, the large amount of outdoor work, and the considerable physical mobility possible, individuals often work far out of the range of their immediate supervisors. As for operators, three-quarters of the time they are working nights or weekends, when there may be only one supervisor on duty in the entire plant.

The chemical workers interviewed all felt that the load of supervision was light and that they were given considerable scope to do their jobs in their own way. A construction laborer reported that he kept looking around him all the time during his first few months with the company, expecting someone to be breathing down his neck. On his previous job he had had to be in front of his machine eight hours a day. The other workers at the chemical company kidded him, and it took him quite a while to get used to the different atmosphere.

This freedom is possible because the work team which runs an individual plant takes over many of the functions of supervision in other technological contexts. A worker will come to work and do his job well, not out of fear of a particular boss, but because he feels the other operators in his crew are depending on him to do his part of the total work. Many of the co-ordinating and administrative functions of supervision fall to the head shift operator, the leader of each plant's work crew. Since the head operator is an hourly blue-collar employee and the most experienced man in the particular department, his guidance is not felt to be oppressive supervision. The fact that he has previously worked at each of the jobs in his department in the course of working his way to the top is an important basis of his authority and respect.

The chemical operator probably has more personal contact with persons in higher levels of supervision than do workers in mass-production industries. These contacts generally are for consultation on production problems and are therefore more satisfying than administrative or disciplining contacts. In automated production, when the workers' function becomes responsibility rather than skill, consultation with supervisors, engineers, chemists, and other technical specialists becomes a regular, natural part of the job

---

[4] In the automobile industry, 14 per cent said their workmates could do a lot better, compared to only 1 per cent of the chemical employees. The sample norm was 7 per cent.

duties.[5] Because the operator is responsible for an important and expensive process, he can initiate interaction with those higher in status. Because he is the person closest to the actual operations, he must be listened to. These facts have great implications for the dignity of the chemical worker. Automobile assemblers and textile operatives may call upon a foreman or maintenance machinist when some mechanism is not working perfectly, but their own advice is rarely consulted by their superiors. Technical consultation with superiors does take place in craft industries, but since craftsmen have a more independent domain, it is built into the system less than in continuous-process technology.

The result is that the social atmosphere of the plant becomes an all-important aspect of the work situation in an automated technology, as Alain Touraine has emphasized. A climate of collaboration is necessary for successful operations because of the interdependence of work teams and the importance of individual responsibility.[6] Because the technology, work organization, and social structure of chemical plants allow the worker to become integrated into the company through his work group and to identify with the enterprise, the quality of supervision is extremely salient. Of course, co-operative relations between workers and supervisors are not automatically determined by a continuous-process technology but depend also on the practices of management and the orientation of the individual foreman. For this reason, the extremely high morale and integrated atmosphere in the Bay plant partly reflect its successful management. We would expect to find some plants in the chemical industry, though not as many as in the automotive industry, with considerably less integration and lower morale.

STATUS STRUCTURE, ADVANCEMENT, AND LOYALTY TO COMPANY

A fourth factor which influences integration in the chemical industry is its status structure. An elaborate system of superior and inferior ranks supports a normative structure because those in higher positions have presumably internalized the goals of the enterprise and more clearly express its values. The existence of achievable higher positions also serves to motivate those of lower status to accept the goals of the organization and to act in accordance with its norms.

The technological requirements of continuous-process production encourage a finely elaborated status structure, since, as we have seen, a balanced skill distribution emerges, made up of employees at all levels of training and responsibility. This differentiation is further developed within each operating department, where the jobs make up an elaborate hierarchy. A typical oper-

[5] Alain Touraine has observed this in the automated workshops at Renault. *L'évolution du travail ouvrier aux usines Renault* (Paris: Centre National de la Recherche Scientifique, 1955).
[6] *Ibid.*, pp. 118–19, 173–83.

ating department consists of seven men in seven different job grades, from a beginning helper to the responsible head shift operator. Each job is a step on a natural ladder of promotion. Workers start in the department at the bottom, and the assumption is that the men will work up, one step at a time, and eventually reach the top position. At each step, there is an increase in training required, job duties (particularly responsibility), pay, and status.

Georg Simmel has written of the "inevitably disproportionate distribution of qualifications and positions" which means that all social organization involves a "contradiction between the just claims to a superordinate position and the technical impossibility of satisfying this claim. . . ." Simmel observes that among the ordinary workers in a factory there are certainly very many who could equally well be foremen or entrepreneurs.[7] The highly differentiated stratification in the chemical plant is possibly one of the best solutions to this problem of the inevitable injustice of all social systems. The elaborate hierarchical arrangement probably allows the maximum number of people to be in positions where there are others below them in rank, and this is another force for social integration.

The high level of advancement which a stratified blue-collar world makes possible is a fifth factor which supports normative integration in the continuous-process industries. The situation differs considerably from that of the automobile, textile, and other industries. Many Bay Company workers commented that in other industries a man is hired to do a particular job and it is assumed he will stay on that job. The job histories of these chemical workers show a great deal of upward movement. Of the twenty-one workers interviewed, twenty had some job advancement; only one had experienced no job change.

A representative case is that of a thirty-three-year-old operator who started with the company thirteen years ago as a bus boy in the cafeteria. After three years he moved into the ammonia plant, where he worked in succession as a janitor, a cylinder painter, and a cylinder-filler. After three years in the ammonia plant, he moved into the methionine plant and began climbing its job ladder. He started as a helper, moved up to finishing operator, then to ion operator, then to mercaptan operator, and finally to his present job as hydantion operator, fifth highest on a ladder of seven jobs. Above him are the acrolein operator and the head shift operator. After reaching these two steps, the salaried position of process foreman is his goal.[8]

[7] Georg Simmel, *Sociology*, trans. Kurt Wolff (Glencoe, Ill.: Free Press, 1950), pp. 300–3.

[8] All in-plant job careers do not show such neat upward progression, however. Another operator had been on eight different jobs in his four years with the company, and much of this movement was horizontal and some even downward. He began as a laborer in the distribution department and then became a helper in the chlorination plant. This was on the bottom of the ladder, but it held the possibility of upward movement. But the latter plant shut down, which sent him back into the yard pool of unskilled labor. He moved back again into distribution and then worked in an experimental plant called the petroleum pond. But this project

In addition, skilled maintenance craftsmen in the continuous-process industries are recruited from the ranks of the less-skilled employees through
formal apprenticeship and training programs. In an auto plant studied by
Robert Guest, only 6 per cent of the maintenance craftsmen had started
their careers on the assembly line:[9] fully skilled craftsmen were hired from
the outside. In direct contrast, at one of the largest oil refineries, 90 per cent
of the 1,000 skilled workers in 1937 had originally started in the plant as
unskilled laborers.[10]

A study of a major oil refinery similarly reports that "the method of
upgrading, whereby all new hires start out in the labor pool and branch
out from there into specialties," contributes to general job satisfaction. "After
a short stay in the labor gang it is almost inevitable that a worker progress.
. . . Under this scheme the majority of our long term respondents have
experienced considerable mobility in the refinery." [11]

The Roper survey results confirm the superior advancement opportunities
in the chemical industry. Seventy-nine per cent of the chemical workers,
compared to only 47 per cent of all workers answered that their jobs led to
promotions if they did them well. This was by far the highest proportion
among the sixteen industries and was exactly twice as large as the proportion
of automobile and textile workers who expected promotion. The second
highest figure, 63 per cent, was in the petroleum refining industry (see
Table 45, Appendix B).[12]

Advancement opportunities for chemical workers exist largely within the
blue-collar manual sector; the route into supervision, engineering, and higher
management is not as open. However, chemical workers may have slightly
better chances of rising out of the blue-collar ranks than workers in other
industries because the industry's rapid growth creates more openings.[13]

---

was completed, and he was sent back into the yard pool. All these changes took place in
two years, after which he moved into his present department at the bottom rung as an
assistant mercury-cell operator. After two years on this job, he moved up to the second step
out of four jobs in the department, as a Bay Company cell operator.

[9] Robert Guest, "Work Careers and Aspirations of Automobile Workers," in Walter Galenson
and Seymour M. Lipset (eds.), *Labor and Trade Unionism* (New York: John Wiley & Sons,
1960), p. 322.

[10] Henrietta M. Larson and Kenneth Wiggins Porter, *History of Humble Oil and Refining
Company* (New York: Harper & Bros., 1959), p. 382.

[11] Union Research and Education Projects, University of Chicago," A Report on the OCAWIU
Organizing Effort and the Representation Election at the Whiting Refinery of the Standard Oil
Company of Indiana" (September, 1956, mimeographed), p. 15.

[12] Among the Bay plant workers surveyed by Davis, 72 per cent felt that opportunities to
get ahead there "were better than with other companies." The majority of the sample, 60
per cent, said advancement was slightly better in their plant rather than much better. Similarly
most of the negative people said "slightly poorer," not "much poorer."

[13] Thirty-six per cent of the chemical workers in the Roper survey said they wanted to become
foremen while the corresponding figure for auto workers was 30 per cent. Of the aspiring
chemical workers, 54 per cent expected to achieve this goal, the highest proportion in any
industry. Only 28 cases are involved in this statistic, which therefore should be treated with
caution. Thus, 19 per cent of the chemical workers were realistically oriented toward supervisory

Jobs in the automobile industry rarely allow a worker to show those quali-ties of skill and leadership that he may possess. Chemical operating and maintenance jobs not only permit their use; they often develop such poten-tialities. This fact and the relative lack of a worker-management cleavage in the industry result in greater feelings of equity concerning the distribution of promotion than exist in other industries. The advancement progress of each employee is reviewed periodically in the continuous-process industries, and this means that misunderstandings and resentments about promotions can be "aired out." In addition, such bureaucratic procedures as seniority provisions and the public posting of job openings also diminish the senti-ments of injustice and inequity. Although individual workers have their own grievances, there seems to be no general feeling that advancements within departments are awarded unfairly, in contrast to the situation ob-served by Chinoy at the ABC automobile plant. However, there is consider-able dissatisfaction about the age limit which kept middle-aged operators out of craft apprenticeship programs. And resentment against the length of time necessary to transfer from shift work to day jobs appears to be common in many continuous-process plants.[14]

The high level of integration in the chemical industry is confirmed by Roper statistics which show that chemical employees, along with garment workers, had the lowest proportion of cynical responses to the question on what qualities get a man ahead. Cynical responses were 24 per cent, com-pared to 39 per cent in the whole sample and 50 per cent in the automobile industry. Sixty-nine per cent of the chemical employees, far more than in any other industry, said that it was one's energy and willingness to work which resulted in advancement. The responses of oil workers to this ques-tion suggest considerably less satisfaction with the norms of distributive justice in that industry. Cynical responses were 43 per cent, which is higher than the all-factory average; refinery workers were considerably more likely to stress seniority as the key factor. Forty-nine per cent of the oil workers mentioned this, compared to 28 per cent of the chemical employees and 25 per cent of all workers (Table 46, Appendix B).[15]

The structuring of advancement opportunities in continuous-process tech-nology enhances the integration and cohesion in these industries; conversely,

---

posts, compared to only 12 per cent of the automobile workers. And 28 per cent of the chemi-cal workers, compared to 20 per cent of the automobile workers, thought that they had good chances of rising above the foreman level (see Table 49, Appendix B). These differences are admittedly quite small.

[14] Union Research and Education Projects, University of Chicago, "Report of a Study on the Organizing Potential of the Bayway Refinery" (1956, mimeographed), pp. 27–28.

[15] Perhaps one reason for this difference between the two continuous-process industries is regional. In the Roper sample, a high proportion of the chemical workers were in the South, presumably concentrated in the Atlantic border states like Delaware and Maryland that have a number of big chemical plants. The oil refinery employees were all in the North, where seniority is more likely to be institutionalized.

the high level of integration increases an employee's motivation to advance and is therefore an incentive toward superior performance. An insightful operator, who had worked in four other industries and developed a comparative perspective, makes this point:

There's more place to advance here than in other places. At the can company I was at the top but there's not much difference between the bottom and the top. In the brickyard there's no difference at all—you stay on the same job all your life. Here the difference between my job and the top job is about $1,200 a year. That makes an incentive to do your best and to get promotions. I guess that's the way the company sees it.

However, I must qualify this highly positive picture. The institutionalization of mobility routes through formal job ladders and the company's encouragement of aspiration and training result, naturally enough, in a high level of expectation of upward movement. In addition, the industry's employment security has been so consistent that workers are not as preoccupied with holding on to their jobs as are the automobile workers and textile workers. When the job is secure, advancement becomes even more important psychically. And since promotions are rarely as rapid as workers would like them, considerable dissatisfaction often results.

The economic downturn of the past few years has decreased the rate of advancements in the industry sharply and thus has aggravated this crisis in expectations. Taking advantage of the general postwar prosperity and its own growth position, the chemical industry expanded very rapidly in the late forties and to a lesser extent in the early fifties. Advancements were quite rapid. When other industries were laying off workers during recent recessions, it was able to avoid unemployment because of its superior economic and growth situation: workers who quit or retired were simply not replaced. However, in this period, advancement has slowed down drastically.

The finding in the 1947 Roper survey that four-fifths of the chemical workers felt their jobs led to promotions would probably not be repeated today: although the superior advancement pattern, compared to other industries, still holds in general. In fact, the very large degree of dissatisfaction with this decline in upward movement is suggested in Davis' 1959 survey. Among eleven characteristics of the job, "opportunity for advancement" was most consistently liked least by the respondents. Yet, 72 per cent of these same respondents admitted that chances to get ahead were better than at other companies.

Despite these recent disappointments, the job security and upward mobility in the chemical industry mean that employment there tends to become a life-long career—in the sense that a white-collar employee or a civil servant has a career. When employment is viewed as a permanent career rather than as a short-term job, loyalty and identification with the organization are enhanced. These attitudes are further supported by the non-manual, clean, and responsible nature of the process operator's work, which gives him something in common with the white-collar employees in his own company and distinguishes him from the mass of factory workers in heavy industries.[16] In short, the conditions of work in the process industries produce a worker who is more middle-class, in situation and perspective, than most blue-collar employees.

We have seen that continuous-process technology results in a distinctive plant social structure, many aspects of which contribute to a high degree of social cohesion and normative integration. It is fortunate that these natural, spontaneous, social processes work in this direction because automated production requires an integrated manual work force for its successful operation. Not only does the responsibility demanded of the operator necessitate more loyalty to the enterprise than when work is standardized, but the constant technological change inherent in continuous-process production also makes an integrated work force essential.

The continuing economic and technical advances in the oil refining and chemical industries would be impossible if workers in these industries were disposed to resist innovation and change, as are many industrial workers. The high degree of integration, the relative lack of conflict, and the high level of job security in the chemical industry provide an atmosphere in which technological change is more accepted by workers and unions than in the automobile industry, where, because of its history of labor-management strife and its irregular employment pattern, workers are naturally suspicious of the motives and effects of technological innovation.[17]

A study of the Opinion Research Corporation found that automobile workers were more likely to oppose automation and fear its consequences than were chemical workers. Fifty-eight per cent of the chemical employees, compared to 43 per cent of the auto workers, felt that "improved machines" were "a good thing for employees." In addition, a consistently higher proportion of automobile workers felt that their company should neither install faster machines nor move in the direction of more automation. Automobile

[16] A possible consequence of career employment in manual work may be the development of a future time perspective, a trait which has been considered characteristic of the middle class rather than the working class. Many Bay plant workers mentioned that they could expect to move up a notch or two at least five years from now because certain top operators were due to retire then.

It is interesting to contrast the end of career lines in the automobile and the chemical industries. Older workers in the automobile industry cannot take the pace of the line and may be forced to take lower-paying jobs such as those of sweepers. The older chemical workers hold down the most skilled and responsible jobs in both the operating and the maintenance departments: younger workers count the years and months until they retire.

[17] The frequency of change also influences attitudes toward it. When major changes are fairly rare, as in the automobile industry, change becomes something which is feared; when change is part of the normal order of events, it becomes considerably more acceptable and less threatening.

workers were more likely to believe that improved machines result in fewer jobs, whereas chemical workers were much more likely to feel that improved machines result in higher wages.[18]

The high level of loyalty and company identification in the chemical industry is confirmed by various survey findings. Chemical workers were more nearly unanimous in the belief that their company was as good or better than any other place to work in their industry than any other group of workers in the Roper study. Ninety-two per cent felt this way, compared to 62 per cent of automobile workers and 73 per cent of all factory workers. (Company loyalty, however, may be somewhat less pronounced in oil refining, where 75 per cent of the workers preferred their own company) (see Table 38, Appendix B). And in a survey of the Opinion Research Corporation, 54 per cent of the chemical workers (the highest figure) said that their company takes a "real interest in its employees," compared to 43 per cent of all manufacturing employees and only 30 per cent of the automobile workers (see Table 15, Chapter 5, p. 111).

The important role which labor unions play in the rule-making process in automobile plants is a reflection of the deep cleavage between workers and management in that industry. In textiles, the lack of union organization is related to the infrequency of worker-company conflicts, due to the traditional orientations of the workers and the homogenous institutions of the southern small-town communities. The chemical industry is also relatively unorganized. Less than 50 per cent of its employees belong to unions. The integration in chemicals is not based primarily on traditional attitudes but is an outcome of continuous-process technology, favorable economic conditions, and worker satisfaction with superior wages and employee benefits. The persistence and strength of many independent, sometimes company, unions in chemicals is another indication of its cohesive industrial community.[19]

AUTOMATED WORK AND SELF-ALIENATION

Since work in continuous-process industries involves control, meaning, and social integration, it tends to be self-actualizing instead of self-estranging. Among chemical employees one finds less of the subjective alienation which is so pronounced for automobile workers on an assembly line. However, as we shall see, the chemical worker's non-alienation is not the same

---

[18] Opinion Research Corporation, *Automation—Friend or Foe of the Workingman?* tabular supplement to *Public Opinion Index for Industry,* XII (1954), No. 6, p. A-1.

[19] For an insightful and thorough analysis of the nature of unionism in the chemical industry and the reasons for the relative lack of organization, see the articles by Arnold Weber: "Union-Management Power Relations in the Chemical Industry," *Labor Law Journal,* IX (1958), 664–8; and "Competitive Unionism in the Chemical Industry," *Industrial and Labor Relations Review,* XIII (1959), 16–35.

as that of the printing craftsman. It is based more on an organizational (company), rather than an occupational, identity, and it reflects some totally new features, principally those of a dynamic technology and a changed rhythm of work.

The dialectic between involvement and monotony.—Basic to the feeling-tone of alienated activity is a heightened awareness of time. Instead of losing himself in a timeless present, the alienated actor is detached and preoccupied with thoughts and images of a future time period when the work will be over and done with. This differs, of course, from the craftsman's image of the future appearance of his product, which serves as a model for his immersion in the work of the present.

Continuous-process production in the chemical industry greatly affects the worker's relation to time because, as we have seen earlier, it results in a new rhythm of work. On the one hand, this work rhythm creates situations that permit a total immersion and present-time involvement rarely found in machine-tending and assembly-line industries; at the same time it also magnifies the problems of boredom and monotony inherent in time consciousness.

Automatic chemical processes are never perfect. From time to time, trouble in the form of problems, unexpected reactions, or actual breakdowns of the mechanism, takes place. Automobile workers typically complain that every day when they come to work, they know exactly what they are going to do every minute of that day. A Bay chemical operator, on the other hand, remarked that when he begins a new shift he never knows what the situation is going to be until he talks to the man he is replacing from the previous shift. He doesn't know whether there will be some impossible bug in the operations and if there is trouble he cannot predict what it will be.

Although operators do not exactly welcome trouble—they prefer smooth operations—the opinion was unanimous that its unpredictable occurrence adds interest, excitement, and challenge to their jobs. Locating the trouble, diagnosing the problem, and restoring the operations to a smooth, trouble-free condition was mentioned as the chief source of accomplishment in work by a large number of operators. Maintenance workers, too, are particularly likely to find trouble-shooting the aspect of their work which is most satisfying to them.

Almost invariably, Bay Company operators indicate that they like this work rhythm. Whereas automobile and textile workers resent greatly the pressure that is constantly on them, none of the chemical operators seem to mind the unusual bursts of activity that are expected of them in a problem situation.[20] This is because they can clearly see the necessity for such stepped-

---

[20] These production crises should be distinguished from the yearly shutdowns and startups of the continuous-process technology, called "turn-arounds," which also require intense activity. There is some evidence that these predictable changes in routine are resented.

up work and because it is not a constant job requirement. Most importantly, these unexpected crises give chemical workers an occasional chance to "go all out," to give all of themselves on the job, an opportunity which, as David Riesman has noted sadly, is denied automobile workers by the very nature of the assembly line. The crisis situation thus permits total absorption in the immediate present; it also adds drama to what otherwise might be a pleasant but drab routine.

On the other hand, the changed work rhythm in continuous-process technology includes long stretches of time with nothing definite to do. If no crises have developed, regular readings and checks take up only half of the operator's time. Monotony, boredom, awareness of time and its slow passage thus become intensified. This is particularly true on night and weekend shifts, when there are no bosses around to ask questions and no maintenance workers to make repairs and pass the time with.

There are a number of ways in which chemical workers deal with this problem of on-the-job leisure. The most important use of time is probably conversation and joking with fellow workers. Operators report that the most popular topics of conversation are politics, outside leisure interests, and books and magazines they have read.[21] Reading is another important activity. As one operator put it, "The men are always reading and will read anything they can get their hands on." Although officially forbidden, the company permits it in practice. However, games such as cards and checkers, which were allowed in the past, have been eliminated because they are potentially too engrossing. Another interesting form of job leisure is experimenting with the automatic controls, which for some operators provides a diverting, non-utilitarian game, which perhaps has educational side effects.

For example, a worker has the responsibility to see that the proportion of a certain chemical in a mixture stays between 32 and 36 per cent, the acceptable tolerance range. He says the instrument indicates that "it's running okay at 33 or 35 per cent. But I want to see if I can get it set at 34. I keep adjusting the controls until it's 34." Such experimentation is a kind of diverting game where the interest hinges on the outcome, and success gives one a feeling of satisfaction and victory.[22] "Playing with those things, it's to your own benefit because you learn the equipment and the controls better," was the way the operator justified this activity.

[21] An operator who had worked in four other industries claims that the conversations of chemical employees are on a level of intelligence far above what is typical in other factories. Although there is no way to prove such a statement, it is plausible because of the relatively high levels of education of Bay Company workers and because the unusual amount of free time on the job gives them opportunity for reading and for more reflective discussion.

[22] I cannot estimate how many operators play with the controls for non-utilitarian purposes, since I did not discover the existence of this practice until halfway through the interviewing. Several other operators also experimented in this way, while an approximately equal number said they never do this "because when things are going all right they should be left alone."

Continuous-process technology thus contains tendencies toward greater interest and involvement and toward greater monotony and boredom. Interviews at the Bay Company suggest that the balance is heavily in the direction of interest: the great majority of workers felt that their jobs were more engrossing than others they had held in different kinds of industries. The Roper interindustry data support this conclusion also. Only 11 per cent of the chemical employees found their jobs mostly or always dull and monotonous, compared to 20 per cent of all factory workers. Fifty-two per cent said their jobs were interesting nearly all the time, and 38 per cent found them interesting most of the time. Only in the craft industry of printing do we find a higher proportion of workers who feel they have interesting jobs (Table 42, Appendix B). In contrast to the automobile workers, even the less-skilled chemical workers find their jobs interesting. Eighty per cent of the unskilled and low-skilled chemical employees found their work interesting, compared to only 48 per cent of the automobile workers in the comparable skill groups.[23]

The alternation between routine and crisis seems to be characteristic of process technology in general, and not only automated processes. In his study of a "hot room" in a steel-rolling plant, which also has a process form of production, Charles Walker quotes a "piercer plugger" whose observations are similar to those of chemical operators:

There's a certain monotony you might not understand. Sometimes you do the same thing 2000 times in eight hours . . . but something can always happen . . . and when it does there's more damn fun than a picnic down there in the mill. There's monotony no end but still there's always the unexpected.[24]

The chance for growth and development.—Continuous-process technology is highly dynamic, and one of the consequences of a changing work milieu is that it challenges the self-estrangement inherent in personal stagnation. Chemical workers stress the fact that even though they have become perfectly competent to handle their jobs they are not through learning because something new comes up all the time. An operator who had been on his job two years told me: "You never know everything that's needed to know on it. I know the basic things. But sometimes I doubt if I know anything. You scratch your head and just wonder when something goes wrong."

To carry on experimental work on new processes and products, chemical companies establish pilot plants, often on a short-time basis, to which regular operators are assigned. Work in such plants increases the diversity of a man's job experience and provides an opportunity for growth and development. Even within regular departments, the frequency with which new equipment

---

[23] On the other hand, 20 per cent of the oil refinery workers found their jobs dull and monotonous all or most of the time, a figure identical with the sample norm.

[24] Charles R. Walker, *Steeltown* (New York: Harper & Bros., 1950), p. 61.

or new processes are introduced means that learning is more or less constant. A young operator, in comparing the chemical plant with his previous job in the paper industry, emphasizes the heightened interest which change and new experience bring about:

A chemical plant is more technical. There are more interesting jobs. There [at the paper factory] you grab a box, it's all manual labor. Nothing to hold you, you do the same thing every day. Here, the operations are constantly changing. It holds your interest. You get something going; you wonder what's going to happen, how it will come out.

A technical and changing work environment obviously requires a different kind of work force than an environment in which jobs and processes are relatively unchanging. A student of labor conditions in the chemical industry writes: "A continuous result of new development is the. regular change in jobs and in methods of work. Modifications of duties on the job and introduction of new types of duties demand workers of fairly high ability." [25] In recent years, chemical companies and oil refineries have generally limited their hiring to high-school graduates, in an attempt to get workers who are intelligent and adaptable. Although many workers are not able to change fast enough to keep up with changing technology, their environment itself tends to produce workers who are more alert, more technically minded, and more adaptable than the average.

In order to help the work force keep up with technological change, companies in the continuous-process industries have instituted extensive training programs. At a major oil refinery in the Bay area, all of the operators had recently completed one week's schooling on the job. In addition, technical courses at evening schools and junior colleges are actively encouraged by management, which often pays a portion of the worker's tuition.[26]

Still, the challenge, interest, and intelligence required in these jobs should not be exaggerated. It is true that automated work is too demanding for men with below-average I.Q.'s, in contrast to repetitive machine and assembly-line work where these employees adapt well. Yet a worker whose intelligence is well above average often finds continuous-process operations insufficiently stimulating. An oil refinery personnel executive told me that he will not place applicants with I.Q.'s of 120 or more in operating jobs.

[25] Edmund H. Lambert, Jr., "Labor and the Chemical Industry" Master's thesis, University of California, Berkeley, 1949, in files of the Institute of Industrial Relations, Berkeley, p. 15.
[26] A U.S. Department of Labor study of the introduction of a catalytic-cracking unit in a petroleum refinery emphasizes the attention given to formal training in the process of technological change. For shift foremen, classroom instruction on a full-time basis began six months before the equipment was put in operation. Stillmen, equivalent to head operators in the chemical industry, were trained three months before the installation. Even for operators and helpers, classes covering the process, controls, and operating conditions were held three days a week, eight hours a day. U.S. Department of Labor, *Studies of Automatic Technology: A Case Study of a Modernized Petroleum Refinery* (Bureau of Labor Statistics Report No. 120 [Washington: U.S. Government Printing Office, n.d.]), p. 18.

Twenty-one per cent of the chemical workers said that their jobs were too simple to bring out their best abilities, in comparison to the 25 per cent dissatisfied among the total sample and the 35 per cent among disgruntled automobile workers. But even among the unskilled chemical employees, only 26 per cent found their jobs too simple, in contrast to 46 per cent of the unskilled auto workers (Table 50, Appendix B).[27]

The automated operator's identity crisis.—Earlier we have seen that work in the printing industry fosters an occupational identity which is approved by the self and by others, whereas work in the textile and automobile industries tends to establish a negative occupational identity. The relative scarcity of objectively alienating tendencies in the continuous-process industries means that work contributes to the employee's sense of self-esteem and worth; however, it is a positive organizational, rather than an occupational, identity which is enhanced under automated work conditions.

The occupation of operator of automated equipment is a very new one. Unlike that of the printer, it has no venerable traditions with which to identify. No generally accepted standards have as yet been developed for judging the absolute and relative level of the process operator's skill, which by its very nature is less visible and tangible than that involved in manual work. Because of the public's lack of familiarity with automated technology, it is probably difficult for the chemical operator to gain the respect of others through identifying with his work—in contrast to the printer or the railroad engineer.

Since skill in the automated plant is new and vaguely defined and there is no societal consensus on its value, it is not surprising that the process operators themselves were ambivalent about the character of their jobs. Virtually all of the workers interviewed said that their tasks required skill, even lots of skill, yet they were unsure of what was involved.[28] Lack of consensus on the relative value of one's contribution to a common enterprise can be a source of insecurity for those whose skill level is ambiguous and a source of hostility toward those groups whose judgments make one's status precarious. During the period of the field work, the Bay Company was conducting a job-evaluation program which assessed the requirements and skill of each job in order to make wage rates more consistent. It is almost in-

[27] Oil workers felt more thwarted than chemical employees in the expression of their abilities. Thirty-five per cent of the refinery employees felt their jobs were too simple for them. I have no satisfactory explanation for this and other evidence in the Roper study that alienation among oil refinery workers is more widespread than among chemical employees. Possibly these differences reflect the higher aspirations of oil workers in this particular study: the refinery workers were northerners, the chemical employees predominantly southerners. Perhaps the key factor is the smaller degree of social cohesion in oil refineries, which tend to be larger and more centralized than chemical plants. It is also possible that the few oil workers in the Roper sample were more dissatisfied than is typical for the industry.

[28] A few asked my opinion of their skill level. They stressed that they had a "different kind of skill," one which "takes brains." One man noted that many workers "just aren't built to be operators."

evitable in such programs that some workers will react strongly when their job classifications are downgraded. The extreme reaction of the operator quoted below is not typical of the plant-wide attitude; however, it does reflect the ambiguous skill level inherent in the nature of process operation:

It takes skill to be an operator. Maybe you've heard of this job-evaluation program that's been going on. Well, our supervisor thinks there's not much skill in our work. The way he described our jobs for the job-evaluation program, it's like he thinks you could train a bunch of chimps and they could do the job. He thinks we're a bunch of idiots. That has caused unhappy feelings.[29]

The ambiguity of the operator's contribution and status is also highlighted by the major structural division within the work force of continuous-process plants, that between the maintenance and production divisions. As the operators put it, "There's a critical line between the day worker and the shift worker."[30] In the past, maintenance craftsmen were attached to a particular operating department, but the establishment of a centralized maintenance division in the Bay Company a few years ago has undoubtedly increased the strength of this natural cleavage and reduced the frequency of work and social relations between employees in the two divisions. Their differing interests are reflected in the union and in contract negotiations. Maintenance craftsmen are considerably more important in the union than operating personnel and are thought by some to be unappreciative of the operator's special needs, such as shift pay differentials.

Three of the four maintenance craftsmen interviewed had worked as operators. They viewed operating work as more routine and monotonous with less variety and challenge. They felt that operators didn't work as hard as craftsmen, who prefer working with tools, objects, and problems, rather than the controls and dials of automatic equipment.[31] The plant-wide status

[29] A study by William F. Whyte of an aviation-gasoline plant provides additional evidence that operators of automatic-process equipment are unusually sensitive with respect to their skill. When a new general superintendent referred to the highly paid operators, who were also trying to get a higher wage classification, as "only watchmen," who, without using any skills, "just have to watch the charts," a developing crisis in worker-management relations came to a head. There was a storm of resentment, a surge of interest in a CIO union which was trying to displace a company union, and a temporary withholding of job information from the engineers. William Foote Whyte, "Engineers and Workers—a Case Study," *Human Organization*, XIV (1956), 3–12.

[30] Since the continuous-process operations are exceedingly costly to start up and shut down and because the capital equipment is so expensive that full use must be gained from the investment, large chemical plants and oil refineries usually operate on a twenty-four hour, seven days a week basis. The manual workers who operate the automatic equipment must therefore work rotating shifts. They are called shift workers, while maintenance and distribution employees who do not have to work nights and weekends are called day workers.

[31] Indeed, some of these images are confirmed by comparing the attitudes of maintenance workers and operators in the Davis survey. Seventy-three per cent of the maintenance and distribution workers report that they are usually very tired or fairly tired, at the end of the day; only 27 per cent were slightly tired or not tired. But only 52 per cent of the operators

of maintenance craftsmen is generally higher, since transfers from operations to maintenance work were quite common and there seemed to be virtually no job changes in the other direction.[32] Interviews with workers in a large eastern oil refinery also revealed that jobs in the mechanical trades are viewed as more desirable than process operations.[33]

The insecure position of the operators was confirmed by their greater sensitivity to this structural cleavage. Maintenance workers were unwilling to admit any feelings of rivalry and competition between the two divisions or to say that one kind of work was more important than the other. The operators, on the other hand, were quite defensive and concerned about their relative positions. They felt that craftsmen looked upon them as just dial watchers who sat around and didn't have any real physical or manual work to do. They defended themselves on two grounds. Most common was the assertion that they got out the products, the lifeblood of the company's operations, and therefore without them the craftsmen would have nothing to do.[34] Further a number of operators felt that their work was inherently more challenging than maintenance: "Once you've learned how to repair a piece of equipment you do it the same way all the time." The tendency for each group of workers to view the other's jobs as more routine is not only curious but shows the important value manual workers place on work which is not standardized.

The joking relationship which has developed between maintenance

---

were very or fairly tired; 48 per cent, almost half, were only slightly tired or not tired at all.

The operators were also more likely to feel that people had to work harder at other companies than at the Bay chemical plant. Eighty per cent felt this way. The maintenance workers, however, were about evenly split between those who felt work was harder at their company and those who felt it was harder at other plants.

There is evidence in Gerald White's history of the early years of Standard Oil of California that the division between the processing operators and the craftsmen has a long tradition in the continuous-process industries. After discussing the extremely long workday of the shift operators in 1907, White continues: "Yet in the oil industry the long work of the shift men was not quite as harsh as it sounds, for looking after the stills was a relatively easy task. The men, moreover, usually managed to nap a little during the night. *Shift work, so some mechanics claimed, was a 'lazy man's job' despite the long hours*" Gerald T. White, *Formative Years in the Far West: A History of Standard Oil of California and Predecessors through 1919* (New York: Appleton-Century-Crofts, 1962), pp. 524–25 (my emphasis).

[32] These men transferred mainly to get off shift work and on to a day schedule, although in every case they were also attracted by the desire to learn a trade.

[33] Union Research and Education Projects, University of Chicago, "Report of a Study of the Organizing Potential of the Bayway Refinery," pp. 28–29.

[34] As one operator expressed it: "The machine shop's people are kind of a clique. They run things around here. . . . There's a critical line between the day worker and the shift worker. The day workers think the shift people are just out here because we're money hungry.

"They figure you're just looking at dials and sitting around, that any guy can do it. (*Spoken with real feeling.*)

"Yes, it takes the form of a lot of kidding but there's seriousness underneath. There is a lot of rivalry between the day and the shift people. If it wasn't for us, they'd have no work to do. We get the product out." (My emphasis.)

workers and operators[35] is a solution to the real tensions that have developed in a situation where two radically different kinds of blue-collar work coexist in the same enterprise. The maintenance-operations cleavage reflects a historical change in the nature of blue-collar skill. The new skills of the automatic operators have been recognized as crucial by management but are not yet viewed as legitimate expressions of manly work in the larger society, whereas traditional craft skill does have this broader implication. Therefore status emulation and uncertainty brings anxiety into the relations between these two types of workers, and the resultant tension is released through ritualized kidding.[36]

The strength of organizational commitment.—With occupational identity so problematic, production workers in the continuous-process industries are drawn toward the company, and this institution tends to become the focus of worker loyalty, in contrast to the situation in craft industries. Ninety-two per cent of the the chemical employees, the highest proportion in the sixteen industries Roper surveyed, said that their company was about the best place to work, compared to 78 per cent of the printers (Table 38, Appendix B).[37] Yet if we look at an indicator of occupational rather than organizational identification, 58 per cent of the chemical workers would seek other trades if they could begin their work life again, in contrast to only 36 per cent of the printers (Table 37, Appendix B).

Loyalty to company is not just a response to a lack of occupational identity but develops from the career orientation to employment in the continuous-process industries. The unusual degree of job security, the many promotion opportunities, and the proliferation of welfare benefits—all encourage identification with the company. In craft industries, such as printing and the building trades, security and welfare are more commonly due to the strength of the union, the association of the occupational community.

According to two case studies, the extraordinary organizational identification of oil refinery workers makes it extremely difficult for a CIO union to gain their allegiance. Ninety-five per cent of the employees in one refinery

---

[35] A craftsman coming into an operating control room is likely to say, "Let's go fellows, get off your ass, and do some work for a change." I have not been able to determine the typical rejoinder of the operator, who seems to be shorter of this kind of verbal ammunition.

I have not meant to imply that the Bay plant or the chemical industry is falling apart at the seams because of this cleavage. The general atmosphere in the plant is very positive; the competition between these workers is usually friendly and not destructive.

[36] The position of the chemical operator is somewhat marginal. In the society as a whole, white-collar work is more highly valued than manual work, but the operator's occupation has not been socially redefined as non-manual. And within the working class, manual work, especially that which involves craft skill, is more highly esteemed. That a certain amount of anxiety should result from this status ambiguity is to be expected.

[37] Again the oil refining industry does not follow the pattern. Seventy-five per cent of these workers were satisfied with their company, 71 per cent would choose a different occupation. Thus, in contrast to chemical employees, the oil workers in the Roper sample seem to be somewhat more discontented with both company and occupation.

said that they would work for the company again if they had to decide once more. The majority also wanted their children to work for the company, though preferably in white-collar rather than manual jobs. Many of these employees save copies of the company magazine for friends and relatives, give them to their children to take to school, or display them prominently in their home.[38] In the other refinery, the researchers report:

Better than half of our respondents have had extensive work experience in other jobs, for the most part in steel mills and in small plants. And by the very nature of the oil industry and the work they are now doing, they find their present jobs more rewarding than in the past. But the respondents do not differentiate as to the nature of the industry or firm, the credit goes to Standard, and its "progressive labor policies." [39]

The chemical worker wants advancement, but the prospect of working all his life for the same company is not threatening. Ely Chinoy found that automobile workers could not face the prospect of spending the rest of their lives on the line with the same company. When asked about their future plans, they were likely to construct rather unrealistic fantasies about quitting and starting up independent businesses. It was therefore with some hesitation that I asked Bay Company workers whether they expected to be with their present employer for "the rest of their working days." Instead of receiving embarrassed responses, most workers indicated that they not only expected it, they hoped to be able to do this. Some who had other occupational goals said that if they did not achieve them it would not be very serious because their present work was so satisfactory. Not only was the urgency of the automobile worker's out-of-plant goals absent, the aspirations of the chemical employees seemed much more realistic than the fantasies described by Chinoy.[40]

Indeed, chemical workers are less likely to quit their jobs than other workers. Quit rates in the oil and chemical industries are among the lowest in all manufacturing. An average of only 1.1 chemical workers per 100 quit their jobs each month between 1946 and 1958, compared to 2.4 automobile workers. The oil refining industry had an even consistently lower quit rate. In the three years between 1959 and 1962 the average rate in chemicals was 0.7 per 100 workers a month, about half the average for all manufacturing industries. Of twenty-one factory industries, only two, oil refining and

[38] Union Research and Education Projects, University of Chicago," Report of a Study of the Organizing Potential of the Bayway Refinery," pp. 28–29.

[39] Union Research and Education Projects, University of Chicago, "Report of the OCAWIU Organizing Effort," p. 21.

[40] A study of oil refinery employees reports exactly the same attitudes as in the Bay Company and also makes a similar contrast to Chinoy's findings. Union Research and Education Projects, University of Chicago, "Report of a Study of the Organizing Potential of the Bayway Refinery," p. 34.

primary metals (iron and steel), had slightly lower rates (see Table 30, Appendix A). One Bay Company employee mentioned the permanency of the work force as a factor which slowed down the rate of advancement. "Jobs are too good; nobody quits," he said, somewhat regretfully.

SOCIAL INTEGRATION THROUGH RESPONSIBLE FUNCTION: A NEW SOURCE OF DIGNITY AND NON-ALIENATION IN BLUE-COLLAR WORK?

For chemical workers, then, work means much more than the pay check, the major factor binding automobile assembly-line workers to their job. Certainly the instrumental purpose of work is important for chemical employees, as it must be for all except perhaps a minority of creative artists and intellectuals; the critical difference is that the job includes many features which are inherently fulfilling. It was for intrinsic, immediate, job-content reasons that most chemical workers interviewed preferred their present work over past jobs in other industries; in contrast, the X plant workers studied by Walker and Guest preferred automobile-industry employment only for such extrinsic considerations as pay and security. Since the intrinsic nature of the work—its challenge, learning opportunities, and social function in production—is meaningful to an employee in a continuous-process chemical plant, the job is therefore not solely the means to an end which it tends to be in other industrial settings. The chemical worker is less likely to be subjectively alienated than the automobile worker.

In stressing the unique combination of technological, economic, and social forces which counteract alienation in the chemical industry, I do not want to unduly exaggerate the well-being and happiness found in these work environments. There are undoubtedly many chemical companies where workers are more dissatisfied than at Bay, a plant with a remarkably high degree of morale and social cohesion. Even in the latter plant, one meets a number of workers who are clearly alienated and express marked negative feelings about the work of an automated operator. It was my impression—unchecked by systematic statistics—that young, highly intelligent, and ambitious workers were the most likely to be dissatisfied. They viewed the work as insufficiently challenging, advancement opportunities as too long range, and probably also resented general working-class status and income. The over-all argument is simply that there are proportionately fewer of these alienated workers in continuous-process industries.

The printing craftsman also tends to be a non-alienated worker. However, the content, the conditions, and the consequences of non-alienation are not the same in craft and continuous-process industries. The printer's freedom is based on his traditional manual skill and the control over his work environment inherent in the use and possession of such skill. He has an independence and a sense of security which is based on the scarcity of craft skills, on his occupational identity, and on a powerful union. Of all modern workers, his status is most similar to that of the old medieval craftsman.

The chemical worker's freedom is the result of an automated continuous-process technology and constant technical change, rather than tradition. Based on the responsibility required by the non-manual work of controlling an automatic technology, it reflects new conditions and job requirements which result from the needs of management rather than the consequences of the worker's superior power position. Although in this sense chemical employees are more dependent on their companies than printers, the responsibility for automated production confers a new source of dignity and worth on manual employment—a possibility not foreseen by many students of alienation, who assess manual work by the yardstick of traditional craftsmanship.

8

ALIENATION AND FREEDOM
IN HISTORICAL PERSPECTIVE

The industry a man works in is *fateful* because the conditions of work and existence in various industrial environments are quite different. The print shop, the textile mill, the automobile plant, the chemical continuous-process operation—all important factory milieux in the present-day situation—illustrate the far-reaching diversity and pluralistic quality of American industrial life. The comparative analyses of these four industrial settings in the previous chapters show that an employee's industry decides the nature of the work he performs eight hours a day and affects the meaning which that work has for him. It greatly influences the extent to which he is free in his work life and the extent to which he is controlled by technology or supervision. It also influences his opportunity for personal growth and development—to learn, to advance, to take on responsibility. His industry even affects the kind of social personality he develops, since an industrial environment tends to breed a distinctive social type.[1]

In this study I have attempted to show how each dimension of alienation —powerlessness, meaninglessness, isolation, and self-estrangement—varies in form and intensity according to the industrial setting. There is thus no simple answer to the question: Is the factory worker of today an alienated worker? Inherent in the techniques of modern manufacturing and the principles of bureaucratic industrial organization are general alienating tendencies. But in some cases the distinctive technology, division of labor, economic structure, and social organization—in other words, the factors that differentiate

---

[1] From this point of view there is something misleading in the spate of such generalized titles as *Industrial Man, Blue Collar Man,* etc. It seems more appropriate to speak of "industrial men" or "blue-collar men," phrasings that do not connote such a uniformity of condition. Theodore Purcell's *Blue Collar Man* (Cambridge, Mass.: Harvard University Press, 1960), for example, is based on a study of workers in only one industry, meat-packing. Compare also William L. Warner and Norman H. Martin, *Industrial Man* (New York: Harper & Bros., 1959); Clark Kerr, *et al., Industrialism and Industrial Man* (Cambridge, Mass.: Harvard University Press, 1960); and Alex Inkeles, "Industrial Man: The Relation of Status to Experience, Perception and Value," *American Journal of Sociology,* LXVI (1960) 1–31.

individual industries—intensify these general tendencies, producing a high degree of alienation; in other cases they minimize and counteract them, resulting instead in control, meaning, and integration.

The method of comparative industrial analysis therefore illustrates the diversity and pluralism within modern manufacturing, highlights the unequal distribution of alienation and freedom among the factory labor force, and exposes the causal factors underlying these variations. In addition, it permits a historical perspective on the long-run changes in the relation between the manual worker and his work. Because of the uneven movement of modernization trends, industries coexist today that in a sense "belong" to different periods in the history of manufacturing. The four industries compared in this study vary in the degree of mechanization of technology, rationalization of division of labor, concentration of economic structure, and bureaucratization of social organization. By comparing the consequences of these variations in the four contexts, one gets a sense of the historic implications of long-range developments for alienation and freedom in the factory. The case study of the automated chemical industry is valuable in pointing to possible future changes in the balance between freedom and alienation.

In this final chapter I shall summarize some of the findings of the investigation, bringing together the four industrial situations that up to now have been analyzed in separate discussions. The major focus will be on the historical significance of the industrial comparisons, but in addition I shall consider some questions for public policy and for theory in industrial sociology that emerge from this study of alienation in the factory. Let us begin with a consideration of the impact of technological change on the nature of manual work.

THE THREE TYPES OF BLUE-COLLAR WORK

As technology has developed higher levels of mechanization, there has been a shift in the job requirements of the factory employee. In printing and other craft technologies, traditional manual skill, the manipulation of "hard" materials by hand and with simple tools, is the dominant type of work. In continuous-process technology (oil refineries and heavy chemical plants), the mechanization of production and materials flow has reached the point where process operators neither see the product nor work on it directly with their hands. Instead they monitor the automatic control dials, inspect machinery, adjust valves, and record the data that describe the operations of the automated system. The dominant job requirement is no longer manual skill but responsibility. In place of the *able workman,* required when the worker's role in the productive process is to provide skills, a *reliable employee,* capable of accepting a considerable load of responsibility, is now needed in the automated industries.

Traditional manual skill and "non-manual" responsibility differ in their basic qualities,[2] but both require considerable discretion and initiative. They therefore contribute to the dignity and self-respect of the factory worker. Unfortunately, the transition from one to the other is neither direct nor immediate. Craft technology rarely "evolves" into automated technology. The industries most characteristic of the middle stages of manufacturing development utilize machine and assembly-line techniques. Both these intermediate technologies bring about jobs that generally demand little manual skill or responsibility and thus epitomize the historic process that has been called "deskillization."

The textile and automobile assembly industries illustrate two different ways by which this deskillization has taken place. In the machine industries, traditional skill is undermined by the development of technology; in assembly-line production it is eliminated by the rationalization of work organization, by an extremely elaborate subdivision of labor. Both the expansion of technology and the growing subdivision of labor ultimately depend on the replacement of the unique product characteristic of craft industries by the more standardized product of mass production.

The erosion of traditional skill has largely completed its course in American industry, and present trends now suggest that such skill will increase in importance in the shrinking blue-collar sector. Traditional craft industries still play an important role in the economy and may enhance their significance even in a future automated society. The building construction industry, based largely on a traditional craft technology and traditional manual skill, is the largest single employer of blue-collar workers in the United States today. And a more affluent and educated public, reacting against the standardization of values and products in a mass society, may increase its future demand for unique and individuated articles.

Furthermore, automated manufacturing paradoxically increases traditional craft skill, which is applied, however, to maintenance problems rather than production work. Since automation involves a considerable increase in intricate plant machinery and technical processes, considerably more repairmen in various trades are needed to maintain this equipment. In the largest oil

---

[2] The difference between these two modes of work is implied in Elliott Jaques' distinction between skill and *nous,* a Greek word which means mind or reason. Skill, according to Jaques, "is the capacity of a person to exercise sensory and perceptual judgment in carrying out the discretionary aspects of his work. . . . Skill is made up of the capacity to respond intuitively to the sense of touch, sight, hearing, taste, smell, or balance, and physically to guide and manipulate one's work according to the sense or feel of the job in the course of doing it." *Nous,* on the other hand, is the "capacity to exercise mental judgment" in carrying out the discretionary aspects of work. It "is made up of the capacity to weigh up available information, to sense what other information, if any, ought to be obtained, and mentally to proceed on the basis of what feels like the best course of action where many factors in the situation are only unconsciously assessed, and some of the factors—perhaps even the most important ones—are simply unknown." Elliott Jaques, *Equitable Payment* (New York: John Wiley & Sons, 1961), pp. 81–82.

refineries and heavy chemical plants, there are as many or more maintenance employees than production employees. Within automated factories, two radically different kinds of blue-collar work coexist, each with its competing claim to skill and status.[3]

On the other hand, technological change at present is probably reducing the relative importance of low-skilled machine and assembly-line work in the labor force. Automation is eliminating unskilled factory jobs at a faster rate than they are being created through the further deskillization of craft work. Still, many industries with machine and assembly-line technologies will maintain them and not automate, for both technical and economic reasons. The product market in the shoe industry, for example, does not readily permit the standardization of styles, sizes, and shapes which makes automation economically feasible.[4] In other industries, including motor vehicles, the manner in which the product is constructed makes the automation of assembly operations extremely difficult technologically. Thus, there is no immediate prospect for the total elimination of unskilled manual operations in old industries. Furthermore, some new industries may begin manufacturing their products by means of the older technologies, since it can take considerable time to develop the standardized product and consumer volume that permit a higher level of mechanization.

In the complex and diversified manufacturing sector of an advanced industrial society, at least three major kinds of blue-collar factory work exist at the same time: the traditional manual skill associated with craft technology; the routine low-skilled manual operations associated with machine and assembly-line technologies; and the "non-manual" responsibility called forth by continuous-process technology.[5] Although craft skill will continue to play a significant role, the shift from skill to responsibility is the most important historical trend in the evolution of blue-collar work. The relative decline of unskilled, standardized jobs is, in the long run, a positive development;[6] however, a considerable amount of the routine work that negates the dignity of the worker will very likely persist in the foreseeable future.

TECHNOLOGY, FREEDOM, AND THE WORKER'S SOUP

Of the several dimensions of alienation, the impact of technology is greatest with respect to powerlessness, since the character of the machine system

[3] Some of the tensions involved in this situation are discussed in chapter 7, pages 159–62.

[4] James Bright, *Automation and Management* (Boston: Harvard University Graduate School of Business Administration, 1958), pp. 30–37.

[5] These types correspond exactly with the three stages in the evolution of manual work that Alain Touraine has distinguished at the Paris Renault Automotive Works. *L'évolution du travail ouvrier aux usines Renault* (Paris: Centre National de la Recherche Scientifique, 1955).

[6] Only in terms of the nature of manual work, of course; the loss of jobs resulting from these technological changes is a more serious matter to the individual worker than any historical improvement in the dignity of labor.

largely determines the degree of control the factory employee exerts over his sociotechnical environment and the range and limitations of his freedom in the work situation. In general, the long-run developments in this area parallel the historical evolution in blue-collar work. The interconnection between traditional manual skill and control is so intimate that theoretical distinctions between the two concepts become blurred: the very definition of traditional skill implies control over tools, materials, and pace of work. It is therefore no surprise that printers and other workers in craft technologies command a variety and degree of freedom unrivaled in the blue-collar world.

Machine technology generally reduces the control of the employee over his work process. Workers are rarely able to choose their own methods of work, since these decisions have been incorporated into the machines' very design and functioning. In the textile industry, pace and output are determined by the machine system and the organization of tasks; for the most part, operatives simply respond to the rhythms and exigencies of the technical system instead of initiating activity and exerting control.[7] In the assembly-line technology of the automobile industry, the worker's control is reduced to a minimal level. The conveyer-belt apparatus dictates most movements of the operative and pre-empts many of his potential choices and decisions.

An apparently trivial situation, the homely "case of the worker's soup," strikingly illustrates how a continuous-process technology restores the personal freedoms of the employee. This incident also points out the disparity in atmosphere between assembly-line and automated work environments. When asked about the possibilities of setting his own work pace, a chemical operator mentioned that the men often warm up a can of soup on a hot plate within the automated control room where they are stationed. Suppose this soup is on the stove, ready to eat, just at the time that's officially scheduled for the operator's round of instrument readings, an activity that takes about thirty minutes. "You can eat the soup first and do the work later, or you can take the readings earlier than scheduled, in order to have the soup when it's hot," reported this operator. In other words, the nature of production work in an automated technology makes it possible for the employee to satisfy personal and social needs when he feels like it, because he can carry out his job tasks according to his own rhythm. The automobile assembly-line worker who gets a craving for a bowl of soup is in an entirely different situation. He must wait for his allotted relief time, when another worker takes his place on the line, and if he still wants soup at that time he will

---

[7] On the whole, powerlessness increases with growing mechanization within this group of industries. In the less-developed shoe and apparel industries workers operate individual machines, and they usually are able, therefore, to control both the pace at which they work and the quantity of their output. Since they can stop and start their own machines, they are also relatively free to leave their work stations for brief periods.

probably drink it hurriedly on his return from the lavatory. Ironically but fittingly, his will be the "automated" soup, purchased from a commercial vending machine, since there is no room and no time for hot plates and cans of soup on an automotive conveyer belt.

If we shift from this consideration of long-run historical developments to look at the broad range of industrial environments today, it appears that only a minority of blue-collar workers are as controlled and dominated by technology or supervision as are automobile and textile workers. It is likely that most workers have jobs that permit them to set their own work pace, at least within limits—although adequate evidence on this point is lacking, unfortunately. Because of enlightened personnel policies and because an affluent society can afford a relaxed atmosphere at the point of production, most workers are free from intensive pressures on the job. Among all the factory employees in the Roper study, only 24 per cent said they had to work too fast. And because of prosperity, a more employee-oriented management, and the policing function of labor unions, the great majority of workers today are free from close and arbitrary supervision, a means of control that was quite prevalent a generation or two ago.

On the other hand, one aspect of control over the immediate work process is generally lacking in factory work: the freedom to choose the techniques and methods of doing the job. Predetermination of these decisions by engineers, foremen, and time-study men is the norm in mass-production industry. Probably only craftsmen and the few blue-collar operators in the new automated industries have much opportunity to introduce their own ideas in the course of their work. This general absence of opportunities for initiative is suggested by the fact that 51 per cent of the Roper factory workers said they could not try out their own ideas on the job—this was the only question relating to the objective work situation on which more than half of the respondents were dissatisfied.

Inherent in the idea of responsibility as the worker's job requirement is a degree of control over that area of the work process that is his domain. A long-run decline in powerlessness is therefore to be expected because of the character of automated technology and the nature of manual work in highly mechanized systems. But the unusual degree of freedom in industrial chemical plants is not simply a consequence of these factors. The economic expansion and general prosperity of the industry contribute much to the relaxed atmosphere on the job. Therefore automated industrial technology will not automatically guarantee freedom and control, since some automated firms and industries will be under economic stress in that far distant future when automation will be the dominant technology. In addition, automated technologies will take many forms, and variations within automated industries will result in different modes and levels of freedom.

DIVISION OF LABOR AND MEANING IN WORK

Along with the progressive mechanization of technology, another important historical trend in industrial development has been the increasing subdivision of labor within more and more rationalized systems of work organization. This has intensified the alienation of meaninglessness, making it more difficult for manual workers to find purpose and function in their work. There are hopeful signs in continuous-process plants, however, that automation is reversing this long-run development also.

Meaninglessness is rare in craft industries, because the products are unique rather than standardized and because the division of labor remains on the elementary level of craft specialization. Even the unskilled laborer shoveling cement on a building site is making a contribution toward the construction of a particular and tangible structure. His work is organized by the building problems of the individual site, and therefore he develops a task-completion orientation rather than a cyclical-repetitive approach to the job. In addition, craftsmen tend to work on large parts of the product: linotype operators set the type for all the pages of a book or magazine; hand compositors work on the whole page.

The increasing division of labor characteristic of both machine and assembly-line industries tends to undermine the "substantive rationality" natural to the craft organization of work. Product standardization in the mass-production industries means that work involves a repetitive cycle rather than a succession of distinctive tasks. Work organization further limits the employee to one segment of the product and a small scope of the process involved in its manufacture. Textile operatives, for example, are confined to one room in the mill, which contains a department carrying out only one process of the dozens required for the completion of the product, and in that room they generally perform only one or two of the total number of productive tasks. In automobile assembly, the proportion of product worked upon and the scope of operations becomes even more minute. And the operative's sense of purpose and function is reduced to a minimum when he attaches steering columns all day long and has nothing to do with any part of the automobile besides his own restricted specialty. It is highly ironic, and also tragic, that workers are confined to the most limited task assignments in the very industry where they know the most about the product and the processes because of the *expertise* gained working on their own cars.

Fortunately, however, fractionization of work does not continue to increase in a "straight-line" fashion as technology develops higher and higher levels of mechanization. The most characteristic feature of automation is its transfer of focus from an individual job to the process of production. The perspective of the worker is shifted from his own individual tasks to a broader series of operations that includes the work of other employees. Since automated processes are integrated and continuous rather than divided in the way that labor is divided, the responsibility of one employee for his share of a plant's process is inevitably linked to the responsibility of other workers.

Since the decentralized subplants that make up a continuous-process factory manufacture different products and since automated technology has reduced the number of workers necessary for each process, each man's job assignments and responsibilities differ from those of his workmates. Therefore each operator senses that he is contributing a unique function to the processing of his department's product, even though the product is standardized and remains the same from day to day. The unique function of each operator is enmeshed in a network of interdependent relations with the functions of others. And responsibility as a job requirement demands thinking in terms of the collective whole rather than the individual part. For all these reasons, automation results in a widening of the worker's scope of operations[8] and provides new avenues for meaning and purpose in work.

There is little meaninglessness in craft production because each craftsman makes a contribution to a unique *product*. In continuous-process production there is little alienation of this type because each operator contributes a unique *function* in the processing of a standardized product. Meaninglessness is most intensified on the automobile assembly line because both the product and the function of the individual worker is so highly standardized. Whereas the conveyer belt represents an extreme in this situation, as well as many others, the alienation of meaninglessness is probably more widespread and serious than that of powerlessness among the general labor force today, since the elaborate division of labor within the typical factory makes it difficult for most employees to relate their jobs to the larger purposes and goals of the enterprise.

TECHNOLOGY, TIME PERSPECTIVE, AND INVOLVEMENT

In the course of industrial development, there has probably been a tendency for manual work to become inherently less engrossing and for instrumental, external considerations to gain in importance over intrinsic task satisfactions. It is difficult for the manual worker to identify with the standardized products of mass-production industries or to become deeply involved in their manufacture. Therefore, like meaninglessness, self-estrangement in the work process tends to be a more common state among factory workers today than the alienation of powerlessness. But it is a mistake to view self-alienation simply as a generalized predicament of the factory worker in modern society, since its intensity depends on the specific conditions of industrial technology and the division of labor.

[8] Bright, *op. cit.*, pp. 183–84.

The nature of an industry's technology and its division of labor determine the rhythm of the manual worker's job and the characteristic orientation toward time that he experiences in the course of his work. They thus influence the degree to which the worker can become involved and engrossed in work activity and the degree to which he is likely to be detached or alienated from his immediate tasks. Craft technology and traditional manual skill create an unique-task work rhythm in which there is involvement in the present situation on the basis of images of the future completion of the product or task. The skilled worker must be emotionally engaged in the immediate activity of molding raw materials and solving problems of construction; craft work does not permit the barter of present-time gratifications for future rewards. On the other hand, the unskilled routine jobs in the standardized machine and assembly-line industries foster a repetitive-cycle work rhythm, a detachment from present tasks, and a concern with the future cessation of the activity itself, rather than the completion of specific tasks.[9] Since the intrinsic activity of the work in these industries tends to result in monotony rather than any immediate gratifications, the meaning of the job is largely found in instrumental future-time rewards: wages, fringe benefits, and, when present, economic security.

Continuous-process technology and the work of monitoring automatic equipment results in still another rhythm, one that is new and unique in factory settings. It is the variety and unpredictability of the "calm-and-crisis" mode of time experience that is probably most liberating. There are periods of routine activity when such tasks as instrument-reading and patrolling are carried out, periods of waiting and relaxing when the routine work is done and operations are smooth, and also periods of intense activity when emergency breakdowns must be controlled. In the two calm situations there is probably much detachment and monotony, coupled with an habituated attention to the potential occurrence of something extraordinary; however, in the crisis periods, total involvement in the immediate present results.[10]

Continuous-process technology offers more scope for self-actualization than machine and assembly-line technologies. The nature of the work encourages a scientific, technical orientation and the changing character of the technology results in opportunities for learning and personal development for a considerable section of the blue-collar labor force. In contrast, work in machine and assembly-line industries is rarely complicated by problems and difficulties that might challenge the worker's capacities and shake him out of his routine and thus offers little potential for personal development.

[9] The difference in time orientation between craft and machine-assembly tasks corresponds closely to Hannah Arendt's distinction between work and labor. *The Human Condition* (Chicago: University of Chicago Press, 1958).

[10] The unpredictability of problems and emergencies prevents even the smooth periods from becoming totally routine.

The effect of these technological variations on involvement in work can be seen when employees in each of these industries are asked whether their jobs are interesting or monotonous. The great majority of all factory workers consider their jobs interesting; the significant point is the pattern that relative differences in monotony take. As we advance up the scale of industrial development, the proportion of workers who find their jobs dull increases from a scant 4 per cent in the printing industry, to 18 per cent in the textile industry, and to 34 per cent in the automobile industry (and to 61 per cent of those unskilled auto workers concentrated on the assembly line). But in the chemical industry, only 11 per cent complain of monotony, which suggests that automation may be checking the long-run trend toward detachment and self-alienation in factory work.

INDUSTRIAL STRUCTURE, SOCIAL ALIENATION, AND PERSONALITY

The historical development of mechanized technology and rationalized work organization has influenced social alienation as well as powerlessness, meaninglessness, and self-estrangement, because these trends have affected industrial social structure. Different technologies result in variations in the occupational distribution of the industrial labor force, in the economic cost structures of the company, and in the size and layout of the factory. These factors, in turn, affect the degree of integration and cohesion in an industry and the extent to which factory workers feel a sense of belonging in an industrial community. Because of variations in industrial social structure, industries differ in their modes of social control and sources of worker discipline, and distinctive social types and personalities are produced that reflect the specific conditions of their industrial environment.

Craft industries are usually highly integrated on the basis of the traditions and norms of the various occupational specialties, and social alienation is low because of the skilled worker's loyalty to, and identification with, his particular craft and trade union. Skilled printers, like workers in the building trades and other craftsmen, are relatively independent of their companies, since the market demand for their skills gives them mobility in an industrial structure made up of large numbers of potential employers. The occupational structure and economic organization of craft industries thus make the work force autonomous from management, rather than integrated with it or alienated from it. This autonomy is expressed in the skilled craftsman's characteristic (and characterological) resentment of close supervision. Since the management control structure has little effective power and since craft technology is too undeveloped to be coercive, the locus of social control in these work settings is the journeyman's own internalization of occupational standards of work excellence and norms of "a fair day's work." Work discipline in craft industries is therefore essentially self-discipline. The industrial environment produces a social personality characterized by an orientation to craftsmanship and quality performance, a strong sense of individualism and autonomy, and a solid acceptance of citizenship in the larger society. Satisfied with his occupational function, the craftsman typically has a highly developed feeling of self-esteem and a sense of self-worth and is therefore ready to participate in the social and political institutions of the community as well as those of his craft.

Because machine industries have low-skilled labor forces, occupational groups have less identity and autonomy. Therefore they rarely provide a basis for social integration. The unskilled worker in these industries is more dependent on his employer, and the company thus tends to be the central institution in the industrial community. A characteristic of machine industries that usually contributes to social integration is the large number of female employees. Male workers feel that their status is higher and that they are recognized as more important than the women. They have somewhat increased chances for promotion into the minority of jobs with skill or responsibility. Women, who tend to be more satisfied than men with the prevailing unskilled routine jobs, "cushion" the occupational floor in machine industries, raising the ceiling slightly for the men who might otherwise be frustrated in low positions.

In southern textiles, unique historical and geographical factors have been critical in producing a social structure that is more cohesive and highly integrated than most machine industries. With the mills located principally in small towns and villages, the industrial community centered around the factory is almost identical with the local community itself. Southern textile towns are traditional societies that are highly integrated, and commitment to mill employment seems to follow naturally from the strong loyalties to family, church, and locality. Social control is thus centered in the folkways of the community and the paternalistic domination of management. Factory discipline is not based on the internalized motivation characteristic of printers but stems from a number of largely external sources. These include a mechanized technology and subdivided work organization that is more coercive than that of the craft industries and the rather close supervision of foremen and other management representatives. Of course social control is also rooted in the tendency of the tradition-oriented textile worker to accept management authority and the industrial status quo. The typical social personality produced by this industrial environment is almost diametrically opposed to that of the craftsman. In addition to submissive attitudes toward authority, the textile worker tends to have little autonomy or individuation and to have a low level of aspiration, which includes an indifferent attitude to the meaningfulness of his work. The low estimate of self-worth and the absorption in the relatively narrow confines of kinship and church counter any expression of citizenship and participation in larger social worlds.

Two consequences of assembly-line technology and work organization, the "massified" occupational distribution and extremely large factories, are the critical elements underlying the social structure of the automobile industry. The mass of workers are at a uniform level of low skill, and the majority of men in assembly plants are paid almost exactly the same rate. The relative lack of occupational differentiation by skill, status, or responsibility creates an industrial "mass society" in which there are almost no realistic possibilities of advancement. The industry therefore lacks a built-in reward system for reaffirming its norms and integrating the worker into a community based on loyalty to the company. Social alienation is further intensified because automobile workers are low skilled, without strong occupational identity, and loyalty to an independent craft is not possible for most employees.

In addition, the technology and elaborate division of labor require a large physical plant and a sizable work force. As a rule, the larger the factory, the more tenuous is the employee's sense of identification with the enterprise and the greater the social and sympathetic distance between him and management. The automobile assembly plant stands at the apex of the historical development toward larger and larger factories: the proportion of workers employed in plants with more than 1,000 persons is 21 per cent in printing, 25 per cent in textiles, and 82 per cent in the transportation equipment industries! Automobile production may be the ideal example of an industry where large plants and firms have most contributed to the extreme development of an impersonal work atmosphere and to the breakdown of sympathetic communication and identification between employees and management.

In these circumstances, social control rests less on consensus and more on the power of management to enforce compliance to the rule system of the factory, a power sometimes effectively countervailed by the strong labor union, which has a legitimate mandate to protect certain interests of the workers.[11] The compelling rhythms of the conveyer-belt technology and the worker's instrumental concern for his weekly pay check are more important to him than internalized standards of quality performance or an identification with organizational goals in providing the discipline that gets work

[11] The above formulation somewhat exaggerates the power conflict in the industry; the union also participates in the setting of the rules and, in a sense, aids the company by helping to secure the worker's compliance to them. To some degree this creates a basis for consensus. A system of norms has emerged from the conflict between the two organizations. Their past and present confrontations over such issues as union recognition, working conditions, wages, disciplinary rules, and grievances has created a framework of reciprocal expectations and obligations, even within a general atmosphere of mutual distrust and hostility.

done in an orderly fashion. The social personality of the auto worker, a product of metropolitan residence and exposure to large, impersonal bureaucracies, is expressed in a characteristic attitude of cynicism toward authority and institutional systems, and a volatility revealed in aggressive responses to infringements on personal rights and occasional militant collective action. Lacking meaningful work and occupational function, the automobile worker's dignity lies in his peculiarly individualistic freedom from organizational commitments.

AUTOMATION AND SOCIAL INTEGRATION

Social alienation is widespread in the automobile industry because of the marked anomic tendencies inherent in its technology and work organization. In the chemical industry, on the other hand, continuous-process technology and more favorable economic conditions result in a social structure with a high degree of consensus between workers and management and an integrated industrial community in which employees experience a sense of belonging and membership. Social alienation is absent because of the combined effect of a number of factors: of first importance are the balanced skill distribution and the differentiated occupational structure that markedly contrast with the non-stratified structure in automotive plants.

Continuous-process technology results in a wide variety of occupational categories, and it requires workers at all levels of skill and responsibility. Because oil refineries and chemical plants produce an assortment of products and by-products, there are many different processes taking place in individual plant buildings, each of which has a work crew composed of slightly different job positions. Unskilled laborers are needed, as are large numbers of process operators at moderate, as well as high, levels of responsibility, and skilled maintenance craftsmen are also in demand. Such a status system is a socially integrating force, since it provides many high positions to which employees may aspire, and the successful workers most exemplify the values and standards of the company. When possibilities for greater rewards of higher pay and status exist, workers are motivated to perform well and internalize the goals of the enterprise.

Secondly, automation reverses another long-run trend, that of increasing factory size, and results also in a distinctive change in plant layout in these industries. A reduction in the number of employees in a plant operation is due partly to automation itself and partly to the companies' conscious decentralization policies. (Chemical and oil firms seem to prefer many medium-sized plants rather than a few giant operations.)[12] More importantly, the decentralization principle is applied to a single factory. In steel mills, auto-

---

[12] Only 40 per cent of the chemical workers and 53 per cent of the oil workers are employed in establishments with more than 1,000 persons, compared to 82 per cent of automobile workers.

mobile assembly plants, textile mills, and print shops, the departments that carry out the various stages of the production process all exist under the same roof—so that there is, in essence, only one plant. But though chemical plants and oil refineries are spread out over a large terrain, they are decentralized into a large number of individual buildings or subplants that are spatially separated from each other. In each of these a different product is made or a particular process is carried out by a crew of operators who have collective responsibility for the total operation, as well as individual responsibilities for certain parts of it. These "Balkanized" units and the work teams attached to them serve as centers of employee loyalty and identification and give work in the continuous-process industries a cohesive "small plant" atmosphere, even though the employer is actually a large national corporation. These small work teams are an effective source of work discipline. Men perform up to standard because they do not want to let down their workmates or their department. Collective control by the working crew will probably become more important in many industries besides continuous-process ones, since team responsibility is the natural outgrowth of the integrated process inherent in automated technology per se.

Informal work groups are even more important to the worker and more central a factor in over-all morale in machine and assembly-line technologies because the unskilled, repetitive jobs lack intrinsic gratifications and make social satisfactions more imperative. Unfortunately, cohesive work groups are a problematic outcome in these technologies, because, unlike process production, they do not naturally result in team operations or collective responsibility. In many simple machine and light-assembly industries, individual employees work very close to others who do similar or identical jobs, and informal cliques are formed which maintain norms of production and provide a sense of belonging and cohesion. In the textile industry, however, workers with multimachine assignments are spread out at great distances in very large rooms, so that no working groups can be formed. Similarly, automobile assembly production, with its serial operations, places each worker next to a different set of workers, so that stable groups with clear and distinct identities do not easily form.

A third factor contributing to social integration in the continuous-process industries is the changed character of automated work. The difference in the nature of work performed by production workers and managers has been one of the most significant factors underlying class conflict within the factory.[13] But with automation, the work of the blue-collar process operators

[13] The traditional distrust and mutual feeling of distance between men who work with their hands and tools and those who work with their "brains" and paper is probably as old as the division between literate and non-literate strata that emerged with the invention of writing. The tendency for white-collar employees to identify with the management rather than with the factory workers is partly due to the feeling that their clean, non-manual work gives them more in common with their employers.

becomes very similar to that of the white-collar staff—it is clean, includes record-keeping and other clerical tasks, and involves responsibility.[14] Thus automation may eliminate the "innate" hostility of men who work with their hands toward "pencil-pushers" and administrators. And, conversely, white-collar employees will probably gain an enhanced understanding of, and respect for, the work of blue-collar men, since the office staff's contact with the plant and its production problems increases in automated firms, due to the greater need for checking and consultation.

The cohesive social structure in the continuous-process industries is further supported by the economic basis of automated production. As industrial technology becomes more mechanized, the cost structure of the enterprise changes. Since the investment in expensive machinery rises sharply in automated industries and the number of production workers declines, the proportion of total cost that is capital equipment increases and the proportion of labor cost decreases. A capital-intensive cost structure means that heightened efficiency, increased output, and higher profits can more easily be attained through exploitation of technology rather than the exploitation of the worker. The hard-pressed textile firms and to a lesser extent the automobile assembly plants, with their relatively low levels of mechanization and high labor costs, attempt to remain competitive by getting as much as possible out of each worker. The cost structure furthers the tendency to use the workers as "means," as commodities in the classic Marxist sense. The economic base of automated technology allows a more enlightened management to view the workers as human beings, as partners in a collective enterprise, who, because of their responsibility for expensive machinery and processes, must be considered in terms of their own needs and rights.

In addition to the structural economic relations that result from the nature of automated production, contingent economic conditions have also contributed greatly to social integration. Heavy chemicals has been a highly prosperous growth industry. Economic prosperity has permitted large chemical companies to provide their employees with a regularity of employment and long-range job security that is not possible in less stable industries. Since security of employment is the fundamental precondition of a worker's commitment to his company and industry, economics is therefore basic to the cohesion and consensus in chemicals. A second precondition of employee loyalty and identification is an opportunity to advance and improve one's status. The long-term growth in the industry has brought with it the expansion of plants and labor force, making advancement, as well as per-

---

[14] Of course, automated operators are responsible for machinery and technical processes, which is not true of the work of most white-collar people. The close relationship to, and deep interest in, machinery is part of the manual worker's "natural" mentality in an advanced industrial society. In time this aspect of the job will presumably serve to make the automated employee's outlook similar to that of the engineer rather than the clerk, supervisor, or salesman.

manent employment, a meaningful reality. Economic prosperity has furthered social integration in still another way: it has permitted a relaxed atmosphere on the job and co-operative rather than strained and conflict-laden relations between workers and supervisors. In direct contrast, the economic fluctuations in the automobile industry mean that irregular employment is common, a fact that profoundly militates against an atmosphere of consensus and good will.

Due to all these factors, the social personality of the chemical worker tends toward that of the new middle class, the white-collar employee in bureaucratic industry. As a new industry whose important growth has been in the period of the large-scale corporation, heavy chemicals has been able to provide its blue-collar workers with the career employment (permanency, regular promotions, company benefits) that has generally been the fate only of white-collar people. The automated operator's work—light, clean, involving the use of symbols, and resulting in regular contact with engineers, salesmen, and supervisors—is also somewhat similar to that of the office employee. And his mentality is not far different; he identifies with his company and orients himself toward security. Like the white-collar man, this security comes from his status as an employee, from his dependence on the benevolent and prosperous company, rather than his own independence. Generally lukewarm to unions and loyal to his employer, the blue-collar employee in the continuous-process industries may be a worker "organization-man" in the making.

Of course the high degree of consensus and cohesion in the chemical industry is not typical. Nor is the situation in automobile assembly, where social alienation is so extreme, characteristic of the average manufacturing establishment. On the whole, social alienation is not as widespread in American industry as meaninglessness and self-estrangement are. The majority of blue-collar workers are committed to their roles as producers, and are loyal (although within limits)[15] to their employers. This is supported by the findings in the Roper study that 73 per cent consider their company as good or better than any other place to work in their industry; only 17 per cent said other companies were better, and 10 per cent were undecided. Although the development of technology through the assembly line has reduced the cohesion of industrial social structure, other long-term trends have probably lessened the social alienation of factory workers that was so prevalent in the early period of industrialization. Modern bureaucratic organization is based on universalistic standards of justice and fair treatment, and its system of

---

[15] Loyalty to the company does not preclude persistent loyalty to labor unions and occasional opinions that the interests of these organizations may conflict, as the proponents of the "dual loyalty" thesis have pointed out. Compare Ross Stagner "Dual Allegiance as a Problem in Modern Society," *Personnel Psychology*, VII (1954); Lois Dean, "Union Activity and Dual Loyalty," *Industrial and Labor Relations Review*, VII (1954) and Purcell, *op. cit.*, pp. 248–62.

rules has enhanced the normative integration of industry. The long period of economic prosperity and its concomitants—steady employment, higher wages, better living standards, and promotion opportunities—have profoundly contributed to the secular decline in the worker's class consciousness and militancy, a development that reflects the growing consensus between employees and employers and the increase in the worker's feeling that he has a stake in industry.

ALIENATION TRENDS: THE LONG VIEW

The historical perspective on alienation and freedom in the factory reveals a clear and consistent pattern. Because secular developments in technology, division of labor, and industrial social structure have affected the various dimensions of alienation largely in the same direction, there is a convergence of long-range trends in the relation of the factory worker to his work process. Alienation has traveled a course that could be charted on a graph by means of an inverted U-curve.

In the early period, dominated by craft industry, alienation is at its lowest level and the worker's freedom at a maximum. Freedom declines and the curve of alienation (particularly in its powerlessness dimension) rises sharply in the period of machine industry. The alienation curve continues upward to its highest point in the assembly-line industries of the twentieth century. In automotive production, the combination of technological, organizational, and economic factors has resulted in the simultaneous intensification of all dimensions of alienation. Thus in this extreme situation, a depersonalized worker, estranged from himself and larger collectives, goes through the motions of work in the regimented milieu of the conveyer belt for the sole purpose of earning his bread. Assuming that the industries compared in this book are to some degree prototypes of the historical epochs of manufacturing, the dominant and most persistent long-range trend is an increase in alienation and a corresponding decline in freedom.

But with automated industry there is a countertrend, one that we can fortunately expect to become even more important in the future. The case of the continuous-process industries, particularly the chemical industry, shows that automation increases the worker's control over his work process and checks the further division of labor and growth of large factories. The result is meaningful work in a more cohesive, integrated industrial climate. The alienation curve begins to decline from its previous height as employees in automated industries gain a new dignity from responsibility and a sense of individual function—thus the inverted U.[16]

---

[16] This does not imply that future developments in automation will result simply in a continuation of the major trend toward less alienation. Automated technology will take many forms besides continuous-process production, and the diversified economic conditions of future automated industries will further complicate the situation.

The four industries that have been studied in this investigation are useful in pointing to these broad historical tendencies. Since they are only four cases out of the much broader spectrum of manufacturing industries, however, their analysis does not permit conclusive generalizations as to the absolute degree of alienation existing among American factory workers today. They tend to represent the extreme developments rather than the modal situation. For most factory workers the picture is probably less black and white than for workers in the automobile and textile industries, where they tend to be highly alienated and the printing and chemical industries, where freedom and integration are so striking. Were one to hazard the alienation score sheet of the typical factory worker, the results would probably be quite mixed: a high degree of meaninglessness and self-estrangement, a low degree of powerlessness and social alienation.

Still, studying the worker from the viewpoint of the intellectual observer with his own values and conceptions of freedom and self-realization, we must conclude that alienation remains a widespread phenomenon in the factory today. But we must also approach the problem from the perspective of the worker. The distribution of alienation and freedom in the typical score card suggested above is probably fairly consonant with the values and aspirations of the blue-collar labor force today. People with limited educations are most concerned with being free from restrictive and oppressive conditions. The absence of opportunities to develop inner potential, to express idiosyncratic abilities, and to assume responsibility and decision-making functions, may not be a source of serious discontent to most workers today. For this reason, empirical studies show that the majority of industrial workers are satisfied with their work and with their jobs.

SOLUTIONS TO ALIENATION IN WORK

It is fashionable to argue that work alienation is not an important present or potential problem because work has lost its former position as "the central life-interest," particularly for manual workers.[17] It is the hope of many that the opportunities for self-expression and creativity denied by modern technology and bureaucracy can be found again in the freely chosen pursuits of leisure time. The leisure argument is supported by the technological trends that are reducing the necessary number of hours each employee must work to produce the nation's goods and services and also by the tendency for higher levels of education to increase people's awareness of the many avenues of self-expression available in learning, the arts, community affairs, and the world of hobbies and sports. The problem with the leisure solution is that it underestimates the fact that work remains the single most

[17] Robert Dubin, "Industrial Workers' Worlds: A Study of the Central Life Interest of Industrial Workers," *Social Problems*, III (1956), 131–42.

important life activity for most people, in terms of time and energy, and ignores the subtle ways in which the quality of one's worklife affects the quality of one's leisure, family relations, and basic self-feelings.[18] Finally, the very fact that alienation is distributed unevenly in the labor force means that the implicit policy of emphasizing leisure as a solution to the problems of unfree work involves a basic inequity—a division of society into one segment of consumers who are creative in their leisure time but have meaningless work and a second segment capable of self-realization in both spheres of life.

For this reason, a free society must face the present question of alienating and dehumanizing work, particularly its extreme expressions. It is curious that public policy, which has been increasingly concerned with those aspects of industrial life formerly protected by the sanctity of private enterprise, has up to now failed to examine the quality of the work of the American citizen. There is a need for the introduction of new and even radical ideas based on a knowledge of concrete situations in particular industries and the recommendations of public committees representing management, unions, and academic research.

A number of companies, most notably the International Business Machines Corporation (IBM), have attempted to counter the historic trend toward a greater division of labor by systematically enlarging the content and responsibilities of their jobs. In one IBM department, production machinists who had formerly simply operated drill presses or automatic screw machines were given the added responsibilities of sharpening their tools, setting up their machines, and inspecting their machined parts—jobs which had been previously done by specialists. This program not only "introduced interest, variety, and responsibility" and increased the importance of the product to the worker, it also improved the quality of the product and reduced costs.[19] Other companies have introduced job rotation, a policy that permits the worker to move from one subdivided job to another, adding variety to his work and expanding his knowledge of the technical organization.

Job enlargement and job rotation have been introduced on a number of automobile assembly lines with some success in reducing the oppression of the conveyer belt and the monotony of the work. But because of the intensity of alienation in its various dimensions in this work environment, such minor modifications of the work organization are not sufficient. It is with

[18] The impact of work on other areas of life is still not well understood, but considerable impressionistic evidence suggests that it is highly significant.

[19] The IBM experience is summarized by Charles R. Walker, "The Problem of the Repetitive Job," *Harvard Business Review*, XXVIII (1950), 54–58; an article which has been reprinted in Walker, *Modern Technology and Civilization* (New York: McGraw-Hill Book Co., 1962), 119–27. See also F. L. W. Richardson, Jr. and C. R. Walker, *Human Relations in an Expanding Company: A Study of the Manufacturing Departments in the Endicott Plant of the International Business Machines Corporation* (New Haven: Yale Labor and Management Center, 1948).

respect to the assembly line itself that the basic values underlying industrial organization need reassessment. The conveyer belt is the most "rational" method of building automobiles according to the value standard of efficiency only if the human factor is left out.[20] But in any genuine appraisal of this mode of production the intangible and unmeasurable costs to those involved in the work must be balanced against traditional economic costs.

Precisely because the automation of assembly operations involves such difficult technical problems, there is a need for joint research by industrial engineers and social scientists into new methods of automobile production that are advanced socially as well as technologically. A crash program of research in industrial design and job analysis is needed, oriented to the goals of worker freedom and dignity as well as the traditional criteria of profit and efficiency.[21]

The UAW, which has made no small contribution to the auto worker's dignity, deals with the problem of the assembly line by attempting to reduce in as many ways as possible the number of hours a man spends on such a line in his lifetime. Their 1960 contract demands included reduction of the age of retirement to 60, an increase in the number of holidays and in the length of vacations, and a proposal to cut the work week to thirty or thirty-five hours. The purpose of all these progressive demands was to "spread the work," even inhuman work, in an industry with economic troubles which faces greater mechanization. There is no thought of modifying the assembly line itself. As Carter Goodrich noted forty years ago, unions have been mostly concerned with the problem of maintaining the *jobs* of their members, and therefore they have been relatively unconcerned about the *kind of work*

---

[20] A most persuasive analysis of the conflict between efficiency and human values in industry is Daniel Bell's "Work and Its Discontents," in *The End of Ideology* (Glencoe, Ill.: Free Press, 1960), pp. 222–62.

[21] Most promising in this direction is the theoretical approach and research on "job design" developed by Louis Davis and his associates. In one study Davis, Canter, and Hoffman investigated the criteria by which a number of manufacturing firms assign jobs to production workers and conclude that "by adhering to the very narrow and limited criteria of minimizing immediate cost or maximizing immediate productivity, [they] design jobs based entirely on the principles of specialization, repetitiveness, low skill content and minimum impact of the worker on the production process. Management then frequently spends large sums of money and prodigious efforts on many programs that attempt to (a) counteract the effects of job designs, (b) provide satisfactions, necessarily outside the job, which the job cannot provide, and (c) build up the ego satisfaction and importance of the individual which the job has diminished." Louis E. Davis, Ralph R. Canter, and John Hoffman, "Current Job Design Criteria," *The Journal of Industrial Engineering*, VI (1955), p. 6.

In another important article, "Toward a Theory of Job Design" (The Journal of Industrial Engineering, VIII [1957], 305–9), Davis argues that higher economic productivity and lower total costs will result from specifying work content in terms of twenty-three criteria that differ considerably from those industry employs today. Davis' criteria overlap almost completely with the definitions of non-alienation for each of the dimensions of alienation analyzed in my own study. Although Davis does not utilize the alienation concept and terminology explicitly, he seems particularly impressed with the importance of the meaninglessness dimension.

their people do.[22] With the realistic fears of unemployment brought about by further technological change, it seems likely that this "blind spot" in union outlook might continue another forty years.

An enlightened public policy could also increase the southern textile worker's opportunity for freedom and dignity. In contrast to the automobile industry, the problem in textiles is based less on technological factors and more on the industry's social institutions, particularly its conservative management. The pluralistic power distribution that more and more characterizes modern industries is lacking. And the mill hands' tentative movements toward establishing organizations of independent expression and representation are consistently suppressed by the industry's antiunion policies. As the federal government increasingly intervenes to protect and extend the civil rights of Negroes in the South, there will be a greater precedent for intervention to guarantee the free operation of labor unions, an essential element in industrial citizenship. A strong labor union would not only reduce the powerlessness and improve the working conditions of textile employees; it would also be an important force toward the modernization of this traditional industry.

TOWARD A SOCIOLOGY OF INDUSTRIES

Policy recommendations aimed at reducing the manual worker's experience of alienation must take into account the specific conditions in an industrial environment and not assume that the situation of the employee is the same from one factory to the next. Here industrial sociology can be useful if it provides a theoretical perspective and methodology that is sensitive to the diversity of industrial work situations. On the whole, this discipline has lacked a systematic, comparative approach to the study of variations within modern industry. It has operated, by and large, with an undifferentiated global image of industrial life. The theoretical focus is usually on a "typical" individual firm or economic organization or on "industry in general," the whole complex of more or less mechanized production systems.

The present study of alienation in the factory has emphasized the importance of individual industries and groups of similar industries, as units of economic and social organization. As a beginning attempt it has been limited in a number of ways, investigating only four cases among the much larger universe of factory industries and neglecting completely blue-collar non-factory industries, white-collar work, and employment in the service industries—work settings which have been growing in numbers and importance. Further, the industries chosen probably represent the extremes of technical and social conditions and levels of alienation, a fact which has

[22] Carter Goodrich, *The Miners' Freedom* (Boston: Marshall Jones Co., 1925).

facilitated the location of theoretical relationships but does not enable us to draw conclusions about particular industries not covered in this study or about industry in general. What is needed now is a more complete and comprehensive treatment of the entire range of industrial work milieux.

A systematic, self-conscious sensitivity to the diversity of industrial environments would make it possible to arrive at a more complete, balanced, and empirically based knowledge of the conditions of work in American society today, since the absence of this perspective permits the frequent generalization from case studies of sociotechnical systems (such as the automobile assembly line) which are highly unrepresentative of the total panorama of work situations. The "sociology of industries," as a subfield, could also advance the development of theory in industrial sociology as a whole, since comparative industrial analysis provides a method by which variations in the social institutions of work and personal experiences of employees can be linked to variations in technology, economic conditions, and social organization.[23]

Finally, I have also attempted to demonstrate the usefulness of the alienation perspective in clarifying our understanding of the complexities of the modern social world. This idea, developed by Marx in his early writings, can be expressed in systematic concepts and propositions that raise important analytical, as well as sociopolitical, questions. I hope to have shown that these questions can be partially answered through empirical research (especially of a comparative nature) without eliminating the humane value orientation that has informed the historic usage of this body of thought, for the moral power inherent in the alienation tradition has been its view of man as potentiality. A social scientist must emphasize a sober, non-romantic understanding of man as he is, in terms of present levels of aspirations and achievements. But we cannot assume that men are only what they are at present or what they themselves desire to become. There is a need to fuse an empirical, realistic approach with the valuable humanistic tradition of alienation theory that views all human beings as potentially capable of exercising freedom and control, achieving meaning, integration, social connection, and self-realization. There is always a strain between empirical tough-mindedness and human relevance in social research, and in such areas as the study of alienation in work it is especially essential that this conflict be overcome.

[23] One must guard against the weaknesses of this approach as well as stress its advantages. Just as industrial sociology fosters an undifferentiated view of industry in general and tends to ignore differences among industries, the "sociology of industries" exaggerates the unity of an individual industry and necessarily underplays the important variations within that industry, as well as its similarities to other industries. Our understanding of the conditions and causes of alienation in manual work would also be furthered by an intensive investigation which focused on the variations in worker freedoms and job attitudes among the firms within any one of the four industries I have considered.

APPENDIXES

A. TABLES OF COMPARATIVE INDUSTRIAL STATISTICS

TABLE 18

CAPITAL INVESTMENT PER PRODUCTION WORKER,
MANUFACTURING INDUSTRIES, 1956*

INDUSTRY	INVESTMENT PER WORKER
Oil refining	$110,000
Tobacco	32,600
CHEMICALS	28,600
AUTOMOBILES	18,900
Primary metals (iron and steel)	16,800
Food	16,200
Paper	15,800
Rubber	15,500
Instruments	14,300
Machinery	14,200
Stone, clay, and glass	12,500
Transportation equipment	11,700
Miscellaneous manufacturing	11,500
Electrical	11,400
PRINTING	11,000
Fabricated metals	9,700
TEXTILES	8,800
Lumber and wood products	8,000
Furniture	6,500
Leather	4,400
Apparel	3,600
All manufacturing industries	$15,000

* Source: National Industrial Conference Board, *Economic Almanac, 1960* (New York: National Industrial Conference Board, 1960), p. 216.

TABLE 19

VALUE ADDED BY MANUFACTURING PER PRODUCTION WORKER,
BY INDUSTRY, 1954*

INDUSTRY	VALUE ADDED PER WORKER
CHEMICALS	$12,772
Oil refining	11,965
Tobacco	10,415
Furniture	8,541
Primary metals	8,390
AUTOMOBILES (includes other transportation equipment)	8,169
Food	8,135
Machinery	8,003
Instruments	7,809
PRINTING	7,787
Stone, clay, and glass	7,770
Rubber	7,722
Electrical	7,718
Fabricated metals	7,451
Miscellaneous manufacturing	6,427
Paper	5,771
Lumber	4,936
Leather	4,592
TEXTILES	4,577
Apparel	4,325
All manufacturing industries	$7,490

* Source: Alfred Leroy Edwards, "An Analysis of Industrial and Geographic Variations in Value Added by Manufacture per Employee" (Ph.D. dissertation, State University of Iowa, 1958), p. 24.

TABLE 20

PROPORTION MAINTENANCE AND REPAIR EXPENDITURES OF ALL PAYROLL
EXPENDITURES FOR MANUFACTURING INDUSTRIES, 1958*
(In Millions of Dollars)

INDUSTRY	TOTAL PAYROLL	MAINTENANCE PAYROLL	PER CENT ON MAINTENANCE
Oil refining and coal	$ 1,150	$ 501	44
Primary metals	7,019	2,000	28
CHEMICALS	4,096	909	22
Pulp and paper	2,734	514	19
Instruments	571	97	17
Stone, clay, and glass	2,354	391	17
Lumber	2,110	292	14
Food	7,143	777	11
Rubber	1,310	149	11
TEXTILES	3,183	354	11
Tobacco	284	24	9
Transportation equipment (includes AUTOMOBILES)	10,486	986	9
Fabricated metals	7,019	450	8
Electrical	5,133	360	7
Machinery	9,050	624	7
Furniture	1,432	69	5
Leather	1,157	55	5
PRINTING	4,301	172	4
Apparel	3,664	98	3
All manufacturing industries	$76,379	$9,011	12

* Source: U.S. Department of Commerce, *Statistical Abstracts of the United States, 1961* (Washington: U.S. Government Printing Office, 1961), p. 788.

TABLE 21

INDEXES OF ECONOMIC CONCENTRATION FOR
MANUFACTURING INDUSTRIES, 1954*

INDUSTRY	CONCENTRATION RATIO
Tobacco.	100.0
Oil refining.	99.1
AUTOMOBILES.	96.3
Transportation equipment.	83.2
Iron and steel.	81.1
Electrical.	72.2
Instruments.	69.9
CHEMICALS.	59.4
Stone, clay, and glass.	57.9
Rubber.	51.2
Machinery.	31.1
Food.	22.4
Fabricated metals.	19.3
TEXTILES.	11.9
Furniture.	7.3
Apparel.	5.7
Paper.	5.0
Leather.	2.3
PRINTING	2.3
Lumber and wood.	1.5

* Source: U.S. Congress, Joint Economic Committee, *Post-war Movement of Prices and Wages in Manufacturing Industries*, by Harold M. Levinson, (Study Paper No. 21) [Washington: U.S. Government Printing Office, 1960], p. 7. How the concentration ratios were computed: "The total values of product shipments in each 4-digit industry (within the given 2-digit classification) showing a 50 per cent or more concentration ratio for the 8 largest companies constituted the numerator. The denominator represented the total value of product shipments for the entire industry. The resulting concentration ratios, therefore reflect the proportion of the total value of product shipments in each 2-digit group represented by 'concentrated' 4 digit industries (those in which the 8 largest firms accounted for 50 per cent or more of the total value of product shipments in 1954) in that group" (*Ibid.*).

TABLE 22

AVERAGE NUMBER OF EMPLOYEES PER ESTABLISHMENT,
BY INDUSTRY, 1955*

INDUSTRY	NUMBER OF WORKERS
AUTOMOBILES (includes other transportation equipment industries).	334
Iron and steel.	218
Rubber.	191
Electrical.	177
Tobacco.	171
Petroleum and coal products.	142
TEXTILES.	134
Paper.	112
Instruments.	87
Leather.	78
CHEMICALS.	69
Machinery.	64
Fabricated metals.	48
Stone, clay and glass.	48
Apparel.	40
Miscellaneous manufacturing.	40
Food.	40
Furniture.	36
PRINTING.	25
Lumber and wood.	18

* Source: Computed from U.S. Department of Commerce, *Statistical Abstracts, 1959*, pp. 794–95.

TABLE 23

PROPORTION OF FACTORY WORKERS EMPLOYED IN SMALL, MIDDLE-SIZED, AND LARGE PLANTS, BY INDUSTRY*

INDUSTRY	PER CENT OF TOTAL LABOR FORCE EMPLOYED IN PLANTS OF VARIOUS SIZES					
	1–99 Employees	100–249 Employees	250–499 Employees	500–999 Employees	1,000 plus Employees	Total: Per Cent
Large-plant Industries						
Transportation equipment (includes AUTOMOBILES)	3.9	3.7	4.4	6.3	82.0	100.3
Primary metals..........	8.9	7.8	11.3	12.2	59.7	99.9
Rubber.................	9.4	7.5	9.1	14.3	59.6	99.9
Electrical..............	10.6	9.3	12.2	15.4	52.4	99.9
Petroleum and coal.......	10.9	12.0	13.1	11.5	52.5	100.0
Instruments............	13.8	9.9	11.3	13.1	51.9	100.0
Medium-sized-plant Industries						
TEXTILES...............	14.7	17.7	21.3	21.4	24.7	99.8
Paper..................	18.2	23.7	21.5	17.5	19.1	100.0
Machinery..............	21.7	12.0	11.7	14.6	39.9	99.9
Leather................	22.4	23.5	33.9	15.8	n.a.†	94.6‡
CHEMICALS.............	23.2	13.0	11.8	12.2	39.9	100.1
Stone, clay, and glass.....	29.3	19.6	18.5	12.4	20.2	100.0
Small-plant Industries						
Fabricated metals........	32.7	17.9	16.0	15.2	18.1	99.9
Miscellaneous manufacturing.........	37.2	16.1	11.6	11.9	23.2	100.0
Food...................	38.9	22.7	14.6	10.1	13.7	100.0
Furniture...............	42.3	21.6	16.1	10.6	n.a.†	90.6‡
PRINTING...............	42.3	17.0	11.3	8.9	20.6	100.1
Apparel................	47.9	24.6	15.7	7.8	n.a.†	96.0‡
Lumber and wood........	61.5	18.8	10.8	6.3	n.a.†	97.4‡
All manufacturing industries..............	25.6	15.2	13.5	12.1	33.6	100.0

* Source: U.S. Department of Commerce, *Statistical Abstracts, 1959*, p. 794.
† Data not available.
‡ Total per cent is considerably less than 100 because the number of employees in the largest plants is not available.

TABLE 24

NUMBER OF EMPLOYEES AND PRODUCTION WORKERS, BY INDUSTRY, 1960*

INDUSTRY	NUMBER OF EMPLOYEES	NUMBER OF PRODUCTION WORKERS
Machinery	1,637,000	1,137,000
Food	1,473,000	1,022,000
Electrical	1,305,000	865,000
Apparel	1,216,000	1,086,000
Primary metals	1,186,000	957,000
Fabricated metals	1,079,000	834,000
TEXTILES	946,000	852,000
PRINTING	894,000	573,000
CHEMICALS	875,000	539,000
Transportation equipment	861,000	547,000
AUTOMOBILES	781,000	613,000
Lumber and wood	644,000	577,000
Paper	562,000	448,000
Stone, clay, and glass	550,000	444,000
Miscellaneous manufacturing	501,000	398,000
Furniture	389,000	324,000
Leather	365,000	322,000
Instruments	350,000	226,000
Rubber	259,000	199,000
Petroleum and coal	182,000	116,000
Tobacco	88,000	78,000
All manufacturing industries	16,337,000	12,265,000

* Source: U.S. Department of Commerce, *Statistical Abstracts, 1961*, pp. 208–10.

TABLE 25

PROPORTION FEMALE OF ALL EMPLOYEES, BY INDUSTRY, 1960*

INDUSTRY	PER CENT
Apparel	80
Leather	51
Tobacco	49
TEXTILES	43
Miscellaneous manufacturing	40
Electrical	38
Instruments	33
PRINTING	28
Food	27
Rubber	25
Paper	21
Ordnance	19
CHEMICALS	18
Fabricated metals	17
Furniture	16
Stone, clay, and glass	16
Machinery	14
AUTOMOBILES (includes other transportation equipment)	11
Petroleum and coal products	7
Lumber and wood	7
Iron and steel	6
All manufacturing industries	27

* Source: U.S. Department of Commerce, *Statistical Abstracts, 1961*, p. 213.

TABLE 26

SKILL DISTRIBUTION OF BLUE-COLLAR WORKERS, BY INDUSTRY, 1950*

INDUSTRY	PER CENT			NUMBER OF WORKERS
	SKILLED CRAFTSMEN AND FOREMEN	SEMISKILLED OPERATIVES	UNSKILLED LABORERS	
Industries with High Skill Distributions				
PRINTING......................	70	26	3	394,000
Transportation equipment........	57	37	6	331,000
Machinery.....................	44	50	6	884,000
Industries with Balanced Skill Distributions				
Oil refining....................	38	46	16	146,000
Iron and steel..................	37	38	25	781,000
Non-ferrous metals..............	34	53	13	240,000
Instruments....................	34	62	4	125,000
Fabricated steel.................	31	59	10	520,000
CHEMICALS.....................	30	52	18	340,000
Furniture......................	30	62	8	258,000
Industries with Low Skill Distributions				
AUTOMOBILES...................	29	64	7	675,000
Electrical......................	25	64	10	560,000
Miscellaneous manufacturing.....	23	73	4	320,000
Food..........................	21	64	15	956,000
Stone, clay, and glass...........	20	58	22	351,000
Rubber........................	20	76	4	163,000
Paper.........................	19	68	13	356,000
Industries with Very Low Skill Distributions				
TEXTILES.......................	12	82	6	1,061,000
Tobacco.......................	10	80	10	78,000
Leather........................	8	88	4	319,000
Apparel.......................	7	92	1	923,000
Sawmills and planing...........	7	15	78	149,000
All manufacturing industries......	26	62	12	10,572,000

* Source: Calculated from U.S. Department of Commerce, Bureau of the Census, *Industrial Characteristics*, (Special Report P-E No. 1D, [Washington: U.S. Government Printing Office, 1955], pp. 38–40).

TABLE 27

PROPORTION OF MALE WAGE AND SALARY WORKERS
WHO WORKED FIFTY WEEKS OR MORE IN 1949,
BY INDUSTRY*

INDUSTRY	PER CENT
Oil refining	87.6
CHEMICALS	79.2
PRINTING	77.8
Professional equipment	77.8
Paper	75.6
Electrical	75.5
Food	74.2
Tobacco	74.0
Rubber	73.5
Machinery	72.3
Stone, clay, and glass	68.6
Fabricated metals	68.5
TEXTILES	68.1
Miscellaneous manufacturing	67.9
Transportation equipment	67.7
Furniture	63.3
Leather	62.1
AUTOMOBILES	57.4
Apparel	56.4
Iron and steel	50.2
Lumber and wood	49.0
All manufacturing industries	67.1

* Source: U.S. Department of Commerce, Bureau of the Census, *Industrial Characteristics*, pp. 57–58.

TABLE 28

AVERAGE NUMBER OF WORKERS LAID OFF EACH MONTH FOR LACK OF WORK
PER HUNDRED EMPLOYEES, BY INDUSTRY, 1958–1961*

INDUSTRY	YEARLY AVERAGES				AVERAGE: 1958–61
	1958	1959	1960	1961	
Transportation equipment (includes AUTOMOBILES)	3.8	3.6	3.6	3.5	3.6
Food	2.5	2.4	3.6	3.7	3.1
Fabricated metals	3.1	2.7	3.1	2.9	3.0
Miscellaneous manufacturing	3.1	2.3	3.2	3.2	3.0
Tobacco	0.9	0.5	4.5	4.6	2.6
Lumber and wood	2.1	1.7	3.1	2.4	2.4
Apparel	1.8	0.9	3.2	3.1	2.3
Stone, clay, and glass	2.5	1.4	2.4	2.2	2.1
Primary metals	2.6	1.0	3.0	1.7	2.1
Furniture	2.2	1.4	2.1	2.1	2.0
Leather	1.8	1.2	2.1	2.3	1.9
Machinery	2.4	1.2	1.9	1.7	1.8
Rubber	1.8	1.1	2.2	1.7	1.7
TEXTILES	1.8	1.2	1.5	1.3	1.5
Electrical	1.8	0.9	1.6	1.4	1.4
Paper	1.3	0.9	1.2	1.1	1.1
Ordnance	1.8	0.7	0.9	0.7	1.0
Instruments	1.3	0.6	1.0	0.9	1.0
PRINTING	n.a.†	n.a.†	0.8	1.0	0.9‡
CHEMICALS	1.0	0.5	0.9	0.9	0.8
Oil refining	0.6	0.4	0.6	0.6	0.6
All manufacturing industries	2.3	1.6	2.4	2.2	2.1

* Source: "Current Labor Statistics," *Monthly Labor Review*, LXXXIV (1961), 678 and LXXXV (1962), 709.
† No data available.
‡ Average based on two years only.

TABLE 29

UNEMPLOYMENT RATES, BY INDUSTRY, 1958–1961*

INDUSTRY	YEARLY AVERAGES				AVERAGE, 1958–61
	1958	1959	1960	1961	
AUTOMOBILES	21.3	10.1	8.4	13.9	13.4
Apparel	12.0	9.6	10.5	11.4	10.9
Lumber and wood	11.6	8.7	9.1	11.1	9.9
Primary metals	11.4	5.3	7.8	10.9	8.9
Furniture	9.3	6.9	6.9	9.2	8.1
TEXTILES	9.5	7.2	6.3	6.8	7.2
Fabricated metals	9.1	6.5	6.1	6.7	7.1
Stone, clay, and glass	8.7	5.3	6.0	8.1	7.0
Food	8.1	6.7	6.4	7.7	6.8
Transportation equipment	7.2	4.8	5.8	6.8	6.2
Machinery	9.0	4.3	4.7	6.4	6.1
Electrical	8.7	5.4	5.0	6.9	6.0
CHEMICALS	5.1	3.6	3.3	3.3	3.8
PRINTING	4.0	3.2	3.6	3.9	3.7
All manufacturing industries	9.2	6.0	6.2	7.7	7.3

* Source: "1961 Statistical Supplement," *Monthly Labor Review* (Washington: U.S. Government Printing Office, 1961), p. 3. "The base for the unemployed rate includes the employed classified according to their current job, and the unemployed, classified according to their latest civilian job, if any. It excludes the unemployed persons who never held a full-time civilian job" (*Ibid.*).

TABLE 30

AVERAGE NUMBER OF WORKERS QUITTING JOBS VOLUNTARILY EACH MONTH PER HUNDRED EMPLOYEES, BY INDUSTRY, 1958–1961*

INDUSTRY	YEARLY AVERAGES				AVERAGE, 1958–61
	1958	1959	1960	1961	
Apparel	1.7	2.5	2.3	2.0	2.1
Lumber	1.7	2.3	2.3	1.9	2.1
Leather	1.5	2.1	2.2	2.1	2.0
Miscellaneous manufacturing	1.2	1.8	1.9	1.8	1.7
TEXTILES	1.2	1.6	1.6	1.6	1.5
Furniture	1.1	1.7	1.7	1.5	1.5
PRINTING	n.a.†	n.a.†	1.5	1.4	1.5‡
Food	0.9	1.2	1.7	1.6	1.4
Electrical	0.9	1.3	1.2	1.1	1.1
Ordnance	0.8	1.1	1.0	1.4	1.1
Paper	0.8	1.2	1.2	1.0	1.1
Tobacco	0.9	1.1	1.0	0.9	1.0
Instruments	0.7	1.0	1.1	1.0	1.0
Fabricated metals	0.8	1.1	1.1	1.0	1.0
Rubber	0.6	0.9	1.1	1.1	0.9
Transportation equipment (includes AUTOMOBILES)	0.8	1.0	0.9	0.8	0.9
Stone, clay, and glass	0.7	0.9	1.1	1.0	0.9
Machinery	0.6	0.9	0.9	0.8	0.8
CHEMICALS	0.5	0.7	0.8	0.7	0.7
Primary metals	0.4	0.7	0.6	0.5	0.6
Oil refining	0.3	0.4	0.5	0.5	0.4
All manufacturing industries	0.9	1.3	1.3	1.2	1.2

* Source: *Monthly Labor Review*, "Current Labor Statistics," LXXXIV, 677 and LXXXV, 708.
† No data available.
‡ Average based on two years only.

B. TABLES OF WORKERS' JOB ATTITUDES, BY INDUSTRY

(From Roper-Fortune Survey of Factory Workers)

TABLE 31

PROPORTION OF FACTORY WORKERS WHO FEEL JOBS ARE STEADY, BY INDUSTRY*

INDUSTRY	PER CENT			NUMBER OF RESPONDENTS
	Can Have Job	Might Lose It	Don't Know	
CHEMICALS................	94	2	4	78
Oil refining................	92	4	4	51
PRINTING..................	92	1	8	116
Paper.....................	91	1	8	105
Apparel...................	89	3	8	270
Non-ferrous metals..........	88	3	9	89
Food......................	85	7	8	296
TEXTILES..................	84	4	12	410
Furniture.................	83	7	10	259
Stone, clay, and glass........	83	8	9	109
Sawmills and planing........	77	11.5	11.5	68
Iron and steel..............	76	14	10	409
Machinery.................	75	14	11	295
Leather...................	74	9	17	129
AUTOMOBILES..............	73	21	6	180
Transportation equipment....	68	19	13	94
All factory workers........	81	9	10	2,957

* Question: "Do you think you can have your present job as long as you want it, except for temporary layoffs— or do you think there is a good chance that the job won't last as long as you want it to?"

TABLE 32

PROPORTION OF FACTORY WORKERS EXPECTING A LAYOFF, BY INDUSTRY*

INDUSTRY	PER CENT			NUMBER OF RESPONDENTS
	Yes	No	Don't Know	
AUTOMOBILES..............	29	60	11	180
Transportation equipment....	24	65	11	93
Stone, clay, and glass........	18	66	16	108
Iron and steel..............	18	66	16	410
Apparel...................	15	69	16	271
Furniture.................	14	70	16	259
TEXTILES..................	14	73	13	409
Food......................	13	69	18	297
Non-ferrous metals..........	12	74	14	89
Machinery.................	10	68	22	294
Leather...................	9	82	9	129
Sawmills and planing........	8	74	18	68
Paper.....................	3	79	18	106
PRINTING..................	3	90	7	114
Oil refining................	2	90	8	51
CHEMICALS................	2	90	8	78
All factory workers........	14	71	15	2,956

* Question: "Do you think you are likely to be laid off temporarily at any time during the next six months?"

TABLE 33

PROPORTION OF FACTORY WORKERS WHO FEEL JOBS MAKE THEM
WORK TOO FAST, BY INDUSTRY*

INDUSTRY	PER CENT	NUMBER OF RESPONDENTS†
AUTOMOBILES	33	177
TEXTILES	32	399
Apparel	31	256
Sawmills and planing	27	68
Leather	25	127
Food	24	295
Furniture	23	258
Iron and steel	23	405
Machinery	23	290
Paper	19	103
Non-ferrous metals	17	89
Stone, clay, and glass	15	109
CHEMICALS	12	76
Transportation equipment	11	93
PRINTING	10	111
Oil refining	6	51
All factory workers	24	2,907

* Question: "Does [your job] make you work too fast most of the time or not?"
† Note: The don't know responses have been eliminated, since they were an insignificant proportion of all responses.

TABLE 34

PROPORTION OF FACTORY WORKERS WHOSE JOBS MAKE THEM
TOO TIRED, BY INDUSTRY*

INDUSTRY	PER CENT	NUMBER OF RESPONDENTS†
TEXTILES	38	387
Apparel	38	269
Iron and steel	34	399
AUTOMOBILES	34	178
Non-ferrous metals	33	88
Paper	31	98
Machinery	30	290
Food	29	290
Furniture	29	256
Stone, clay, and glass	26	106
Leather	24	128
Sawmills and planing	24	67
Transportation equipment	20	93
CHEMICALS	19	77
Oil refining	14	52
PRINTING	12	113
All factory workers	30	2,891

* Question: "Does [your job] leave you too tired at the end of the day, or not?"
† See note to Table 33.

TABLE 35

PROPORTION OF FACTORY WORKERS WHO FEEL THEY CAN TRY OUT OWN IDEAS ON JOB, BY INDUSTRY*

INDUSTRY	PER CENT	NUMBER OF RESPONDENTS†
PRINTING	79	112
CHEMICALS	64	75
Transportation equipment	63	90
Oil refining	59	49
Furniture	59	255
Non-ferrous metals	57	89
Paper	56	96
Sawmills and planing	54	·68
Food	48	292
Apparel	47	265
AUTOMOBILES	47	177
Machinery	45	290
Iron and steel	43	402
Stone, clay, and glass	39	109
TEXTILES	38	398
Leather	32	127
All factory workers	49	2,896

* Question: "Does [your job] really give you a chance to try out ideas of your own, or not?"
† See note to Table 33.

TABLE 36

PROPORTION OF FACTORY WORKERS FREE TO LEAVE WORK FOR THIRTY MINUTES, BY INDUSTRY*

INDUSTRY	PER CENT	NUMBER OF RESPONDENTS†
Stone, clay, and glass	91	107
Leather	86	128
PRINTING	81	106
Furniture	81	259
Non-ferrous metals	81	00
Transportation equipment	80	93
Apparel	73	263
Machinery	73	291
Oil refining	68	50
Iron and steel	63	404
AUTOMOBILES	60	176
CHEMICALS	58	77
Paper	57	100
Sawmills and planing	55	66
TEXTILES	49	406
Food	47	289
All factory workers	66	2,903

* Question: "Is yours the kind of job on which someone would have to take your place if you had to leave your work for a half an hour or so, or could you let your work go for a half an hour and catch up on it later?"
† See note to Table 33.

TABLE 37

PROPORTION OF FACTORY WORKERS DESIRING DIFFERENT OCCUPATIONS, BY INDUSTRY*

INDUSTRY	PER CENT			NUMBER OF RESPONDENTS
	Yes	No	Don't Know and Depends	
Leather.....................	71	20	9	129
Sawmills and planing........	71	24	6	68
Oil refining.................	71	27	2	51
AUTOMOBILES...............	69	23	8	180
Iron and steel...............	65	25	10	407
Machinery..................	65	29	6	293
Furniture...................	64	29	7	259
Apparel....................	63	35	2	265
CHEMICALS.................	58	29	13	78
Non-ferrous metals..........	55	36	9	88
TEXTILES...................	54	37	9	409
Food......................	51	34	15	296
Stone, clay, and glass.......	48	25	27	108
Transportation equipment....	48	48	3	93
Paper.....................	37	49	14	102
PRINTING..................	36	50	13	107
All factory workers........	59	32	9	2,933

* Question: "If you could go back to the age of 15 and start life over again, would you choose a different trade or occupation?"

TABLE 38

PROPORTION OF FACTORY WORKERS SATISFIED WITH COMPANY, BY INDUSTRY*

INDUSTRY	PER CENT			NUMBER OF RESPONDENTS
	Own Company as Good	Other Places Are Better	Don't Know	
CHEMICALS.................	92	8	0	78
TEXTILES...................	84	10	6	413
Transportation equipment....	82	14	4	94
Machinery..................	79	17	4	296
PRINTING..................	78	14	8	118
Food......................	76	14	10	299
Oil refining.................	75	23	2	52
Sawmills and planing........	74	19	7	68
Apparel....................	74	16	10	273
Paper.....................	71	16	13	106
Furniture...................	69	23	8	262
Leather....................	66	17	17	132
Stone, clay, and glass.......	65	11	24	109
Iron and steel...............	63	21	16	410
AUTOMOBILES...............	62	25	13	180
Non-ferrous metals..........	57	28	15	90
All factory workers........	73	17	10	2,980

* Question: "For a person in your trade or occupation, do you think your company is about as good a place as there is to work, or do you think there are other places that are better?"

TABLE 39

PROPORTION OF FACTORY WORKERS WHO FEEL JOBS
ARE ESSENTIAL, BY INDUSTRY*

INDUSTRY	PER CENT	NUMBER OF RESPONDENTS
Sawmills and planing.............	96	65
TEXTILES........................	95	390
Oil refining.....................	94	49
AUTOMOBILES....................	94	179
CHEMICALS......................	93	78
Machinery.......................	93	297
Paper...........................	92	105
Furniture........................	90	260
Non-ferrous metals...............	90	90
Iron and steel....................	90	410
Apparel.........................	89.5	273
Transportation equipment..........	85	93
PRINTING.......................	84	115
Leather.........................	82	130
Food...........................	80	297
Stone, clay, and glass.............	71.5	109
All factory workers.............	89	2,965

* Question: "Is your job really essential to the success of the company, or not?"

TABLE 40

LENGTH OF SERVICE, BY INDUSTRY*

INDUSTRY	PER CENT			NUMBER OF RESPONDENTS
	5 Years and Over	One to 5 Years	Less than One Year	
Paper.....................	61	32	7	103
Iron and steel..............	60	26	14	407
Machinery.................	54	31	15	292
AUTOMOBILES..............	52	21	27	180
TEXTILES..................	50	31	19	409
Transportation equipment....	49	32	18	93
Non-ferrous metals.........	48	36	16	88
Stone, clay, and glass.......	47	38	15	108
Oil refining................	47	35	18	51
Apparel...................	45	35	20	266
Food......................	40	39	21	295
Sawmills and planing........	40	25	35	68
Leather...................	39	38	23	129
CHEMICALS................	38	50	12	78
Furniture..................	35	36	29	259
PRINTING..................	35	50	15	107
All factory workers........	48	33	19	2,933

* Question: "How long have you been working for your present employer?"

TABLE 41

PROPORTION OF FACTORY WORKERS WHO CAN THINK
OF OTHER THINGS WHILE WORKING, BY INDUSTRY*

INDUSTRY	PER CENT	NUMBER OF RESPONDENTS†
Apparel	54	266
TEXTILE	54	398
Oil refining	52	52
Furniture	48	256
Non-ferrous metals	46	90
Food	45	286
Sawmills and planing	40	67
Machinery	40	283
Iron and steel	37	408
AUTOMOBILES	37	178
CHEMICALS	36	77
Leather	35	124
Stone, clay, and glass	35	107
Transportation equipment	33	93
Paper	31	99
PRINTING	27	116
All factory workers	43	2,900

* Question: "Can you do the work on the job and keep your mind on other things most of the time, or not?"
† See note to Table 33.

TABLE 42

FACTORY WORKERS' RATING OF JOBS AS INTERESTING OR MONOTONOUS, BY INDUSTRY*
(Ranked by Proportions Who Find Job Mostly or Always Dull)

INDUSTRY	PER CENT					NUMBER OF RESPONDENTS†
	Nearly Always Interesting	Mostly Interesting	Mostly Dull	Always Dull	Mostly and Always Dull	
Stone, clay, and glass	24	38	25	14	39	109
AUTOMOBILES	33	33	16	18	34	174
Food	43	32	18	6	24	294
Transportation equipment	50	27	19	4	23	93
Iron and steel	39	38	16	7	23	402
Sawmills and planing	34	46	9	12	21	68
Machinery	46	33	14	7	21	289
Oil refining	45	35	16	4	20	51
Apparel	49	33	14	5	19	270
TEXTILES	45	37	10	8	18	406
Leather	44	38	16	2	18	129
Furniture	53	31	12	3	15	257
Non-ferrous metals	45	43	10	2	12	89
Paper	52	37	9	2	11	100
CHEMICALS	52	38	8	3	11	77
PRINTING	58	37	4	0	4	115
All factory workers	44	35	14	6	20	2,923

* Question: "Which one of these statements comes closest to describing how you feel about your present job: (a) My job is *interesting nearly all the time*. (b) While my job is *interesting most of the time*; there are some dull stretches now and then. (c) There are a few times when my job is interesting but most of it is *pretty dull and monotonous*. (d) My job is *completely dull and monotonous*; there is nothing interesting about it."
† See note to Table 33.

TABLE 43

PROPORTION OF FACTORY WORKERS WHO FEEL
JOBS ARE TOO SIMPLE, BY INDUSTRY*

INDUSTRY	PER CENT			NUMBER OF RESPONDENTS
	Yes	No	Don't Know	
Sawmills and planing........	38	56	6	68
Stone, clay, and glass........	38	50	13	109
AUTOMOBILES...............	35	58	7	180
Oil refining................	35	62	4	52
Iron and steel..............	29	62	9	406
Apparel....................	26	64	10	272
Food......................	24	59	16	298
Leather....................	24	72	4	130
TEXTILES...................	23	67	10	397
Machinery..................	23	65	12	295
Furniture..................	23	67	10	260
Non-ferrous metals.........	22	76	2	90
CHEMICALS.................	21	69	10	78
Transportation equipment....	20	72	8	95
PRINTING..................	16	77	7	118
Paper.....................	9	72	19	106
All factory workers........	25	65	10	2,954

* Question: "Is [your job] too simple to bring out your best abilities, or not?"

TABLE 44

EDUCATION COMPLETED, ROPER FACTORY WORKERS, BY INDUSTRY
(Ranked by Proportions with Some High School and College)

INDUSTRY	PER CENT				NUMBER OF RESPONDENTS
	No Schooling	Grade School	High School	College	
Non-ferrous metals............	0	21	73	6	90
PRINTING....................	0	25	70	6	102
Paper.......................	0	37	58	6	106
Oil refining.................	0	42	50	8	52
Leather.....................	0	43	51	5	120
Food.......................	3	44	51	3	296
Machinery...................	0	46	48	6	296
Transportation equipment......	0	48	50	2	94
Apparel.....................	3	45	49	3	272
Iron and steel...............	2	47	47	3	412
Sawmills and planing..........	1	51	43	4	68
CHEMICALS..................	0	54	40	6	78
AUTOMOBILES................	2	53	40	6	179
Furniture...................	3	54	42	2	262
Stone, clay, and glass..........	10	51	37	1	109
TEXTILES...................	2	67	29	1	410
All factory workers..........	2	48	46	4	2,955

TABLE 45

Proportion of Factory Workers Who Feel Jobs Lead to Promotions, by Industry*

INDUSTRY	Per Cent			Number of Respondents
	Yes	No	Don't Know	
Chemicals..................	79	12	9	78
Oil refining..................	63	31	6	52
Furniture....................	59	32	8	260
Transportation equipment....	57	33	10	93
Paper.......................	55	30	15	106
Sawmills and planing........	54	38	7	68
Non-ferrous metals..........	52	46	2	90
Food.......................	51	32	18	297
Machinery..................	49	44	7	297
Printing....................	48	32	20	112
Iron and steel..............	46	45	10	409
Apparel....................	43	50	7	272
Textiles....................	40	52	8	410
Automobiles................	39	53	8	180
Stone, clay, and glass.......	34	50	17	109
Leather....................	28	53	18	130
All factory workers.......	47	42	10	2,963

* Question: "Does [your job] lead to a promotion if you do it well, or not?"

TABLE 46

Factors Chosen by Workers as Most Important in Advancement in Their Factory*

INDUSTRY	Per Cent							Number of Respondents
	Quality	Energy and Willingness	Seniority	Bosses	Politician	Friend of Boss	All Cynical Answers	
Iron and steel........	47	35	34	28	10	18	56†	407
Automobiles........	51	44	25	23	8	19	50	180
Transportation equipment........	63	51	24	28	13	7	48	92
Furniture...........	61	56	17	28	6	12	46	259
Stone, clay, and glass	51	45	16	28	2	16	46	108
Oil refining.........	41	55	49	29	2	12	43	51
Leather.............	60	57	25	25	9	6	40	129
Food...............	52	55	29	27	5	8	40	294
Machinery..........	57	49	28	21	6	12	39	294
Non-ferrous metals...	67	49	20	26	1	11	38	89
Sawmills and planing	59	31	12	19	3	9	31	68
Textiles............	59	57	28	19	4	8	31	409
Printing............	64	48	23	22	3	5	30	109
Paper..............	67	51	29	21	1	4	26	102
Apparel............	59	56	15	11	6	8	25	271
Chemicals..........	54	69	28	18	1	5	24	78
All factory workers	56	50	25	23	5	11	39	2,940

* Question: "Which one or two things do you believe gives a person the best chance to advance in the plant where you work? (a) the *quality* of his work; (b) his *energy* and *willingness* to work; (c) how long he has been with the company [*seniority*]; (d) how well he gets on personally with his immediate *bosses*; (e) how good a *politician* he is; or (f) whether he is a friend or relative of a high official or foreman [*friend of boss*]." Industries ranked by proportion of total "cynical responses," answers d, e, and f combined.
† Note: Percentages add to more than 100 per cent because most respondents gave several answers.

TABLE 47

PROPORTION OF MALE FACTORY WORKERS WHO FIND JOBS DULL OR MONOTONOUS
ALL OR MOST OF THE TIME, BY INDUSTRY AND SKILL*

INDUSTRY	UNSKILLED		LOW SKILLED		MEDIUM SKILLED		SKILLED	
	Per Cent	Number	Per Cent	Number	Per Cent	Number	Per Cent	Number
AUTOMOBILES.................	61	69†	27	22	16	37	6	31
Sawmills and planing..........	50	22	17‡	6	4	24	7	14
Stone, clay, and glass..........	43	30	63‡	8	46	28	21	28
Machinery....................	43	65	23	29	17	69	6	71
Transportation equipment......	43	21	40‡	5	18	22	14	42
Food........................	41	88	19	31	20	56	4	53
Leather.....................	38	26	33‡	6	4	25	7	14
Iron and steel................	36	113	35	54	20	114	3	93
Paper.......................	33‡	6	25‡	8	19	21	4	26
Furniture....................	30	44	11	27	19	69	6	89
Oil refining..................	30	10	11‡	9	33	15	7	14
TEXTILES....................	27	70	16	37	19	64	3	76
PRINTING...................	25‡	4	0‡	1	7	14	3	79
Apparel.....................	23	13	25‡	8	15	27	3	37
Non-ferrous metals...........	17‡	6	50‡	2	25	20	4	47
CHEMICALS..................	12	17	43‡	7	6	17	0	24
All factory workers..........	38	604	25	260	19	622	5	738

* Skill categories by length of training: unskilled, less than one month; low skilled, one to three months; medium skilled, three months to two years; skilled, more than two years training See question 5, Appendix C for wording.
† Don't know responses have been removed.
‡ Disregard percentage: too few cases.

TABLE 48

PROPORTION OF FACTORY WORKERS WANTING ANOTHER JOB
AT SAME PAY, BY INDUSTRY*

INDUSTRY	PER CENT			NUMBER OF RESPONDENTS
	Yes	No	Don't Know	
Iron and steel...............	34	62	4	405
AUTOMOBILES...............	33	65	2	179
Food.......................	26	71	3	294
Oil refining.................	22	76	2	50
Leather.....................	21	67	12	129
PRINTING...................	21	69	10	107
Machinery..................	21	77	2	293
Transportation equipment....	20	79	1	90
Sawmills and planing........	18	82	0	67
Furniture...................	16	80	4	259
Apparel....................	14	80	6	264
Paper......................	14	80	6	103
Stone, clay, and glass........	13	82	5	108
Non-ferrous metals..........	13	86	1	88
CHEMICALS.................	11	83	6	78
TEXTILES...................	11	86	4	406
All factory workers........	20	76	4	2,920

* Question: "Is there any other job in your company, paying about what your present job does, that you would rather have?"

TABLE 49

PROPORTION OF FACTORY WORKERS EXPECTING TO ADVANCE
BEYOND FOREMAN LEVEL, BY INDUSTRY*

INDUSTRY	PER CENT			NUMBER OF RESPONDENTS
	Chances Not Good	Chances Good	Don't Know	
Leather...................	82	8	10	128
TEXTILES..................	74	11	15	385
Iron and steel..............	73	16	11	403
Apparel....................	70	19	10	267
Machinery.................	67	20	13	292
Sawmills and planing........	66	18	16	68
AUTOMOBILES...............	65	20	15	178
Furniture..................	62	24	14	258
Stone, clay, and glass.......	61	18	22	107
Paper.....................	60	27	13	102
Food......................	59	25	16	294
CHEMICALS.................	55	28	17	78
Oil refining................	55	29	16	51
PRINTING..................	54	21	25	107
Non-ferrous metals..........	52	30	18	88
Transportation equipment....	45	32	24	92
All factory workers........	66	20	15	2,898

* Question: "Would you say the chances are good, or not very good, that you will some day be offered a job above the foreman level in your plant or some other plant?"

TABLE 50

PROPORTION OF FACTORY WORKERS WHO FIND JOBS
TOO SIMPLE, BY INDUSTRY AND SKILL*
(Ranked by Proportion of Dissatisfied Unskilled Workers)

INDUSTRY	UNSKILLED		LOW SKILLED		MEDIUM SKILLED		SKILLED	
	Per Cent	Number	Per Cent	Number	Per Cent	Number	Per Cent	Number
Oil refining.................	70†	10	22†	9	20	15	36	14
Sawmills and planing..........	68	22	43†	7	17	24	29	14
PRINTING....................	50†	8	0†	1	13	15	15	81
AUTOMOBILES.................	46	85	35	23	24	38	16	31
Iron and steel................	43	128	50	56	19	115	11	94
Machinery...................	40	83	23	43	16	76	14	72
Stone, clay, and glass..........	36	36	63†	8	47	30	29	31
Food........................	34	122	20	41	17	66	16	55
Transportation equipment......	33	21	20†	5	9	22	21	42
TEXTILES.....................	33	159	16	77	20	83	11	75
Apparel.....................	32	74	31	52	27	81	16	51
Furniture....................	31	54	20	30	24	74	17	93
Leather.....................	31	45	29	17	23	48	0	15
Non-ferrous metals............	30†	10	67†	6	30	23	8	48
CHEMICALS...................	26	23	57†	7	19	21	8	24
Paper.......................	8	25	17	12	14	28	7	29
All factory workers..........	37	905	29	394	21	759	15	769

* See note to Table 47 for explanation of skill categories. See question 4c, Appendix C for wording.
† Disregard percentage: too few cases.

TABLE 51

SKILL DISTRIBUTIONS OF FACTORY WORKERS IN ROPER SAMPLE, BY INDUSTRY*

INDUSTRY	UNSKILLED		LOW SKILLED		MEDIUM SKILLED		SKILLED	
	Per Cent	Number	Per Cent	Number	Per Cent	Number	Per Cent	Number
Industries with Low Skill Distributions								
AUTOMOBILES	48	85	13	23	21	38	18	31
Food	43	122	14	41	23	66	19	55
TEXTILES	39	159	19	77	21	83	20	83
Leather	36	45	14	17	38	48	12	15
Industries with Balanced Skill Distributions								
Stone, clay, and glass	34	36	8	8	29	30	30	31
Sawmills and planing	33	22	10	7	36	24	21	14
Iron and steel	32	128	15	56	29	115	24	94
CHEMICALS	31	23	9	7	28	21	32	24
Machinery	30	83	16	44	28	76	26	72
Apparel	29	74	20	52	32	81	20	51
Paper	27	25	13	12	30	28	31	29
Oil refining	21	10	19	9	31	15	29	14
Industries with High Skill Distributions								
Furniture	21	54	12	30	29	74	37	93
Transportation equipment	23	21	6	5	24	22	47	42
Non-ferrous metals	11	10	7	6	26	23	55	48
PRINTING	8	8	1	1	14	15	77	81

* See note to Table 47 for explanation of skill categories.

TABLE 52

PROPORTION OF FACTORY WORKERS OPTIMISTIC ABOUT SECURITY ON RETIREMENT, BY INDUSTRY*

INDUSTRY	PER CENT			NUMBER OF RESPONDENTS
	Likely	Unlikely	Don't Know	
CHEMICALS	63	23	14	78
PRINTING	58	27	14	106
Transportation equipment	57	34	9	93
Oil refining	51	37	12	51
Apparel	49	40	11	265
Sawmills and planing	49	43	9	68
Paper	48	28	24	103
Non-ferrous metals	44	44	11	88
TEXTILES	43	37	20	407
Iron and steel	43	42	15	406
Food	42	43	15	296
Furniture	42	48	10	258
Machinery	40	44	16	293
Leather	33	44	23	129
AUTOMOBILES	33	58	9	180
Stone, clay, and glass	26	57	20	108
All factory workers	43	42	15	2,929

* Question: "As it looks now, do you think it is likely or unlikely that you'll be able to retire from work when you are 65 and live the rest of your life in reasonable comfort on your savings, pensions, and social security payments?"

C. THE ROPER-FORTUNE SURVEY QUESTIONNAIRE

1. On the whole would you say that the prices of most things you have to buy are still going up, are now staying about the same, or have started to go down? _____Up _____Same _____Down _____Don't know

2. Would you say that jobs like yours are becoming harder or easier to get around here these days? _____Harder _____Easier _____No change (volunteered) _____Don't know

3. *a*) For a person in your trade or occupation do you think your company is about as good a place as there is to work, or do you think there are other places that are better? _____Own company as good _____Other places are better _____Don't know.

   b) (If "own company as good.") What is it about your place that makes it better than others?

   c) (If "other places better.") Why do you think there are other places that are better?

4. Now I'd like to ask you a few questions about your present job:

	Yes	No	Don't Know
a) First, does it make you work too fast most of the time, or not?	—	—	—
b) Does it leave you too tired at the end of the day, or not?	—	—	—
c) Is it too simple to bring out your best abilities, or not?	—	—	—
d) Does it really give you a chance to try out ideas of your own, or not?	—	—	—
e) Can you do the work on the job and keep your mind on other things most of the time, or not?	—	—	—
f) Is your job really essential to the success of the company, or not?	—	—	—
g) Does it lead to a promotion if you do it well, or not?	—	—	—

5. Which one of these statements comes closest to describing how you feel about your present job? (Hand respondent card.)
    _____ *a*) My job is interesting nearly all the time.
    _____ *b*) While my job is interesting most of the time; there are some dull stretches now and then.
    _____ *c*) There are a few times when my job is interesting but most of it is pretty dull and monotonous.
    _____ *d*) My job is completely dull and monotonous; there is nothing interesting about it.

6. Do you think you are likely to be laid off temporarily at any time during the next six months? _____Yes _____No _____Don't know

7. Do you think you can have your present job as long as you want it, except for temporary lay-offs, or do you think there is a good chance that the job won't last as long as you want it to? _____Can have as long as I want it _____Job may end before I want it to _____Don't know

8. Do you think your company could afford to guarantee the employees their wages for *a full year* with no lay-offs in slack times, or don't you think the company could afford to do this and still remain in business? _____Could afford _____Could not afford _____Don't know and depends

9. *a*) Opinions vary on whether the job of foreman is a job to be wanted or a job to be avoided. We'd like to know how *you* feel about this____would you like to be a foreman some day or wouldn't you care particularly for such a job? _____Like to be a foreman _____Not like to be a foreman _____Depends and don't know _____Not applicable (foreman now)

   b) (If "like to be a foreman.") Do you think things will work out so that you will be a foreman some day, or are the chances not so good that you will become a foreman? _____Will become foreman _____Will not become foreman _____Don't know and depends

10. Suppose there is a foreman's job open in your plant and two people are being considered for it, _ one has worked in the plant twice as long and the other has much more ability. Which one do you think should get the promotion?_____One who has worked twice as long _____One who has much more ability _____Don't know

11. Just considering your own personal impression, which one or two of the things on this card do you believe gives a person the best chances to advance in the plant where you work? (Hand respondent card.) Note: If respondent gives only one answer ask: "Any other?" _____The quality of his work _____His energy and willingness to work _____How well he gets on personally with his immediate bosses _____How good a politician he is _____Whether he is a friend or relative of a high official or foreman _____How long he has been with the company _____None of them

12. Do you think it would be a good idea or a bad idea if the company took a vote in the shop on who should be foreman, and agreed to give the job to the winner? _____Good idea _____Bad idea _____Don't know

13. *a*) Do you have any union in your plant? _____Yes _____No _____Don't know

    b) (If "yes" to 13*a*.) Do you think the union should or should not be consulted before the choice for the job of foreman is made? _____Union should be consulted _____Union should not be consulted _____Don't know *c*) (If "yes" to 13*b*.) Suppose the company wants to appoint one person and the union wants another to get the job. If they can't agree, who should have the final say, the company or the union? _____The company _____ The union _____Don't know

14. Are you a member of a union yourself? _____Yes _____No _____Don't know

15. Would you say the chances are good, or not very good, that you will some day be offered a job above the foreman level in your plant or some other plant? _____Good _____Not good _____Don't know and depends

16. *a*) Which of these statements would you say is most true about the quality of work most of the workers in your shop are doing nowadays? (Hand respondent card.) _____(1) They are doing very good work and couldn't do any better. _____(2) They could do a little better work than they are now doing but on the whole they are doing pretty well. _____(3) They could do quite a lot better work than they are now doing.

b) (If 2 or 3.) Why do you think they aren't doing their best work?

17. Is there any other job in your company, paying about what your present job does, that you would rather have? _____Yes, there is _____No, there isn't _____Don't know

18. If you could go back to the age of 15 and start life over again, would you choose a different trade or occupation? _____Yes _____No _____Don't know and depends

19. As it looks now, do you think it is likely or unlikely that you'll be able to retire from work when you are 65 and live the rest of your life in reasonable comfort on your savings, pensions, and social security payments? _____Likely _____Unlikely _____Don't know

20. How long have you been working for your present employer?

21. What kind of work do you do?

22. How long does a person have to spend in training or experience to be able to handle a job like yours?

23. Is yours the kind of job in which someone would have to take your place if you had to leave your work for a half an hour or so, or could you let your work go for a half an hour and catch up on it later? _____ Can leave without relief _____Cannot leave without relief _____Don't know

24. About how many employees are there in the plant you work in?

D. THE BAY CHEMICAL COMPANY STUDY INTERVIEW SCHEDULE

A. PRESENT JOB AND WORK HISTORY
   1. What is your job title?
   2. How long on the job?
   3. How long at Bay?

4. Could you describe just what you do on your job?
5. What was your last job with a different company?   What industry's that in?   How long?
6. Job before that?   Company?   Industry?   How long?
7. Other job you worked longest on?
8. How does work in the chemical industry differ from work in _____ industry or in _____ industry? (Not talking about how the companies differ so much, but the kind of work, the industry.) Well, what ways better, and what ways worse?
9. When someone asks you what you do for a living, how do you answer?

B. THE WORK ITSELF

Going to ask a few questions about your job, and whenever possible when you answer you could also tell me how it shapes up in comparison with job in _____ industry.

10. How much variety is there in your work?
11. Is it pretty much the same all the time?   Does it give you a chance to try out ideas of your own or not?   Like what?
12. How much skill?   What takes skill?
13. How much responsibility?   Like what?
14. Can you do the job and keep your mind on other things most of the time?
15. Is your job too simple to bring out your best abilities, or not?
16. How interesting is it?
17. Anything in your work give you a feeling of satisfaction or accomplishment?   What?
18. How well do you like the actual work you do?
19. Do you have enough freedom on the job?
20. Do problems ever come up that challenge you in the work?
21. Do you ever feel pushed?
22. Do you know all there is to know about your work, or is there still more to learn?   Like what?
23. Do you need to know any chemistry to be a chemical worker?   On your job?   On others?

OPERATORS ONLY

24. How do you like working with automatic equipment as compared to working more with your hands, small machines or tools?   Why?
25. How do you feel about all the big chemical machines and pipes?   Do you control the operations or do the operations control you?
26. Is there any way you can make a game out of your work?   I mean how can you make time go faster when you're on the job?
27. What product do you make?   What's it used for?   Do any other companies make it also?   Which?   How good is it?

28. Do you ever imagine what it looks like inside the pipes, chemical reactors, other machines?

29. Would it make the job more interesting if you could see it?

30. Is your work as a chemical operator more like the work of a _____ (steel worker, assembly line worker, etc.) or more like the work of a white-collar man in an office?

C. Job Security (All Workers)

31. How secure do you feel your job is?   How does this compare with [industry worked in before]?

32. Why do you feel that things are this way at Bay?   In the chemical industry?

32a. Do you ever worry about layoffs?   Shutdowns?

D. Work Groups and Teams

33. On your job, do you work by yourself or with others?

34. What are the other jobs that are part of your work team or group? Where does your job fit in?

35. Is there as much opportunity to shoot the breeze on this job as others in the plant?   How about as compared to the other industries you've worked in?

36. How's the cooperation, the teamwork among the men?   Compared with other industries?

37. Do you yourself prefer to work in a group or by yourself?

E. Advancement and Aspirations

38. How good are your chances to get ahead?

39. Are they better in the chemical industry or in other industries?

40. What promotions have you had with this company?

41. How high can you go?

42. How high do you want to go?

43. What does it take to get ahead here?   How about in other industries?

44. Any kind of work in plant you'd rather do than your present job?

45. Do you expect to work here the rest of your life?   (This is a delicate question, I want to repeat that everything is confidential.)

46. What would you rather be than a chemical worker?

Miscellaneous

47. Whose work is more important, do you think, that of the operators in the process division or that of the craftsmen in the maintenance departments?

48. Who works harder?

49. Do you think pay scales in the plant are fair?

50. Any rates that are too high or too low?

51. How does company treatment of workers compare with _____ industries?

52. What do you think of the fringe benefits?

53. Anything else you want to say about the job, plant, chemical industry?

INDEX

INDEX

PHOENIX BOOKS
in Sociology